Praise for *Marketing in the Public Sector*

"Professionally, as an academic turned politician, this book—if published a few years earlier—would have made my life much simpler. This book lays out, in detail with concrete examples, how to conduct a grand plan for change. Particularly impressive is the application of different marketing principles along each step of the transition process toward establishing an efficient service-oriented governmental agency."

Somkid Jatusripitak, *Ph.D., Deputy Prime Minister and Minister of Commerce, Royal Thai Government*

"This book is filled with insights for people who want to communicate effectively about government programs, but it should also be on the bookshelf of any government manager who needs to think creatively about how to improve customer service. Every page contains information and ideas that public-sector leaders can, and should, put in their management tool kits."

Christine O. Gregoire, *Governor, Washington State*

"Increasingly, public sector managers have been challenged to 'do more with less.' *Marketing in the Public Sector* demonstrates that marketing is not simply another line-item expense, but rather a set of tools that help public servants allocate resources more effectively and efficiently. The book is chock-full of real-world stories of creative marketers working within diverse organizations, all of whom have come to understand that marketing is not simply advertising or persuasion, but rather a mindset."

E. Marla Felcher, *Ph.D., Adjunct Lecturer in Public Policy, John F. Kennedy School of Government, Harvard University*

"Kotler and Lee are teaching governments to motivate by invitation rather than intimidation. Instead of complaint and reaction, they work to create a culture of contagious cooperation that can replace rulemaking with social consensus. This is a practical manual for un-clogging hearing rooms, cooling tempers, and putting government back on the side of the people who pay for it."

Dave Ross, *CBS News Commentator*

"*Marketing in the Public Sector* provides an excellent planning framework for public sector officers engaged in all levels of marketing and communications. Showcasing real-world examples, it successfully demonstrates the marriage of commercial marketing concepts into public sector practice."

Dr. K Vijaya, *Director, Corporate Marketing & Communications, Health Promotion Board, Singapore*

"Public sector organizations are now faced with an urgent need to stand out from the crowd in order to successfully compete for funding, talent, and influence. Philip Kotler and Nancy Lee have written a unique, practical, and timely book containing comprehensive guidelines and cases that those involved in the marketing of public sector organizations will find absorbing and most useful."

Paul Temporal, *Group Managing Director, Temporal Brand Consulting, Author of* Public Sector Branding in Asia

"Every day, professionals in the public sector deliver thousands of programs and services in increasingly demanding environments. This book is a 'must read' and a standard reference for every public servant engaged in public sector marketing and communications. Congratulations to Kotler and Lee for creating a book that is both educational and practical."

Jim Mintz, *Director, Centre of Excellence for Public Sector Marketing*

Marketing in the
Public Sector

Marketing in the Public Sector

A Roadmap for Improved Performance

Philip Kotler
Nancy Lee

Vice President, Editor-in-Chief: Tim Moore
Associate Publisher and Director of Marketing: Amy Neidlinger
Wharton Editor: Yoram (Jerry) Wind
Acquisitions Editor: Paula Sinnott
Editorial Assistant: Susie Abraham
Development Editor: Russ Hall
Cover Designer: Alan Clements
Managing Editor: Gina Kanouse
Senior Project Editor: Lori Lyons
Copy Editor: Ben Lawson
Indexer: Erika Millen
Compositor: codeMantra
Proofreader: Linda Seifert
Manufacturing Buyer: Dan Uhrig

© 2007 by Pearson Education, Inc.
Publishing as Wharton School Publishing
Upper Saddle River, New Jersey 07458

Wharton School Publishing offers excellent discounts on this book when ordered in quantity for bulk purchases or special sales. For more information, please contact U.S. Corporate and Government Sales, 1-800-382-3419, corpsales@pearsontechgroup.com. For sales outside the U.S., please contact International Sales at international@pearsoned.com.

Printed in the United States of America

Third Printing, January 2008

ISBN 10: 0-13-706086-6
This product is printed digially on demand.

Pearson Education LTD.
Pearson Education Australia PTY, Limited.
Pearson Education Singapore, Pte. Ltd.
Pearson Education North Asia, Ltd.
Pearson Education Canada, Ltd.
Pearson Educatión de Mexico, S.A. de C.V.
Pearson Education—Japan
Pearson Education Malaysia, Pte. Ltd.

Library of Congress Cataloging-in-Publication Data is on file.

We dedicate this book to every current and future
public servant engaged in the pursuit of the common
good—good for government, good for citizens, and
good for the environment. Our intention is for you to
discover the contribution that traditional marketing
principles and techniques can make to improving
your agency's performance. Our hope is you
experience that the real magic of marketing is
(simply) a citizen-oriented approach.

CONTENTS

ACKNOWLEDGMENTS

My thanks go to my wife Nancy for her unfailing support of my work and to the other members of my family; to my Kellogg School of Management colleagues who are always a source of inspiration; and to the city of Chicago, which has taught me much about the role of government in making a city work and prosper.

—*Philip Kotler*

Thank you to all the committed and competent public servants in Washington State who inspire me and others with what happens when we practice the marketing mindset. And a special thank you to my dear husband Terry, who continues to carry my bags, put up the tent, chase off the wolves, put out the fire, and remind me to look at the stars.

—*Nancy Lee*

PART I

INTRODUCTION

1

Improving Public Sector Performance by Seizing Opportunities to Meet Citizen Needs

Let us begin with the end in mind, painted by scenes from a day in a not too distant future—a day in which the interests of citizens, as well as public sector agencies, are served:

In Oregon—Todd checks his morning online newspaper and rereads a headline—to be sure it was for real. "Post Office reports record profits and will hold first-class stamp rates at 39 cents for the next five years." It seems services for small businesses are soaring.

In Kansas—Sophie heads out the door with her fourth-grade daughter eager to see if this "walking school bus program" the school district raves about will really help Allison lose the ten pounds her pediatrician said she should. If successful, it's also supposed to cut the district's transportation costs by fifteen percent.

In Los Angeles—Juanita picks up her carpool partner who jumps in and places their renewed carpool sticker on the windshield, downloaded from an email she received last night from the city. She mentions a new feature on the Web site that also

3

allowed her to reserve their favorite spot in the city's parking garage before leaving home.

In New Jersey—Trent, an operations manager at a construction firm, receives an email notice that the state's Labor and Industry workshop he wanted to attend has been expanded, so he can now get in. He hopes what he heard will be true for his company—that those participating in the workshop had reduced workplace injuries, and that the following year insurance premiums were down.

In Texas—Bobby Joe climbs into his pickup and pauses, gets back out, and glances at the DON'T MESS WITH TEXAS sticker on his own bumper. He decides he didn't put it on there just to keep the bumper from falling apart, so he pulls out his cable and wraps it across the bed to secure his load of wood debris.

In Jordan—Sabbah listens to his 11-year-old son who shares with him the results of a water audit he conducted on their home, an assignment he received in school today. His son then shows Sabbah pictures of water-saving devices they could put in their shower and kitchen sink and tells him how many gallons it might save their family (and their country) each day.

In Capetown—Trudy turns the corner and comes to an abrupt stop as she sees the flashing lights on the street outlining the crosswalk, indicating that a pedestrian has stepped off the curb in front of her car—someone she hadn't seen.

In Finland—Tuomo clamps on the new spikes for his shoes he received yesterday at the community center. Free for many seniors as a part of the country's effort to increase physical activity, they are supposed to help keep him from falling when he shovels his sidewalk clear of snow and ice.

In London—Julia wanders down to the city park on her lunch hour, eager to see the new traveling interactive art exhibit on display there. She can't help but notice the crowds at the new food concession stand on park property, and she hears from the owner that the city will be using revenues from this public/private venture to buy more litter receptacles for the parks and city sidewalks.

> **In Singapore**—Johnson opens a utility bill that includes a message recognizing his household for reducing electrical usage during peak times and, as a thank you, a coupon worth $50 on conservation-related products at a major home supply retail partner.
>
> **In Rome**—Giacomo arrives home from a business trip, eager to tell about an airport he was in that afternoon where he made it through security in record time, as they now have little booths you walk through that don't require you to take anything out of your pockets or briefcase. He also noticed they had less than half the security staff he usually saw at each checkpoint.

On closer examination, you would likely see that this possible world is one where governmental agencies have clearly seized the opportunity to meet citizen needs—in a way that contributes not only to social good but to economic and environmental good as well. By offering quality programs and services, they have increased citizen interest, revenues, and satisfaction. By improving and reporting on agency performance, they have engendered support. By developing infrastructures mindful of citizen inclinations and behaviors, they have increased public health and safety. By communicating effectively, they have motivated voluntary compliance. By providing easy access to services, they have increased utilization and even decreased operating costs. And by forming partnerships with the private sector, they have been able to expand services, improve ambiance, and deliver a few welcome surprises.

We have written this book to support current and future public sector managers and staff in discovering this clear link between meeting citizen needs and improving public agency performance. The focus is on how to use fundamental, proven marketing principles and techniques to accomplish these goals. The aim is to choose goals and actions that serve the Common Good, those that create the greatest possible good for the greatest possible number of people. Good in this public sector context is defined in terms of social good, economic good, and environmental good—measures often referred to as the triple bottom line.

Before turning your attention to marketing's potential contribution, a few questions are first worthy of discussion to provide a backdrop grounded in reality.

What Do Citizens Want and Get from Public Agencies?

Every society needs a public sector, for which the most important function is to define the operating principles of the society. Who is the government? How are governing officials elected or selected? What does the government allow, and what does it prohibit? How is revenue secured to pay for government operations? How do citizens influence their government?

A second role of government is to perform those public services that are critical to the public interest, such as responsibility for defense and the military. National and local governments believe that they should manage essential public services, such as policing, fire control, parks, libraries, zoning, energy, sanitation, road construction, education, and healthcare facilities. Often the argument is made that certain services should be run as natural monopolies—such as the U.S. Army or the U.S. Postal Service—because they must be under a single command or would gain scale efficiencies.

A third role is to provide necessary public services that neither the private sector nor the nonprofit sector want to handle or can handle with existing resources. Thus governments typically provide assistance to the poor independently or in tandem with the agencies in the nonprofit sector.

Because government operations are carried on at a great cost to its citizens, however—consuming in the U.S. more that 40% of taxable income—citizens want them to be conducted efficiently and effectively. We grow up experiencing the efficiency of private enterprise and then want comparable performance from public agencies.

Unfortunately, many are critical of government services and what they perceive as wasteful purchases and practices, a lack of needed services, and a perversion of government by powerful interest groups. Specific complaints are probably all too familiar to you:

- Taxes are high, and we don't get our money's worth.
- Some government agencies pay scandalous prices for common goods, and there are million-dollar overruns on government contracts.

- The nation's public infrastructure (bridges, roads, etc.) is deteriorating in spite of road taxes.
- Public agencies are often slow and inflexible because of excessive bureaucracy and rules.
- Public employees are overprotected even in the face of incompetence or unethical behavior.
- Public school failures lead to poor education that leads to poor jobs that lead to broken families and drug abuse that lead to crime and imprisonment.
- Poorer citizens are given inadequate help to improve their conditions and to escape the cycle of poverty.
- System problems create long waiting times, lost correspondence, dirty streets, and more.
- Inept communications create confusion (e.g., Medicare prescription drug plans).
- Lack of responsiveness creates anger (e.g., FEMA's response to Hurricane Katrina).
- Being out of touch with your citizenry creates programs doomed for failure (e.g., the Susan B. Anthony dollar often mistaken for a "quarter").

Clearly, the public sector needs to improve its real and perceived performance in order to raise the public's confidence and satisfaction—and thereby their support. Without this support, citizens take action such as initiating tax rollbacks and voting for representatives who promise agency change or elimination.

What Tools Currently Used in the Private Sector Can Most Benefit the Public Sector?

One answer to improving performance is to adopt tools that the private sector uses to operate their businesses more successfully. Today many public executives and personnel are "going back to school." They are attending seminars on finance, marketing, purchasing, leadership, entrepreneurship, strategy, and operations. They are taking courses in schools of public administration or in business schools to advance their skills and understanding. They want to avoid obsolescence and dependence on civil service and seniority to protect their jobs or qualify for promotions. They want to restore personal and citizen pride in their employer.

These public servants (and you may be one of them) are reviewing and in some cases adopting such private sector practices as

- Total quality management
- Customer-driven strategy
- Self-managing teams
- Flat organizations
- Visionary leadership
- Re-engineering
- Performance metrics and appraisal
- Incentive systems and pay for performance
- Cost/benefit and cost/effectiveness analysis
- Outsourcing
- E-government and e-information
- Learning organizations
- Lean production

Some people question how far this can go, claiming that government operations are inherently different from business operations. The cry to make government agencies more efficient, effective, and innovative strikes many citizens as a pipe dream. They see too many contrasts between government and business organizations:[1]

- Government organizations often are monopolies; businesses exist in competitive markets.
- Government is constituted to serve the interests of citizens; business aims to maximize investor profits.
- Political leaders are creatures of constituencies, reflecting their interests; business leaders are responsible to boards of directors.
- Government activities typically occur in the public light and receive a great deal of attention in the media; business activities

largely are shielded from the media and take place insulated from public, governmental, and media opinion.

- Citizens belong to interest groups that vary in size, influence, and power; businesses obtain their benefits through lobbyists and directly from political leaders.
- Citizens in most contemporary democracies have a strong distrust of government, are ill informed, and show weak participation; investors and business leaders have a strong interest in their enterprises.
- Units of government often have poorly understood mandates and arenas of action. Their functions evolve haphazardly with considerable duplication and overlap; business enterprises have specific divisions of labor and organizational operations.
- Citizens check actions of political leaders by elections, polls, and media stories; business leaders are ultimately accountable only to their boards.
- Governments are slow moving and subject to checks and balances, public hearings, agency infighting, veto powers; business activities are fast moving, once decision making enters the domain of CEOs and boards.
- Government operations are often underfinanced; businesses can get the funds they need when they can demonstrate that it will lead to an acceptable profit.
- The government in the U.S. is divided into three federal branches, 50 states, and an estimated 83,000 local governments with overlapping responsibilities; business tends to have concentrated, centralized activity at the CEO and board levels.[2]
- Government is involved in virtually every area of life; business is focused on the goods and services it produces.
- Governments distribute, redistribute, and regulate resources; businesses mainly produce and distribute resources.

We argue that these differences are often exaggerated and should not be used as an excuse for inefficiency, ineffectiveness, or waste. Many groups—Common Cause, Citizens for Better Government, The Innovation Groups—are working to improve the efficiency and effectiveness of government operations. A major force has been the book

Reinventing Government: How the Entrepreneurial Spirit Is Transforming the Public Sector by David Osborne and Ted Gaebler.[3] The book contains sweeping proposals for change, exemplified by chapter titles including "Catalytic Government," "Community-Owned Government," "Competitive Government," "Mission-Driven Government," "Results-Oriented Government," "Customer-Driven Government," "Enterprising Government," "Anticipatory Government," "Decentralized Government," and "Market-Oriented Government." Endorsed by prominent governmental leaders and elected officials including Bill Clinton, the book reads like a business textbook on how government could be better run.

Change is inevitable and affects the public as well as the private sectors. All organizations are subject to new challenges and new competitors, any of which might call for a restructuring of the organization or its termination. Public sector agencies do not have a guaranteed life or funding levels. Like businesses, they must read the landscape of changing forces and technologies; they must think strategically; they must envision new modes of efficiency; they must innovate; they must market their merits to the general and particular publics who pay taxes or oversee their activities. You, as a current or future public leader, can contribute to that change management.

What Role Can Marketing Play in Improving the Performance of Public Agencies?

One of the fields that has been most overlooked and misunderstood by public sector personnel is marketing. As a public official, how would you define marketing? You might say that we are talking about "advertising." True, public bodies do some advertising. Witness the flurry of ads to recruit new military personnel. Or you might say that marketing is another word for "selling" and that you associate it with "manipulation." As you will read, this becomes a tactic of last resort when marketing principles and techniques have not been used to develop, price, distribute, and effectively communicate the real value of your offerings.

This negative image of marketing is understandably drawn from observing the unending stream of advertising and sales promotion in the private sector. But to identify marketing with only one of its 4Ps (product, price, place, and promotion), namely promotion, is to miss the power and benefits of marketing thinking. Not knowing marketing is tantamount to not doing marketing research; not defining one's customers, partners, and competitors; not segmenting, targeting, and positioning one's offerings of services; not managing the challenging process of innovating and launching new services; not recognizing new channels for distributing public services; not pricing these services correctly when the agency must recover some of its costs; and not communicating about them in clear, persuasive ways.

Marketing turns out to be the best planning platform for a public agency that wants to meet citizen needs and deliver real value. Marketing's central concern is producing outcomes that the target market values. In the private sector, marketing's mantra is customer value and satisfaction. In the public sector, marketing's mantra is citizen value and satisfaction.

We show that traditional marketing concepts work well in the public sector. They work for the federal government and also for those 83,000 local governments, 50 state governments, and thousands of cities, counties, school districts, water districts, and transportation districts—and around the world.

You can use the matrix in Table 1.1 to get a sense of the marketing intensity of different well-known types of government agencies. The more checks in a row, the more marketing-intensive the agency. Among the high marketing-intensive organizations are the postal service, army recruitment, and public transportation, which count on customer utilization and participation. Among the low marketing-intensive organizations are the IRS and auto licensing services.

Going Forward

Public agencies can benefit from bringing a more conscious marketing approach and mindset to their mission, problem solving, and outcomes. In the following chapters, you will explore these major

TABLE 1.1 The Marketing Intensity of Different Public Agencies

	New Product Development	Pricing	Distribution Channels	Public Relations	Advertising	Sales Promotion	Sales Force	Customer Service
Federal								
Post office	✓	✓	✓	✓	✓	✓	✓	✓
Army recruitment	✓	✓		✓	✓	✓	✓	✓
National Archives			✓					✓
IRS			✓					✓
Local								
Auto license bureau			✓					✓
Police department			✓	✓			✓	✓
Public transportation	✓	✓	✓	✓	✓	✓		✓
Ports	✓	✓	✓	✓			✓	✓

marketing activities more systematically. They are illustrated with vivid examples of public agency effectiveness, efficiency, innovativeness, and responsiveness. You will read inspirational and informative stories of responsive public service leaders and how they are using marketing thinking to contribute to meeting agency goals for

- Increasing revenues
- Increasing service utilization
- Increasing purchases of products
- Increasing compliance with laws
- Improving public health and safety
- Increasing citizen behaviors to protect the environment
- Decreasing costs for service delivery
- Improving customer satisfaction
- Engendering citizen support

The good news is that chances are, some public agency somewhere in the world has solved some problems you are facing by using marketing principles and tools.

In the end you should be convinced that marketing is not the same as advertising, sales, or communications and doesn't have to feel like manipulation. It is these skills and more. It involves a customer (citizen-centered) approach, one that will help address citizen complaints, alter their perceptions, and improve your performance. It is a disciplined approach, requiring you to develop a formal plan by conducting a situational analysis, setting goals, segmenting the market, conducting marketing research, positioning your brand, choosing a strategic blend of marketing tools, and establishing an evaluation, budget, and implementation plan. And you'll learn how to develop a compelling one.

Government can move from being low-tech and low-touch to being high-tech and high-touch and thereby deliver more value for the taxpayer dollar. We believe that government can deliver more quality, speed, efficiency, convenience, and fairness to its citizens. We greatly respect the wishes of public servants to perform professionally in their jobs. This book makes a contribution to the marketing skill set and citizen sensitivities of public servants and thereby to the common good.

2

UNDERSTANDING THE
MARKETING MINDSET

"In a match made in marketplace heaven, the world's busiest Web site and the world's largest postal administration formed a business partnership in 2003 that continues to grow and strengthen to this day. eBay and the Postal Service™ share an important and growing customer segment—the millions of small and home-based businesses scattered across the country. Just one facet of the partnership—the USPS® 'postage solution' technology imbedded into the eBay Web site—generated millions of shipments and significant new revenue for the Postal Service in only its first year of operation.

Today, the Postal Service and eBay share Web sites and software, advertising, and promotions, and the partnership has been a resounding success for both parties. According to the San Jose (CA) Mercury News, at the 2005 eBay Live! Conference, special guest Postmaster John E. 'Jack' Potter received a 'rock star' welcome from eBay President and CEO Meg Whitman and thousands of eBay PowerSellers. 'eBayers let it rip,' the newspaper reported, when Whitman asked the audience, 'How much do we love the Postal Service?' "

Anita Bizzotto, USPS® Chief Marketing Officer

15

FIGURE 2.1   A winning partnership

You may find a few things surprising about this quote—first, that the U.S. Postal Service even has a Chief Marketing Officer! At most, you might have expected a Communications or Public Relations Manager. Consider as well their teaming up with a retail giant. As you read in the opening story of their more than 230-year history, you will notice an infusion of the five earmarks of a successful marketing mindset:

- Adopting a Customer-Centered Focus
- Segmenting and Targeting the Market
- Identifying the Competition
- Utilizing All 4Ps in the Marketing Mix
- Monitoring Efforts and Making Adjustments

While you read, imagine what might have happened if the Postal Service had not developed this mindset and made these changes— changes inevitable for all public agencies to plan for and embrace in this world of technological booms, instant gratification, new and fierce competitors, and unleashed globalization.

Opening Story: The United States Postal Service—A Work in Progress

UNITED STATES POSTAL SERVICE® The history of the Postal Service is more than a story about mail. It is a marketing story, one that began in 1775 when the newly formed Post Office Department established a guiding principle that "every person in the United States—no matter who, no matter where—has the right to equal access to secure, efficient, and affordable mail service."[1] Evidence that this rudder is still guiding the ship appeared on CNN 230 years later in a commercial promoting that customers can now do just about anything at usps.com® that they have been doing at the post office. The tagline touted: "Working for you."

Practicing a Customer-Centered Focus from the Very Beginning

Perhaps Benjamin Franklin planted that seed for a customer-centered mindset when he became the first Postmaster General™ in 1775 and began to organize the service with an emphasis on new and shorter routes and authorization for post riders to carry mail at night to speed service between Philadelphia and New York.

Subsequent Postal Service leaders also listened to their customers and tried to respond. The Pony Express™ was contracted in 1860 to provide speedier service to the Pacific Coast. Before 1863, postage paid only for the delivery of mail from Post Office to Post Office. In 1862, progressive Postmaster General Montgomery Blair advocated that mail be delivered free by salaried letter carriers, arguing that if the system of mailing and receiving letters was more convenient, people would use it more often, and this would increase desired revenues.

And it wasn't until 1896 that rural customers began receiving direct delivery (along with offers for stamps, money orders, and registered letters), with typical reactions similar to the Arizona citizen who wrote: "It looks as if 'Uncle Sam' has at last turned his eye in our direction."[2]

Segmenting and Targeting Markets

Customer segmentation and customization of services is an important part of effective marketing, but many would claim the Postal Service has a tough time implementing programs when they are perceived to "unduly discriminate among customers."[3] It hasn't stopped them, however, from developing product options (e.g., First-Class Mail®, Express Mail®, Standard Mail®, Parcel Post®, etc.) and from implementing programs that meet the needs of and provide superior value to key market segments.

Consider how the Postal Service has taken advantage of personal computers to help small business and home office users. PC Postage™ software products offer customers the ability to purchase postage over the Internet and use their standard desktop printer to print the postage indicia directly onto envelopes or labels for mail or packages. A service called Click-N-Ship® allows customers to pay for postage and print shipping labels from the USPS Web site, and another online service called Carrier Pickup online notification lets them arrange for next-day pickup of the packages by their regular letter carrier at no extra charge. These services are providing this growing market with customer access to postage 24 hours a day, 7 days a week, from the convenience of their home and office computers. As one postal print ad puts it, "The Post Office. Conveniently located on a computer near you" (see Figure 2.2).

Identifying the Competition

According to Postal Service annual reports, First-Class Mail volume declined by 4.6 billion pieces in fiscal years 2002 and 2003, the greatest declines in First-Class Mail since the Great Depression.

Competition had continued to grow for every postal product. United Parcel Service (UPS) and FedEx Corp. had entered the scene as major competitors in the early 1980s, promising to deliver packages to most U.S. addresses before 10:30 a.m. the next morning. Postal shipping and overnight products then improved but lost market share to the new shipping specialists, and the rise of electronic communications and other technologies offered alternatives for conveying statements, payments, and personal messages.

FIGURE 2.2 Postal print ad targeting small businesses and home office users

Franchised mail retailing systems rang an additional alarm. At a Mail Boxes Etc. outlet, for example, a customer could bring in an item, and the staff would efficiently package it, price it, and assure its rapid delivery. The availability of packaging material and packaging service at Mail Boxes Etc. was in great contrast to what a customer could expect to get at the local Post Office and in fact pushed the Postal Service into offering similar services.

To become more competitive, the Postal Service began to change and restructure. In a win-win-win move in 2001, for example, the Postal Service announced a business alliance with competitor FedEx that began with offering FedEx drop boxes at Post Office locations in Charlotte, North Carolina. The partnership has since grown into FedEx drop boxes on postal property, a seven-year, $6.3-billion transportation contract to fly Priority Mail and Express Mail shipments on FedEx airplanes, and Global Express Guaranteed, a premium international shipping product from both companies with date-certain service in one-to-two days to most major markets.

Utilizing the 4Ps in the Marketing Mix

In its *2004-2008 USPS Five-Year Strategic Plan*, the Postal Service commits to continuing its businesslike transformation through the execution of bold strategies developed to improve the value of the mail and mail-related products and services.

In the following section, specific strategies and tactics currently being used by the Postal Service have been organized by the traditional mix of marketing strategies, the 4Ps: Product, Price, Place, and Promotion.

Products and Services

It would be more than interesting to know how Benjamin Franklin, an inventor in his own right, would have reacted in 1775 if he were told about the lineup of products and services offered by the Postal Service in 2005:

- Colorful stamps ranging from the generic American flag to the Black Heritage collection, Sporty Cars, the Northeast Deciduous Forests, and a tribute to Dr. Seuss (Theodor Seuss Geisel) with the varieties available at no extra cost
- Choices of formats for stamps, including books, adhesives, rolls, and even subscriptions
- Ancillary services, including Selective Service registration and applications for passports
- Mailing products, including bubble envelopes, holiday boxes, pre-inked rubber stamps, scales, and embossers
- Specialty items such as stamp lapel pins, Ronald Reagan stamp-art tote bags, NASCAR-themed merchandise (the Postal Service sponsors a race car in the Busch Series), and framed Disney stamp artwork
- Unique services for businesses, including access to custom bids from direct mail shops and comprehensive mailing databases

- Free DVDs on how to protect your household from telemarketing fraud, work-at-home scams, and identity theft
- For holidays, special occasions, and business uses, the ability to design and mail your own holiday cards and postcards, complete with your favorite pictures, personalized messages, and your choice of having the cards printed and mailed for you or having them sent to your home or place of business for mailing
- Opportunities to contribute to social causes through the purchase of stamps, supporting such causes as Breast Cancer Research ($45.6 million raised to date for research since 1998) and Stop Family Violence ($1.8 million raised to date for domestic violence programs since 2003)

Price

In the beginning, postage fees were based on the number of sheets in a letter and the distance a letter traveled, a stark contrast to pricing structures and incentives of today where rates are based on weight, size, shape, desired speed, day of the week, and whether domestic or international bound. And there are options to pay extra for services such as a Certificate of Mailing, Certified Mail™, Delivery Confirmation™, Insured Mail, Registered Mail™, Restricted Delivery, Return Receipt, Signature Confirmation™, and Special Handling.

Incentives are included among the Postal Service pricing tools, with a strategic effort in place to work with the mailing industry and its customers to develop innovative pricing approaches such as the recently approved Negotiated Service Agreements, which allow the Postal Service for the first time to negotiate pricing discounts and incentives for increased mail volume, as well as customized services with individual customers.

Place

Expanding access to improve convenience is perhaps the most aggressive marketing effort to date. Consider the evolution from post riders on horseback in 1773 (with boats, sleds, snowshoes, skis, and mules pinch hitting), to the use of stagecoaches in 1775, rail in 1832, steamboats via the Isthmus of Panama in 1849, and air in 1911 to the access and delivery options we have in 2005.

Today, customers have the ability to go to more than 37,000 retail locations or use one of the new award-winning self-service Automated Postal Centers® (the ATMs of the Postal Service), providing access to frequently purchased products and services in Post Office lobbies without waiting in line, as well as in additional locations such as airports (see Figure 2.3). Kiosks accept payment via debit and credit cards; dispense postage based on weight, desired speed and destination; weigh and rate envelopes, flats, and parcels up to 70 pounds; prepare Express Mail forms; provide certified mail return receipts; and allow you to hold mail and file Change of Address forms.

Then consider the capabilities of the Web site, usps.com, that provides the ability among many service offerings to print postage, request next-day pickup of prepaid Express Mail and Priority Mail packages at no extra cost, purchase a Post Office box, or request that mail be held, forwarded, or redelivered.

FIGURE 2.3 Extending hours and shortening lines through a new distribution channel

Promotion

Although the Postal Service has no official motto, it has several famous inscriptions, including one at the General Post Office in New York City: "Neither snow nor rain nor heat nor gloom of night stays these couriers from the swift completion of their appointed rounds," and one at the site of the Smithsonian Institution's National Postal Museum with a focus on customer benefits versus product features: "Messenger of Sympathy and Love, Servant of Parted Friends, Consoler of the Lonely, Bond of the Scattered Family, Enlarger of the Common Life, Carrier of News and Knowledge, Instrument of Trade and Industry, Promoter of Mutual Acquaintance, of Peace and of Goodwill among Men and Nations."

In terms of a corporate logo, the official seal from 1782 to 1837 featured the figure of Mercury, the fleet messenger of the gods and the god of commerce and travel in Roman mythology; then from 1837 to 1970, the symbol pictured a post horse and rider, speeding with mailbags; and from 1970 to the present, the official seal has been the bald eagle, poised for flight above the words "U.S. Mail." In 1993, a new corporate logo was unveiled, one with an eagle's head leaning into the wind. This has not, however, replaced the 1970 postal seal as the official seal.

The Postal Service uses all advertising media to promote its products and services, including Direct Mail (obviously), broadcast and cable television commercials, newspaper and magazine ads, drive-time radio ads, retail posters and take-aways, Web site banners and email blasts, and even a three-panel outdoor display in New York's Times Square in the fall of 2004. Its campaigns range from specific product, service, and event-driven promotions to seasonal themes on a grand scale. In 2004, it mailed an eight-page, five-inch-by-seven-inch *Shipping and Mailing Holiday Guide* to more than 100 million residential addresses, spelling out postal shipping options and explaining how Americans could go online to send holiday gifts without ever leaving their homes or offices. The tagline? "Quick, Easy, Convenient."

In 2005, the Postal Service launched a grassroots promotional campaign, training and engaging thousands of Postmasters and station and branch managers nationwide to reach out to prospective medium, small, and home-based businesses, first to create awareness about the Postal Service Web site, usps.com, and then to promote postal shipping and advertising tools. Over a span of five months in 2005, Postmasters and managers personally contacted more than 160,000 potential customers and reportedly generated $25 million in annualized revenue for the Postal Service.

Monitoring Customer Behavior and Satisfaction and Making Adjustments

Success measures for the Postal Service included in the *Five-Year Strategic Plan* call for an objective way for postal stakeholders, including Congress and the American people, to evaluate the performance of the Postal Service using valid measures and reliable data.

Systems used include ones to measure customer satisfaction and track service performance. In the third quarter of 2005, the Postal Service announced that it achieved an all-time high score of 96 percent on-time performance for overnight delivery of First-Class Mail, as measured independently by IBM Consulting Services. Customer satisfaction, also independently measured, showed that 93 percent of residential customers rated their experience with the Postal Service as excellent, very good, or good.

Methods are also in place to provide citizen input. As of December 2002, the Postal Service sponsored 212 Customer Advisory Councils, groups of citizens who volunteer to work with local postal management on postal issues of interest to the community. Ideas for improvement can also be submitted on the Web site in a section requesting proposals for new products and services and improved financial performance and enhancements to existing products, services, or operations.

The Marketing Mindset

A **Marketing Mindset**, apparent in the evolution and ongoing transformation of the U.S. Postal Service, begins with awareness of basic principles and is sustained through practice, feedback, and adjustments. This introductory chapter is intended to offer a summary of fundamental marketing theories, those representing the underpinnings of the five principles just introduced. For those of you who have had a marketing course or similar training, it will be a quick review. You will experience a simple transference of principles to the public sector arena. For others who are new to marketing, it will be a brief immersion, with subsequent chapters providing more in-depth discussions of the application of these principles and stories exemplifying each.

Principle #1: Adopt a Customer-Centered Focus

One quick way for you to get a sense of a customer-centered focus is to assume your customer (target audience) is constantly asking the question "What's in it for me?" This is often referred to as the WIFM phenomenon, one that sends successful marketing managers on a relentless pursuit to fully understand and satisfy the wants and needs of target customers better than competitors do.

This customer-centered focus didn't emerge as a strong marketing management philosophy until the 1950s, when it became a core component of the marketing concept, contrasted in the following by Kotler and Keller with alternative philosophies:[4]

- *The Production Concept* is perhaps the oldest philosophy and holds that consumers will prefer products that are widely available and inexpensive, and therefore the organization's focus should be to keep costs down and access convenient. Gas stations in the private sector and garbage collection in the public sector practice this philosophy, at least in part.

- *The Product Concept* holds that consumers will favor those products that offer the most quality, performance, or innovative features. The problem with this focus is that program and service managers often become caught up in a love affair with their product, neglecting to design and enhance their efforts based on customer wants and needs. It is otherwise known as the "build it and they will come" or "make it and it will sell" philosophy, one that may explain the challenges that community transit agencies face as they attempt to increase ridership on buses and that parks and recreation departments face in their attempt to rent out facility space to generate additional revenues.

- *The Selling Concept* holds that consumers and businesses will probably not buy enough of the organization's products to meet goals if left alone, and as a result, the organization must undertake an aggressive selling and promotion effort, one with risky assumptions that customers "talked into buying" today will be glad they did and, even if they're not, will come back for more and won't bad-mouth the company...an unlikely scenario. In some public schools in the U.S., for example, special interest groups are working to ban military recruitment officers from high school campuses, concerned with perceptions of aggressive selling.

- *The Marketing Concept* is in sharp contrast to the product and selling concepts. Instead of a "make and sell" philosophy, it is a "sense and respond" orientation. Peter Drucker went so far as to proclaim, "the aim of marketing is to make selling superfluous. The aim of marketing is to know and understand the customer so well that the product or service fits him and sells itself."[5] In the public sector, the implications are that programs and services that have been designed to meet targeted customer wants and needs will require less promotion (e.g., advertising budgets) because satisfied customers may become "evangelists" for the agency. If a city utility's natural yard care workshop is exciting, and better yet, if those who attend are able to keep their lawn weed-free without the use of harmful chemicals, they are bound to share their enthusiasm about this new-found resource with their neighbors.

- *The Societal Marketing Concept* takes the marketing concept one step further. It holds that organizations should develop and deliver superior value to customers in a way that maintains or improves the consumer's *and* the society's well-being. The societal marketing concept calls upon marketers to build social and ethical considerations into their marketing practices and to weigh potential negative impacts of satisfying consumer short-term wants (e.g., fast food) with long-term societal well-being (e.g., an obesity epidemic). The U.S. Postal Service would exemplify this concept, for example, if it chose the least polluting among competitive delivery vehicles.

A customer-centered focus works for you because it is essential to exchange, a process that involves (stated simply) the voluntary transfer of a product to a customer in exchange for some cost (monetary and/or nonmonetary) paid by the customer. Marketers manage this process with the Exchange Theory in mind, which states that what we offer the target market (benefits) has to be perceived as equal to or greater than what they will have to give (costs).[6] To do this, you'll want to know all costs the target market perceives to the exchange and then create benefits that balance the scale. When the target market perceives that costs outweigh benefits, your task is to increase the perceived benefits, reduce the perceived costs, or both.[7] Without this, the theory proclaims that the exchange won't happen.

To develop customer-centered strategies, you need information (market research) to answer fundamental questions. What costs and barriers do target markets perceive to purchasing a product, utilizing your programs and services, or performing a desired behavior? Costs can be monetary or nonmonetary, and barriers can include everything from a lack of awareness that a product or service exists to a perception of a lack of skills needed to participate in a recommended behavior (e.g., composting). What benefits (WIFM) can they imagine from the exchange, and which of these do they value most, ones that we can then amplify? What, for example, is the most compelling perceived benefit of being tested for HIV/AIDS? Is it a longer life because it would lead to earlier treatment? Is it peace of mind? Or is it the ability to assume responsibility for not spreading the disease?

In addition to understanding what influences our target markets to "buy," a customer-centered focus also recognizes the buying decision process and the marketing role at each phase.

Figure 2.4 shows that the process consists of five stages: *need recognition, information search, evaluation of alternatives, purchase decision,* and *postpurchase behavior.* At the need recognition stage, the customer recognizes a problem or a need. (A parent helping his or her child with a term paper, for example, needs more information on the history of Native American tribes.) It may have been triggered by internal or external stimuli, information a marketer would want to know so that marketing programs can involve these factors. During information search, the consumer engages in finding out more about a potential program, service, or behavior. (At this point, the parent and student do a Google search for optional resources.) Of importance for you is how, where, and from whom target markets obtain information. At the alternative evaluation stage, the consumer uses information to

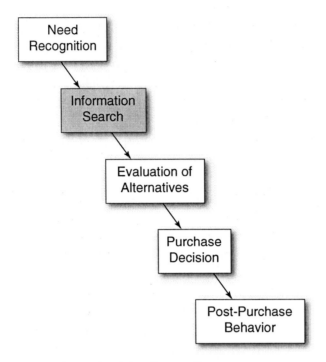

FIGURE 2.4   The Buyer Decision Process[8]

evaluate various options and brands in the choice set. (One of the options that shows up from the Google search is a database from the local public library.) Of most interest here is what options (competitors) are being considered. As implied, the consumer then makes a purchase decision, with the marketer recognizing that an intention (like a fish on the line) may still need to be "reeled in." (The library database is chosen because it emphasizes the age appropriateness of the information, a primary concern for the parent.) And finally, the successful marketer knows that the job does not end when the product is bought, that satisfaction (or dissatisfaction) with the purchase will ultimately impact customer loyalty, positive word-of-mouth, and therefore future sales. (When completed, the parent notes in an optional comment area on the library's Web site that information on one tribe was scarce. They receive an email within twenty-four hours from a librarian directing them to an additional resource.)[9]

Note that although Figure 2.4 implies that consumers pass through all five stages, this happens more when making complex, major decisions than for routine ones. In reality, a person may go straight from need recognition to purchase or may of course never get to the purchase decision.

Principle #2: Segment and Target Markets

Markets are groups of your existing and potential buyers (e.g., mass transit users), and a fundamental premise is that buyers most often differ from each other in one or more ways. They most likely differ in their wants, values, attitudes, resources, geographic location, and even prior experiences with your product or organization. Through market segmentation, organizations divide large, heterogeneous markets into smaller, more homogeneous segments that can be reached more efficiently and effectively with products and services that match their unique needs (e.g., suburban commuters).

Major variables used to segment consumer markets include those that are descriptive, benefit-related, or behavioral in nature. Descriptive factors include *geographics* such as nations, regions, states, counties, cities, neighborhoods, or worksites; *demographic* variables such as age, gender, family size, family life cycle, income, occupation, education, religion, race, and nationality; and *psychographic* factors based on social class, value, lifestyle, or personality characteristics. Benefit segmentation is an effort to distinguish prospects on the basis of different benefits that they might be seeking from a specific purchase. Behavioral segmentation divides a market into groups based on past purchasing or other related behaviors. For example, a campaign to increase HIV/AIDS testing may target women that are already getting an annual pap smear, deciding to work with health care providers to include this test as well.

An additional potential segmentation variable worthy of mention is what is known as the Diffusion of Innovations Theory, the theory that people differ greatly in their readiness to try new products. In a given product area, there are five groups (see Figure 2.5):[10]

- *Innovators* are the most venturesome and adopt new ideas first.
- *Early adopters* are motivated by opinion leaders and adopt new ideas early but carefully.
- *Early majority* are deliberate in their adoption of a new product, acting before the average person.

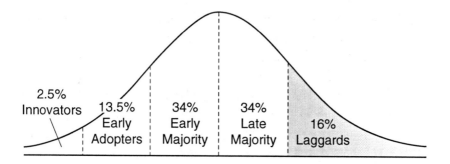

FIGURE 2.5   Segmentation on the basis of relative time of adoption of innovations. Reprinted with the permission of The Free Press, a Division of Simon & Schuster Adult Publishing Group, from *Diffusion of Innovations, Fifth Edition*, by Everett M. Rogers. Copyright © 1995, 2003 by Everett M. Rogers. Copyright © 1962, 1971, 1983 by The Free Press. All rights reserved.

- *Late majority* are skeptical and adopt a new product only after a majority of people have tried it.

- *Laggards* are suspicious of changes and adopt them only when they have become something of a tradition or cultural norm.

In reality, most market segments are described using a variety of variables in an effort to better define target groups.[11] One of the most promising developments in multivariable segmentation is "geodemographic" segmentation, where business information services link U.S. Census data with lifestyle patterns and purchasing behaviors to better segment their markets down to ZIP codes, neighborhoods, and even city blocks.[12]

Business segmenting includes a different set of variables to create homogeneous subsegments. Demographic variables of interest include industry type, location, and company size. Other factors include operating variables (e.g., whether the firm uses advanced technology), purchasing approaches (e.g., centralized or decentralized purchasing), situational factors (e.g., whether the business needs quick and sudden delivery or service) and personal characteristics (e.g., whether the company shows high or low loyalty to suppliers).

After segmenting the market, the organization evaluates and selects segments. Kotler and Armstrong describe major options:[13]

- *Undifferentiated*, a strategy in which a firm decides to ignore market segment differences and go after the whole market with one offer. This might also be considered a mass marketing strategy, one that Henry Ford epitomized when he offered the Model-T Ford in one color, black, or that the Postal Service did in its first century.

- *Differentiated*, where an organization decides to target several market segments and design separate specific offers to uniquely appeal to each one. Tobacco control programs have very different strategies for prevention than for cessation, for example, and for teens versus pregnant women versus seniors wanting to quit.

- *Concentrated* marketing goes after a large share of one or a few submarkets. Public health programs focused on HIV and AIDS, for example, allocate significant resources on very defined segments, such as gay men and African American populations.

In reality, most governmental agencies serve broad markets. Of importance and recommendation here is that you know when the market you serve is differentiated and therefore needs different approaches (e.g., business versus consumer needs for postal services.)

Principle #3: Identify the Competition

The trick in identifying an organization's competition is to avoid what Harvard Professor Theodore Levitt calls "Marketing Myopia." In a seminal article in *The Harvard Business Review* in 1960, he claimed that the railroad industry caused its own decline by insisting, "We're in the railroad business." Had they instead defined the business they were in as the transportation business, they would have seen the competition coming—automobiles, trucks, and airplanes. If they had looked to the customer benefit sought, they would have seen that the market need that the railroads were serving was transportation, not railroading.

At the narrowest level, you can define your competitors as organizations offering similar products and services to the same customers, often at similar prices. These are considered direct competitors. A wider definition would include indirect competitors—those organizations or activities that customers and potential customers use to fulfill the same need. As illustrated in Table 2.1 governmental agencies often have tough competitors.

TABLE 2.1   Examples of Competitors for Public Agency Programs

Agency	Program	Direct Competition	Indirect Competition
Library	Summer Reading Program	Bookstores	Videogames
School Districts	Public Schools	Private Schools	Home schooling
Utilities	Natural Yard Care	Weed & Feed	Neglect/Do Nothing

After defining them, you then find out all you can about these competitors. You must constantly compare your products, prices, channels, and promotion with those of strong competitors, paying close attention to what customers see as the strengths and weaknesses of their offerings. This then becomes a platform for developing marketing strategies, including developing a competitive positioning.

John Zagula and Richard Tong, former leaders at Microsoft, offer "Five Battle-Tested Plays for Capturing and Keeping the Lead in Any Market" in their book *The Marketing Playbook*, providing a straightforward, practical perspective on competitive strategies:[14]

- **The Drag Race Play**—The simplest of the plays, it involves direct competition with one competitor and focuses on "outrunning" them (e.g., Microsoft vs. WordPerfect, and the U.S. Postal System vs. FedEx).

- **The Platform Play**—In this play, you get others to stand with you, defending against common competitors (e.g., Amazon.com's symbiotic relationships with big retailers, and a public utility working with other vendors to offer different types of energy: electrical, coal, gas, wind).

- **The Stealth Play**—Where you "survive by avoiding direct confrontation" (e.g., Enterprise Rent-A-Car deciding not to compete with the travel-related business but rather focusing on capturing and dominating the insurance temporary replacement market, and state troopers distributing alcohol test strips for patrons at local bars on New Year's Eve).

- **The Best of Both Play**—In this more complicated play, you "run up the middle between opposing alternatives" (e.g., Lexus capturing the "Japanese" as well as "luxury" car seekers, and a program in South Africa called "Toot-n-Scoot" where customers who have drunk too much to drive safely are driven home in their car by someone who arrives at the restaurant or bar on a collapsible scooter that fits in the trunk of the drinker's car).

- **The High-Low Play**—Offers the market a high-end as well as mass market option (e.g., Sheraton's premium-priced Hotels and Resorts and Sheraton's mass market offer: Four Points and a public hospital offering single, double, and dormitory rooms).

Principle #4: Utilize All 4Ps Available in the Marketing Mix: Product, Price, Place, Promotion

Detailed descriptions and theories regarding each of the 4Ps of marketing will be presented in Chapters 3 through 7. The principle introduced now is that marketing is more than what most people think when they hear or use the term. When asked what they think of when they think of marketing, most people will mention phrases such as selling, advertising, direct mail, telemarketing, busboards, and outdoor billboards. In truth, these are only a few of the components of only one of the marketing tools to be considered: promotion. In ideal marketing planning scenarios, decisions regarding promotion are not even considered until decisions for each of the other 3Ps have been made, decisions that create the offer to be promoted (product, price, and place).

To develop a common language and understanding of these four tools used to pursue marketing objectives, the following section presents a brief description of each, with examples for public sector agencies.

Product

An organization's products may or may not be tangible objects because a product is frequently defined as anything that can be offered to a market to satisfy a want or need, which can include *physical goods* (food waste composters offered by a utility), *programs* (small business workshops), *services* (public transportation), *experience* (tours of the White House), *events* (Earth Day), *people* (city councils), *places* (parks), *organizations* (public schools), *information* (library Web sites), and *ideas* (water conservation).[15]

In developing product plans, major variables for you to consider are those related to *quality, design, features, options, size, name,* and *packaging.* For example, a public library will make the obvious product decisions regarding choices of books, reference materials, and periodicals. Offerings at many libraries, however, have expanded enormously to now include options to check out audio books, music CDs, videos, and DVDs, select books in large type, take advantage online databases and ebooks, and attend special lectures, community forums, and even film screenings. You will even find in some libraries espresso stands and teen cafes. You should also consider as part of the library's product strategy additional components that affect customer satisfaction and appeal such as the number and location of personnel for assistance, the look and feel of library cards, and atmospherics such as building layouts, lighting, colors, chair comfort, and artwork.

Price

Most likely you think of price as just the amount of money paid for a product or service. In reality, it also includes other values that consumers "give up" in the exchange process. Given this, the real price a customer pays also includes nonmonetary costs such as their time, effort, psychological risks (e.g., taking car keys from a friend who has been drinking), or any physical discomforts that may be experienced (e.g., wearing a seatbelt).[16]

Continuing our example of libraries, monetary pricing decisions will include prices for checking out books, materials, and other resources (free in most cases), any fines and payment schedules for late returns, and costs for workshops, programs, or special training. To meet agency goals in terms of visits to libraries, checking out materials, participation in programs, and customer satisfaction levels, the marketer will also consider strategies (often through the use of product and place variables) to reduce costs (e.g., ways to reduce time to check out a book or effort to find a parking spot).

Organizations know that the prices they set will affect the demand for their product. For-profit organizations try to set prices that will maximize their profits. Public agencies have quite a different set of goals, ranging from pure subsidy to partial or full cost recovery to creating some surplus over costs. You will read more about these differing pricing objectives in a later chapter.

Place

Place strategies include important decisions regarding where, when, and how customers will access the offer, most often referred to as the distribution channel. Convenience of access is often one of the most important considerations for customers when deciding among competitive alternatives, both direct and indirect. Perceptions of convenience will be determined by a variety of variables such as physical locations, days of the week and hours open for business, purchasing options (e.g., online), and delivery options (e.g., overnight).

For libraries, place considerations are numerous, from physical locations, parking, hours, days of the week open, and placement of after-hour return boxes to whether materials can be reserved online and maybe even mailed to your home. And thinking even more progressively, what about installing drive-through windows where customers can return and pick up materials from their cars? After all, banks, coffee stands, fast food restaurants, cleaners, and pharmacies have come to depend on them to compete and create satisfied customers.

Promotion

Promotions are often described as persuasive communications (versus information or education-oriented ones), and an organization's communication strategy includes a custom blend of advertising, personal selling, sales promotion, public relations, and direct marketing (e.g., direct mail, email, and telemarketing). The communicator's real job is to ensure that the target audience members know about the offer, believe they will experience the stated benefits, and are inspired to act.[17]

Promotional activities for libraries include elements from each of these categories. Consider a summer reading program targeting elementary students in a county. Promotional vehicles might include advertising (billboards), personal selling (school librarians mentioning the program to students), sales promotion (banners to attract the attention of parents dropping off and picking up children from school), public relations (stories and calendar listings in local newspapers), and direct marketing (postcards to households in targeted ZIP codes).

A Final Word: The 4Ps versus The 4Cs

It should be acknowledged that these four Ps represent the sellers' view and language for the marketing tools used to influence and facilitate exchange.[18] The buyer has a different perspective, as suggested by Robert Lauterborn:[19]

Four Ps	Four Cs
Product	Customer solution
Price	Customer cost
Place	Convenience
Promotion	Communication

Principle #5: Monitor Efforts and Make Adjustments

In Chapter 1, "Improving Public Sector Performance by Seizing Opportunities to Meet Citizen Needs," we raised many challenges (even demands) faced by governmental agencies to increase efficiencies and effectiveness to improve performance. The marketing functions and activities within public sector agencies are no exception to this responsibility, which leads us to ensuring that systems are in place for evaluating marketing efforts and making any implicated adjustments. It is a control process, designed to maximize the probability that the organization will achieve its established short-run and long-run marketing objectives, as illustrated clearly by Andreasen and Kotler in Figure 2.6.

As suggested, critical components of the system begin with a clear understanding of objectives and goals. Then you acquire tools to measure outcomes; after measuring the outcomes, you conduct rigorous analysis of these outcomes and identify explicit steps for needed course corrections. Then the cycle repeats itself.

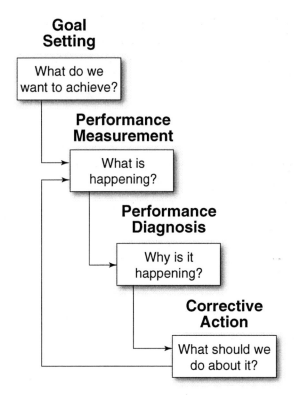

FIGURE 2.6 The Control Process[20]

Numerous tools are available for use in this process, which will be discussed in detail in Chapter 12, "Monitoring and Evaluating Performance." Referring back to our library example to illustrate a few, this systems approach might include monitoring total circulation and then stimulating book usage through newspaper articles or subscription email alerts for new arrivals when desired volume levels are not met. Or it could involve analyzing the circulation of each of the library's major departments during different parts of the day or week to determine where additional efforts are needed to support established objectives. At a more complex level, it could attempt to look not just at circulation but at who was taking out books and develop strategies to bring the number of teenagers utilizing services to established goal levels. It could also include mechanisms to solicit customer comments, measure levels of customer satisfaction, and determine critical areas for improvement that would make goal attainment more likely.[21]

Moving from Here

The American Marketing Association defines marketing as "an organizational function and a set of processes for creating, communicating and delivering value to customers and for managing customer relationships in ways that benefit the organization and its stakeholders."[22] This chapter has made the case that marketing can and has contributed to governmental agency goals, objectives, and missions and that five fundamental principles are key to successful efforts, ones that have guided commercial marketers for decades. In the next eight chapters, we explore the application of these principles to assisting public agencies in eight performance arenas:

Chapter 3	Developing and Enhancing Popular Programs and Services
Chapter 4	Setting Motivating Prices, Incentives, and Disincentives
Chapter 5	Optimizing Distribution Channels
Chapter 6	Creating and Maintaining a Desired Brand Identity
Chapter 7	Communicating Effectively with Key Publics
Chapter 8	Improving Customer Service and Satisfaction
Chapter 9	Influencing Positive Public Behavior: Social Marketing
Chapter 10	Forming Strategic Partnerships

PART II

APPLYING MARKETING TOOLS TO THE PUBLIC SECTOR

3

DEVELOPING AND ENHANCING POPULAR PROGRAMS AND SERVICES

"As you may be aware we received great news from the government after I dropped our petition in to 10 Downing Street. They have now promised to spend £280 million to improve school dinners across the country. This is a huge victory for all dinner ladies, parents and most importantly for the kids to whom it matters the most. This outcome is entirely the result of your sheer commitment to support this campaign, sign the petition and to encourage a fellow 270,000 to sign as well so ... CONGRATULATIONS AND BIG LOVE TO YOU ALL!! ... Jamie O xx"

Jamie Oliver, a celebrity chef in the U.K.
Posted April 13, 2005 on www.feedmebetter.com

One of the most important marketing functions in the commercial sector is that of product management. It is just as important in the public sector, especially for those of you who are program managers. Some say product management first appeared at Procter & Gamble in 1929, when one of the company's soaps, Camay, was not doing well, and a young executive was assigned to give his exclusive attention to this product alone.[1] It worked, and the company as well as other consumer product industries created the role of the product manager, who was responsible for developing competitive strategies for the product, preparing annual marketing plans, working with advertising agencies, supporting the product among the sales force and distributors, gathering continuous intelligence on the product's performance and customer satisfaction, and signaling any opportunity for new product development or needed improvements to existing ones.[2]

In this chapter, you explore basic definitions and components of an agency's product and then focus on product management functions most relevant in the public sector, those of *developing and enhancing programs and services.*

You begin with an inspirational story, selected this time to illustrate the need for and impact of product improvement, depicting how governmental agencies can sometimes be nudged to make these changes and how smart it can be for you to pay attention and respond to these wake-up calls. You also consider the power of one, in the citizenry as well as in the government, to create social change.

Opening Story: School Meal Revolution in the United Kingdom

The International Obesity Taskforce estimates that one in ten school-age children, a total of 155 million worldwide, are overweight and that 30 to 45 million of these students are classified as obese.[3] Significant economic as well as social costs are associated with this epidemic. In the U.K., for example, it is estimated that obesity and diet-related illnesses in the total population are costing the National Health Service more than $12.7 billion annually.[4] To underscore the problem in this country further, recent surveys show that nearly one in five British children is obese and 40 percent of teenage girls are iron-deficient.[5]

Where do governmental agencies begin to tackle this one? And what does marketing have to contribute? The following story from the U.K. suggests that a marketing mindset, especially one with attention on program improvement, can contribute a lot.

Challenges

In March and April of 2005, newspaper headlines wrapped the globe; the world was intrigued with what had happened at 10 Downing Street on March 30th.

"Jamie gives school meals the wooden spoon"[6]
The Sydney Morning Herald, March 24, 2005

"TV chef transforms U.K. school meals"
United Press International, March 22, 2005

"Chef's Naked Truth on School Food"
The Australian, March 22, 2005

"Chef whips U.K. school cafeterias into shape"
The New York Times, April 25, 2005

The "warrior" drawing worldwide attention was a 29-year-old celebrity chef in London with a television program, a best-selling cookbook, a charity foundation that supports unemployed youth— and a mission. He wanted to replace the fatty, salty, greasy, processed, sugary food served in dining halls in Britain's schools (food he called rubbish) with freshly cooked, nutritious meals, ones loaded with natural ingredients, fruits, and (hidden) vegetables. His project, Feed Me Better, captured the attention of a country apparently growing fatter and unhealthier because of its poor diet and sedentary ways and a government wanting to do something about it.[7]

His quest for change and crusade for new rules began with visits he made to schools on behalf of his charity where he discovered, as described by *The New York Times*, "lunches virtually inedible, made up of dishes like gristly sausage rolls and frozen shapes calling themselves fish, chicken and pork. Baked beans and French fries were ubiquitous; vegetables were virtually extinct."[8] He was quoted as asking, "Who's in charge of this?"

Strategies

Over the next year, Jamie Oliver acted more like a marketer than a chef, one with concrete *goals* (changing the rules and increasing resources), a clear sense of the *target audience* (the school children themselves), his *key influencers* (the dining hall staff called Dinner Ladies), and his best potential *partners* (teachers and parents). He had a keen understanding of the *barriers* he would need to overcome (the good taste of bad food and the systems in place to produce it) and *benefits* he would need to amplify (health and better school performance). He developed and implemented an *integrated promotional strategy* utilizing most media vehicles and types, including mass media, printed materials, special events, an award-winning Web site, and a compelling direct response campaign to gather petition signatures.

He even started with a pilot project, persuading one school district in London to give him a chance to demonstrate that school menus could be healthier without costing more. A *New York Times* article posted on the *International Herald Tribune Online* described a few surprises for the pilot: "The cooks, used to dealing mainly with frozen nuggets, balked at the extra work involved in preparing things like seven-vegetable pasta sauce from scratch." One little boy, tasting what he said was his first-ever vegetable, threw up on the table.[9]

Oliver then did what any good marketer would do and resorted to desperate tactics designed to persuade target audiences, including dressing up like a giant corn-on-the-cob, singing a pro-vegetable song, giving out "I've tried something new" stickers, even "tossing a chicken carcass into a blender along with bits of skin, fat and bread crumbs, whizzing it around, and showing off the result: stomach-turning mush that, when shaped and cooked, could pass for the nuggets they had been eating."[10] In the end, he won the loyalty of the children, the praise of the teachers and parents, and the attention of millions of viewers of his four-part television series who were watching, including one Prime Minister Tony Blair.

Those viewers who were inspired to find out more or do something for their own school could visit the Feed Me Better Web site where they were provided an arsenal of options to start a revolution of their own: information on how school meal contracts work, status of schools in their district regarding efforts to improve meal nutrition, details on how the pilot school district was able to change things, factoids about school meals, access to recipes that had been featured on the television series and at the pilot school district, and a Feed Me Better starter pack providing ideas on getting school involvement with classroom learning activities. Visitors were encouraged to lobby their elected officials to increase the minimum amount of money spent per child per day, clarify current nutritional standards for school dinners to create more effective inspections and to raise standards, make nutritional health a part of the national curriculum for all primary schools in England and Wales, and ensure that the needs of big business are not put before those of the health of the children (see Figure 3.1). For six weeks in early 2005, visitors were encouraged to sign a petition to be delivered to 10 Downing Street.

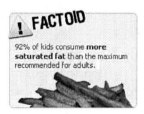

FIGURE 3.1   A factoid appearing on the Feed Me Better Web site

Rewards

Outcomes from the pilot were encouraging, with teachers telling Oliver that their students were more alert and able to concentrate better and that behavior improved markedly among those who had opted for the healthier new dishes.[11] Parents reported their children were having fewer asthma attacks.[12] A promise came from the Greenwich Council (the pilot school district) to replace fast food with fresh food menus for 20,000 students and from the caterer that they would be taking Turkey Twizzlers off the menu,[13] an item that rocked viewers of the television series when they found out it contained one-third meat and water, pork fat, rusk (re-baked sliced white bread), colorings, and flavorings.[14]

On the morning of March 30th, 2005, Jamie Oliver met with Tony Blair and presented a petition with more than 271,000 signatures, ten times more than the 20,000 he thought he would get when he started out six weeks earlier (see Figure 3.2). Considered a wake-up call and mandate for reform, soon afterward Blair announced that he had set aside more than £280 million, about $536 million, to improve school meals.[15]

This national commitment received considerable press and praise, including the following quote in the *British Medical Journal:* "Jamie

FIGURE 3.2   Chef Jamie Oliver delivers a message for school cafeteria reform from 271,000 UK citizens to 10 Downing Street. (Photo © Tom Hostler 2005)

Oliver has done more for the public health of our children than a corduroy army of health promotion workers or a £100 million Saatchi & Saatchi campaign."[16]

Perhaps the most public display of respect for Oliver's work came from a reader of *The Daily Telegraph* who wrote in about the effort asking, "Could Jamie Oliver have a word with the airlines?"[17]

Product: The First "P"

Product, as a term in the public sector is not familiar to many who are more likely to associate the label with tangible goods in the private sector, ones such as soap and tires. In marketing theory, however, this term is broadly interpreted and refers to anything that can be offered to a market by an organization or individual to satisfy a want or need. It does, of course, include physical goods and services, but it also refers to an array of additional organizational offerings being "sold," including events, people, places, the organization itself, information, and ideas. Parallels between the private and public sector are drawn in Table 3.1.

TABLE 3.1   Examples of Product Types in the Private and Public Sectors

Product Type	Private Sector	Public Sector
Physical Goods	Plasma Television	Passports
Services	Hair Salon	HIV/AIDS testing at a Community Health Clinic
Events	Baseball Game	Fourth of July Parade
People	Lance Armstrong	Secretary of State
Places	Tuscany	Yellowstone National Park
Organizations	Microsoft	Census Bureau
Information	CNN	Identity Theft Protection
Ideas	Retirement Savings	Exercise

In addition to product types, a few traditional terms are also worthy of distinction:

- *Product Quality* refers to the performance of the product (e.g., accuracy of an HIV/AIDS test).

- *Product Features* refers to a variety of product components. The number of days (or hours) it takes for an HIV/AIDS test result is a product feature, with rapid testing considered by many a welcomed new option. At a national park, features would include items such as electrical hookups for recreational vehicles, nature hiking trails with plant labels, boat launches, and information kiosks.

- *Product Style and Design* are important product components as well, with style relating more to tangibles (e.g., the aesthetics of an airport's retail store corridor) and design referring more to functionality and ease of use of the product (e.g., the location and traffic patterns of retail shops relative to departure gates).

- *Product Line* refers to a group of closely related products that are offered by an organization, ones that perform similar functions but are different in terms of features, style, or some other variable.[18] A water utility, for example, may offer or promote a variety of water-saving devices including low-flow toilets, low-pressure showerheads, rain barrels, cisterns, and soaker hoses.

- *Product Mix* consists of all the distinct product items that an organization offers, often reflecting a variety of product types, ideally selected to support the agency's mission and strategic objectives. For example, Silicon Valley Power, a city-owned electric utility, has a strategic platform developed in cooperation with the City of Santa Clara Government and City Council that not only includes electrical power generation and improvements in transmission and distribution but also embraces careful monitoring of energy use "so that no resources are wasted."[19] Their product mix appears aligned with this platform and is designed to provide a host of products that will assist as well as motivate both residential and commercial customers to conserve energy (see Table 3.2 and Figure 3.3).[20]

TABLE 3.2   Product Mix for Silicon Valley Power, City of Santa Clara

Product Type	Silicon Valley Power Product Examples
Physical Goods	Energy-saving products featured in a "Plug-ins Catalog" including items such as energy-efficient light bulbs, compact fluorescent floor lamps, lamp timers, electricity monitors, low-voltage thermostats, refrigerator thermometers, and exterior wall lanterns
Programs	Neighborhood solar programs, promoting the installation of solar electric systems
Services	Online meter monitoring for commercial customers, which includes analysis of real-time energy use
Events	Community group meetings for customer input and feedback
People	Meter readers and customer service representatives
Places	Online services and a new power-generating facility
Organizations	Silicon Valley Power, a city-owned electric utility
Information	A Consumer Guide to Home Energy Savings
Ideas	Electrical conservation

Developing an array of products such as those offered by this utility has advantages and implications for many organizations in the public sector, if not all. Perhaps most important is the reality that customers of any given agency have a variety of wants and needs, and most would consider it unlikely that they could be met satisfactorily with a single offering, or even a single type of offering. In their book *Reinventing Government,* Osborne and Gaebler describe the implications and likely future for product mix decisions in the public sector:

FIGURE 3.3   Cover of product catalog

"A time will come when people won't believe that the poor in America once had to visit 18 different offices to get all the benefits to which they were entitled. And a time will come when people won't believe that parents in America once could not choose the public schools their children attended. By the evidence piling up across this land, that time will come sooner than most of us think. In a world in which cable television systems have 50 channels, banks let their customers do business by phone...one-size-fits all government cannot last."[21]

Product Levels

Traditional marketing theory identifies three levels of a product, a model acknowledging that from the customers' perspective, a product is more than its features, style, and design. It must include the bundle of benefits that customers expect to experience when they buy and use the product. This platform is helpful in conceptualizing and designing the product strategy because it stimulates discussions and leads to decisions that create the foundation for the offer.

The *core product* is seen as the center of the total product. It consists of the major needs that will be fulfilled, wants that will be realized, and problems that will be solved by consuming this product. It is the real reason the customer is buying the product and is determined by the customer's answers to such questions as, "What's in it for me to buy this product?" You'll want to keep in mind that people don't buy drill bits. They buy quarter-inch holes. They don't buy cosmetics. They buy hope. They don't buy a room they can rent while away from home. They buy a good night's sleep. And they don't buy stamps. They buy delivery of a card to Mom in time for Mother's Day.[22]

The *actual product* is more obvious and includes aspects such as product quality, features, packaging, style, and design. It also includes any brand name used. Ideally, as always, each of these decisions is made based on customer needs and preferences, taking into consideration alternative (competing) products.

For illustration, consider the features of a service called E-ZPass, an electronic toll collection service operating in several states on the East Coast of the United States. When a prepaid account is established, customers receive a small tag containing an electronic chip that they attach to the windshield inside their car. Each time a customer accesses a toll facility where E-ZPass is offered, that customer can use an E-ZPass lane. An antenna at the plaza reads the vehicle and account information, and the appropriate toll is then electronically debited from the prepaid account, eliminating the need to slow down to find and deposit cash, tickets, or tokens. A record of transactions is included in a periodic statement.[23] This innovation has helped to improve traffic flow and reduce the needless burning of fuel in cars that are waiting to pay a toll.

The *augmented product* includes additional features and services that add value to the transaction beyond customer expectations. Most consider this product level an optional one, with some even labeling it as the "bells and whistles" category. You don't have to have it. In many cases, however, it can be the key differentiator from the competition (e.g., a community college that offers special tutoring for those for whom English is a second language). For campaigns related to public behavior change (social marketing), it may be exactly what is needed to provide encouragement (e.g., a walking buddy match for a college campus physical activity campaign), remove barriers (e.g., a map of jogging trails), or sustain behaviors (e.g., a daily journal for recording physical activity).

Table 3.3 provides a variety of examples illustrating these product levels in the public sector.

TABLE 3.3 Product Levels with Public Sector Examples

Agency or Organization	Core Product (Benefit)	Actual Product	Augmented Product
Transit System	Transportation	Buses	Bike racks on buses
Community College	Education	Classes	Special tutoring for those for whom English is a second language
Emergency Preparedness	Safety	Activities to prepare homes for earthquakes	Distribution of special wrenches to be kept by gas shut-off valves
Water Utility	A chance to take advantage of a natural resource	3000-gallon cistern, in either green or black	A stiff brush for cleaning out the cistern, reducing potential hatching of mosquito larvae
City Police Department	Theft prevention and recovery of stolen property	Responding to notice of a car theft	Providing discount coupons for vehicle steering wheel locks

As a way to summarize the three product levels, note all the possible options available in developing an HIV/AIDS testing product platform.

At the *core* product level, potential benefits of testing to highlight for target audiences include increased peace of mind that comes from knowing one's HIV status, positive or negative; an opportunity to be responsible for personal actions by avoiding spreading the disease to others; if pregnant, getting early treatment for an unborn child; and potential for a longer life and a higher quality of life, as early medical treatment may contribute to both. There are also several options for *actual* products, the tests themselves: blood tests, oral tests, urine tests, rapid tests, home test kits, and tests "packaged" as part of an annual checkup. And finally, potential *augmented* products (which as mentioned earlier may increase the likelihood that someone gets tested) would include services such as counseling, support groups, referrals to medical treatment for HIV, and recommendations for protecting oneself in the future.

Decisions among options at each of these product levels are based on the unique profiles of target audiences—their demographics, geographics, current behaviors, barriers, and motivators. Assume, for example, that the target audience for an HIV/AIDS testing campaign is pregnant women who may be at risk for HIV/AIDS. A product strategy for this market might be designed as illustrated in Figure 3.4.

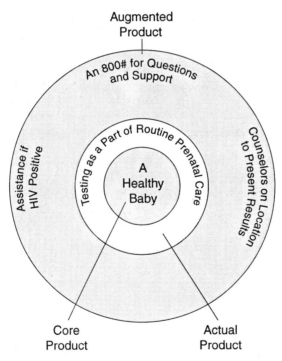

FIGURE 3.4   Product platform for an HIV/AIDS testing campaign

Product Development

A systematic approach should guide the development and launch of new programs and services in the public sector. The challenge is to remain cognizant of important steps without becoming bogged down by them and to allocate sufficient, but not excessive, resources to the process.

Kotler and Armstrong suggest eight major stages in new product development, illustrated in Figure 3.5 and described in the following section.[24]

1. *Idea Generation*. Ideas for new products can come from a variety of sources including employees, special interest groups, elected officials, internal committees assigned to new product development, other governmental agencies, and of course, current and potential customers (e.g., the petition for new menus and ingredients in school meals delivered to Tony Blair, signed by 271,000+ citizens). They can be generated in a variety of ways, including brainstorming sessions, suggestion boxes, and annual awards for new ideas. It is also worthy of attention for you to note that in the private sector, important sources for new product ideas include the company's distributors and suppliers as they have that critical frontline perspective of the marketplace. This applies to the public sector as well (e.g., ideas that contract firms have for shortening lines at airport security). Many organizations maintain a competitive watch, allowing them to take advantage of insights that others may have on customer needs and to be prepared for new competitive offerings. When searching for ideas, Osborne and Gaebler would probably advocate that we take an anticipatory

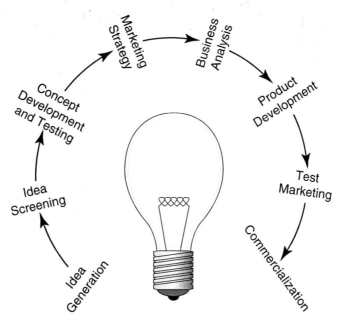

FIGURE 3.5   Major stages in new-product development[25]

approach, searching as much (if not more) for programs and services that are preventive in nature (e.g., ways to prevent wildfires) as we do for ones that are curative in nature (e.g., new firefighting equipment).[26]

2. *Idea Screening*. As ideas are presented or discovered, your task now, as Kenny Rogers sings, "is knowin' what to throw away and knowing what to keep."[27] Criteria for evaluating ideas are varied but must include references to the agency's mission, goals, and resources as well as the unfulfilled wants and needs of customers, zeroing in on those ideas that best meet both requirements.

A state's taskforce on litter prevention, for example, may be considering numerous potential efforts to reduce and prevent littering: new litter bags with Ziploc tops to address customer concerns with spillage from drink containers; drive-up deposits for litter at truckers' weigh stations, eliminating the need for special stops; distribution of smokeless car ashtrays for cigarette butts; or working with a contractor to develop new and improved cables to help secure pickup loads. In the screening process, the idea of new litter depositories for truckers might emerge as the best idea to take to the next level as it addresses a customer need, a major litter problem on roadways, and because it is within the purview of the agencies on the taskforce to make happen.

3. *Concept Development and Testing*. At this stage, you will create a detailed description of the idea, envisioning potentials for each of the three levels of the product platform: options for potential customer benefits, features and design elements for the actual product, and ideas "for extras" comprising the augmented product. Concepts are then tested with the target audience, first to see whether the concept is of interest and then to explore reactions to initial ideas and suggestions for increased appeal.

For a city water utility planning to subsidize and sell rain barrels to interested residential customers, for example, focus groups might be conducted to determine whether the major perceived benefit of the barrels is "a chance to make use of a natural resource" or whether it is more appealing as "a way to save on water bills" and whether a recycled Greek olive barrel is more or less appealing than a new plastic barrel.

4. *Marketing Strategy*. You now develop an initial marketing strategy that describes preliminary thoughts regarding target markets, planned product positioning, and additional marketing mix elements (pricing, distribution, and promotion). It will also project potential market sales, which in the case of public sector agencies refers more to anticipated utilization rates or participation levels.

A marketing plan for a new online service developed in 2003 in Washington State designed to divert unwanted building materials and large household items from landfills highlights steps in this process. The service was developed by the state's Department of Ecology, and a preliminary marketing strategy was outlined by a planning group that included representatives from participating counties around the state. Primary target markets for posting and purchasing building materials were identified as construction and demolition contractors, and for large household items, people having garage sales were among those targeted. The service was positioned as an inexpensive and easy way to dispose of materials and large household items that were perhaps headed for the dump but really "too good to toss" (see Figure 3.6). All items posted were to be priced under $99, and media channels were anticipated to include, among other things, mailings to registered contractors, posters, newsletters, and utility bill inserts.

5. *Business Analysis*. Evaluating the business attractiveness of the proposal is your next task, focusing on calculating total anticipated costs for the program and weighing these against any monetary and nonmonetary benefits to the organization.

A new youth tobacco Quitline, for example, might have made it to this stage in the development process because a state Department of Health could have seen it as meeting both a market need (teens who are smoking and want to quit) and an organizational goal (reduction in youth tobacco use). Experience with an adult Quitline may have helped planners to develop a preliminary marketing strategy. A cost-benefit analysis, however, might cause rethinking as the costs

FIGURE 3.6   Logo used for Washington State's online materials exchange program[28]

for new protocols, extended hours preferred by the teen population, special staff training, and a separate toll-free number are actually determined. When weighed against the actual number of youth anticipated to call, the projected cost per "quit" might be seen as too costly. An alternative idea to develop a youth-dedicated Web site with links to counselors, an idea that was perhaps tabled in the screening stage, might be reexamined, especially after factoring in a finding that more teens were likely to visit a Web site than to call a phone center.

6. *Product Development*. To this point, your new product idea has existed only in words, perhaps illustrated with a few graphics. After passing the business analysis, steps are taken to develop a prototype of the service or physical object, sometimes with more than one version. Prototypes are then tested for functionality, thereby ensuring quality performance.

The water utility mentioned earlier that was developing a program to distribute rain barrels might order and assemble several manufacturer options and select special parts for hookup and mosquito protection. It wouldn't be unusual then for a program manager or someone on staff at the utility to try out the options in their own backyard and report back on which ones worked best and any flaws or cumbersome features that need to be resolved.

7. *Test Marketing*. This step, thought of by some as a pilot, takes the new product to a more realistic market setting. This gives the marketer a chance to test and then refine the target market, the offer (product, price, and place), and promotional strategies. In addition to improving chances for success (market adoption) when the product is launched on a broader scale, this effort may also help reduce costs of rollouts by pointing to strategies that might be eliminated or improved going forward.

This approach might be used for a campaign to promote smoke-free homes and cars where children are present, utilizing a packet of materials sent home from school to parents. In the packet might be several items including a refrigerator magnet, pledge card for a smoke-free home, and air freshener for a car with statistics regarding the effect of secondhand smoke on children in cars, with a reminder message to smoke outside. Of interest at the end of the pilot phase would be whether parents actually put the magnet on the refrigerator, signed and posted the pledge card, and hung the air freshener from the rearview mirror. If evaluation showed, for instance, that very few used the air freshener, or that the air freshener was interpreted by some to mean it was okay to smoke in the car, this budget item could be eliminated upon campaign rollout.

8. *Commercialization*. The organization now decides whether to launch the new program into the market and if so, when and where.

In the public sector, the AMBER Alert System is a relevant example. The program first started in Dallas-Fort Worth, Texas in 1996 when broadcasters in the area teamed with local police to develop an early warning system to help find abducted children, a legacy they created for a 9-year old girl, Amber Hagerman of Arlington, Texas, who was abducted while riding her bicycle and later found murdered. AMBER (America's Missing: Broadcast Emergency Response) Alerts are emergency messages broadcast when a law enforcement agency determines a child has been abducted and is in imminent danger. The broadcast provides information on the physical description of the child and anything known about the abductor's appearance and vehicle. Nine years later, in February 2005, the Department of Justice announced that Hawaii became the 50th state to complete its statewide AMBER Alert plan (see Figure 3.7).[29]

FIGURE 3.7   The AMBER Alert program that started in one state is now in all 50.[30]

Product Life Cycles

When launched, you hope your product will then enjoy a "long and happy life." Unfortunately, this is rarely the outcome. In fact, as with new parents, the work has just begun. To deal with this issue conceptually, marketers often refer to a theoretical model called the Product Life Cycle, illustrated in Figure 3.8, which identifies four distinct stages that the product may go through: Introduction, Growth, Maturity, and Decline. Corporate marketing and brand managers are most interested in the sales and corresponding profits at each stage. In the public sector, *participation and usage levels* are more relevant than sales; *retained earnings* are more applicable than profits. The usefulness to program managers in the public sector is that each phase has its own unique set of characteristics and challenges and therefore implications for strategic actions. Signals that a product is at a particular "stage in life" are described in the following section, as are recommended strategies to employ.[31]

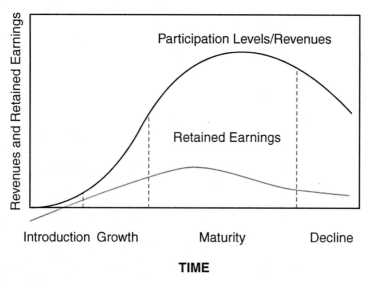

FIGURE 3.8   Product Life Cycle Theory[32]

1. *Introduction*. As might be expected, this first phase is most often a period of slow adoption and participation rates as the product (program or service) is introduced in the market. You and others should not be surprised if costs are high relative to outcomes. In fact, this should be anticipated, and expectations for this should be established ahead of time with key publics, including administrators and funders. At this launching stage, resources need to be focused on informing citizens of the new offering and on getting them to try it, an effort often requiring promotional spending and additional staff time to get the word out (e.g., the promotional efforts necessary to educate people about AMBER Alerts and the appropriate and helpful citizen response).

2. *Growth*. This stage is marked by more rapid market acceptance, thus improving somewhat the rate of return on promotional and staff resource allocations. Ideally, it is an exciting time, as early adopters spread the word and the early majority follows. To support this momentum, turn your focus now to ensuring that the offer meets customer needs and expectations, including product performance (e.g., a new rapid transit system arriving and departing on time) and properly functioning distribution channels (e.g., a Web site for information on transit schedules). For managers, the goal at this stage is to sustain rapid growth by continuing to build brand awareness and loyalty. As noted in Figure 3.8, expenditures of resources are still likely to be high relative to "sales" because upfront development costs are still being "paid for" (e.g., costs for developing the light rail system in the first place).

3. *Maturity*. At some point, the rate of sales growth will slow, and the product will enter a stage of relative maturity, a stage that can and often does provide high profitability when upfront developmental and marketing costs have been returned. Several factors may have contributed to the leveling of sales, including the possibility that the most likely potential customers for the current offer have "already bought it," meaning they are currently using a service (e.g., community transit) or participating in a program (e.g., recycling). You can try several potential modifications to current marketing strategies to sustain product viability: market modification, in an attempt to appeal to new markets for existing products; product modification, an effort to increase usage/sales among current customers and/or to attract new ones; or other marketing mix modifications including changing pricing structures, distribution channels, and/or promotional efforts.[33]

At a city that has a Port Authority managing an airport and a seaport, for example, "sales" are measured and revenues are impacted by the number of passengers arriving and departing at an airport, the number of cargo containers handled at the seaport, the number and value of leases for dock space, and the number of cruise passengers traveling through terminals. At a mature stage, usage and correlating revenues might be sustained, even boosted somewhat, by product modifications (e.g., upgrades to terminals), market modifications (e.g., appealing to recreational boat owners for leasing available dock space), pricing (e.g., requiring vendors at airport terminals to have street pricing, where prices charged must be comparable to those found outside the airport), distribution channels (e.g., availability of online reservations for cargo containers), or promotional strategies (e.g., soliciting the business of international cruise lines or visiting Pacific Rim companies to pursue trade opportunities).

4. Decline. For a program at this stage, sales are on a downward drift. Most options for growth have been explored and tried at the mature product stage. The question that you wrestle with now is whether to withdraw the program from the market or to just scale it down. Decisions will rest on a number of factors, including whether there is continued funding for the program in spite of participation levels (e.g., federal grants for community-based physical activity programs); whether assessments indicate that the decline is temporary due to extraordinary circumstances (e.g., military recruitment during a time of war); or whether the agency, in spite of participation levels, has a mission or mandate to continue to provide the offering (e.g., free immunizations).

You will want to note that this cycle and bell-shaped curve is only conceptual in nature and that some products are introduced and then die quickly, some have only a short growth spurt, others enjoy a long mature stage, and a few thought to be slowly declining are suddenly "brought back to life."

Product Enhancement

Though product enhancement activities are similar to those conducted when developing a new product, it is worthwhile to recognize this as a distinct and important effort, one with a role for marketers, or at least those with a marketing orientation. The role is to sense customer satisfaction levels with current offerings and to help determine what product improvements would increase satisfaction and product performance.

A school reform effort in Philadelphia, one of the nation's largest school districts, provides an inspiring example.

James Nevels, Chair of the Philadelphia School Reform Commission, shared an inspirational story that appeared in *Forbes Magazine* in March 2005. When he started chairing the commission in 2002, he led the district in defining their customers exclusively as the 200,000 children they served, and the challenge was to improve their learning (in marketing terms, the product's performance).

Efforts to improve performance included some that might be expected, such as standardizing curriculums so that all students would learn what had been determined as most crucial for success and would make transferring between schools easier. Elementary school students began spending two hours a day on reading and 90 minutes on math, double what they spent before. Less expected was the initiation of benchmark testing every six weeks in elementary and middle schools and every four weeks in high schools, helping teachers to decide which students needed more dedicated time for a subject and which ones were ready for advanced instruction. They reduced class sizes and added academic coaches.

And there were unexpected, bold strategies as well, ones addressing the learning environment. They adopted one of the toughest codes of conduct in the nation, one that extended to acts committed after school hours and off school grounds: "If a bully beats up a classmate at a bus stop on a Saturday, we will suspend him. In the past he wouldn't even have received a reprimand. A high schooler who damages property or commits an assault will be removed from his neighborhood school and sent to an alternative education high school." In addition, they placed a district police officer in every school and invested millions in metal detectors and video cameras.

The results indeed signaled improved performance. After two years of reform, Nevels reported that between 2003 and 2004 the percentage of the city's public school students scoring "proficient" or better on state exams increased an average of eight percentage points in reading and math for fifth graders and eleven points for eighth graders.[34]

Packaging

As mentioned earlier in the chapter, decisions regarding the *actual product* may include those related to packaging, typically referring to the container or wrapper for the product, its contents, and labeling and printed information. This may include the product's primary container, any secondary package that is thrown away when the product is about to be used, and the shipping package. Traditionally, the primary function of the package was to contain and protect the product. Nowadays, however, it is considered an important marketing tool as well. Consider, for example, the distinctive and elaborate packaging of a condom product in Nepal.

> In collaboration with His Majesty's Government of Nepal Ministry of Health and Department of Health Services (HMG), Population Services International (PSI)/Nepal developed and implemented a campaign promoting the use of the Number One condom, launched in April of 2003. In order not to stigmatize the brand, it was decided that the brand should be established broadly across the youth segment before focusing on the target population—high-risk and vulnerable groups. The packaging colors (fluorescent yellow), hip style, and bold graphics are certainly aligned with this strategic intent (see Figure 3.9). Distribution

FIGURE 3.9   Outer package for PSI condoms distributed in Nepal in cooperation with His Majesty's Government of Nepal

channels for the condoms included traditional outlets such as pharmacies and drugstores and more non-traditional ones such as community health fairs, dance restaurants, and massage parlors. In the first seven months of distribution, 3.51 million Number One condoms were sold.[35]

Summary

You can revisit the basic principles and theories regarding product development and improvement presented in this chapter by taking a walk (in time) around the Louvre, a crown jewel of the French government.

Located in Paris and managed by the French state, the Louvre is one of the largest and most famous museums in the world. As a former residence of the kings of France, it was not even originally intended to become a museum. The museum that now inhabits the Louvre Palace has existed for over two hundred years and was first opened to the public in 1793, consisting primarily of the former royal collections of paintings and sculptures. Its *product types* today are varied and include Asian, Egyptian, Greek, and Roman antiquities; sculptures from the Middle Ages to modern times; furniture and objects of art; and of course, paintings representing all the European schools. The *product line* of paintings alone includes some of the most famous in the world, works of artists like Renoir, Rembrandt, Rubens, and Leonardo da Vinci.

Consider its *product levels*. At the *core*, visitors are most likely seeking and will experience a variety of benefits: those that are emotional in nature (e.g., wonder, pleasure, inspiration) as well as those that are more intellectually gratifying (e.g., a sense of history, an understanding of art and art history). The *actual* products are the exhibits themselves, with some that are permanent collections and some that are only at the museum temporarily. *Augmented* products and services enhance the visitor's experiences, including lectures, concerts, tours, information centers, audio guides, benches for prolonged viewing, and even a shopping arcade and a food court.

History points to significant efforts in terms of *product development:* efforts to conceive and develop new exhibits such as one

featuring the masterpieces from Italy that arrived with great ceremony in 1798.[36] Consider *product enhancements* to address a
mature stage in the museum's life cycle such as the Grand Louvre
Project, which spanned almost twenty years (1981–1999) and
involved enlarging and modernizing the Louvre Museum and the
Decorative Arts Museum.[37]

You can consider the museum itself the *package* since it is in the
truest sense of the word the container for the product. This
could also include the acreage and gardens where the museum
is located in the heart of Paris on the banks of the Seine as well
as the somewhat controversial modern glass pyramid in the central courtyard that has served as its entrance since 1989, which
has proven remarkably effective in accommodating the large
numbers of visitors and providing a welcoming reception; it
even has become a relatively beloved landmark of the city.

4

SETTING MOTIVATING PRICES, INCENTIVES, AND DISINCENTIVES

"When we launched the Click It or Ticket campaign in Washington State, part of me worried we were opening Pandora's box—Pandora's really BIG box! Focus group participants (comprised of people who said they didn't wear their seat belts) told us they hated the Click it or Ticket slogan. They raged at the moderator, 'You do that and I'll call the Governor!' I worried I'd have to defend it in front of legislative hearings. Still, I knew our more positive, coaching messages like 'We love you, buckle up' had run their course. The state's seat belt use rate had hovered near 80% for six years running. With 550 to 600 vehicle occupant deaths yearly, only a very different, more aggressive seat belt campaign would change the behavior of the remaining holdouts."

Jonna VanDyk
Communications Program Manager
Washington Traffic Safety Commission

If you could eavesdrop into conference rooms, elevators, or even a manager's internal dialogue, you might hear the following similar concerns and dilemmas regarding pricing in the public sector:

- What should we charge our utility customers for purchasing these rain barrels to collect runoff water? We know our costs, but will they pay it? If we have many left over, this idea is a goner.
- If we don't get more families moving to our town, the school district is saying they will have to consolidate the elementary school students with the high school students. What in the world will bring families here? We don't even have a movie theater!
- We didn't meet our goals for new military recruits again this month. I thought the increased bonuses would do more for us than this. How high do we have to go?
- We still have less than half of the dogs and cats in this county licensed. Is the $20 fee that unreasonable? Do we really have to resort to increased enforcement? That's going to cost a bundle in overtime.

In the following opening story, of specific interest is the role that marketers play in cases like this where existing fines and laws don't seem to be motivating target audiences. They probably know about these penalties. They just don't believe they will be caught or that they will actually be fined. Marketers are masters at managing perceptions and knowing when that is what is needed.

Opening Story: Click It or Ticket

Sometimes a slogan says it all. Sometimes that can make all the difference.

The National Highway Traffic Safety Administration (NHTSA), under the U.S. Department of Transportation, was established in 1970 and is responsible for reducing deaths, injuries, and economic losses resulting from motor vehicle crashes. *Click It or Ticket* is one of their success stories.

Challenges

Just in the year 2000 alone, the failure of a substantial portion of the driving population to buckle up (around 20 percent across the nation) caused 9,200 unnecessary fatalities and 143,000 serious injuries and cost society $26 billion in easily preventable injury-related costs including medical care and lost productivity.[1]

Reasons for not wearing a safety belt vary, especially by demographics. Hispanics, for example, have lower than average safety belt rates (estimated at 63 percent vs. 80 percent in the general population[2]) with several potential explanations identified by NHTSA. Due to higher poverty rates, Hispanics may tend to drive older vehicles that don't have seat belts or whose seat belts don't work. They often have larger families, with cars that don't have enough seat belts for all the passengers. Those living in rural areas frequently drive pickup trucks, and it is not uncommon for children and other family members to ride in the back of the truck unrestrained. And recent immigrants may not be acquainted with the use of seat belts or child safety seats and might not be familiar with the laws and regulations in the U.S.[3]

Teens are another important targeted demographic group, having the highest fatality rate in motor vehicle crashes, with one key reason being that this age group has lower safety belt use rates than adults.[4] In 2003, 57 percent of 16- to 20-year-old passenger vehicle occupants killed in crashes were not wearing a safety belt.[5] Reasons that teens give for not buckling up are perhaps not surprising: some say it is not cool to be safe; it's fun to be rebellious; it's okay as long as they're in the back seat; it's unlikely they will be in a crash, and even if they were, it wouldn't kill or seriously injure them. They feel invincible.

Agencies working to increase seat belt usage rates also address additional challenges, including opinions of an often quite vocal part of the community who declare that in a free society, each person has the discretion to make his or her own choices, regardless of what others think of the wisdom of those decisions.

Strategies

Click It or Ticket had its beginning in North Carolina, and because of its success in getting citizens to buckle up and stay buckled up, it was hailed as a model for the nation (see Figure 4.1).[6]

FIGURE 4.1   North Carolina's seat belt campaign slogan and logo

The *Click It or Ticket* model supports and encourages states to implement special safety belt checkpoints, assign patrols to special enforcement duties, and adopt a primary seat belt law. A primary law allows law enforcement officers to write a ticket if they simply observe an unbelted driver or passenger. Under a secondary law, an officer cannot ticket anyone for a safety belt violation unless the motorist is stopped for another infraction. Primary laws have been proven effective in increasing safety belt use, with average belt use in states with primary laws at 84 percent in 2004, compared with 73 percent in states without primary laws.[7]

Additional campaign components vary by state but usually include use of the *Click It or Ticket* slogan (see Figure 4.2), promotional efforts such as advertising (often during an established national timeline for activities), signage, earned media (publicity), and partnerships with local agencies, schools, and private sector companies.

FIGURE 4.2   Tennessee's slogan and logo[8]

Rewards

These *Click It or Ticket* efforts helped to increase the national belt use rate to a record high, at 80 percent in 2004. In 2005, the top states were Arizona, California, Hawaii, Michigan, Oregon and Washington, all with rates of 90 percent or higher.[9] Rates are calculated scientifically using trained spotters who count the number of motorists in a given area who are wearing seat belts, using a refined methodology that provides reliable data.[10]

NHTSA estimates that each percentage-point increase in safety belt use represents 2.8 million more people buckling up, approximately 270 more lives saved and 4,000 injuries prevented annually.[11] In 2000, the deaths and serious injuries prevented by safety belts resulted in savings of nearly $50 billion in injury-related costs. And for those who claim this is a personal issue, not a taxpayer's one, this fact should be shared. The general public pays nearly three-quarters of all crash costs, primarily through insurance premiums, taxes, delays, and lost productivity.[12]

NHTSA has conducted evaluations to determine which components of the *Click It or Ticket* model are critical for success. The results of a May 2002 program evaluation, for example, confirmed that intensive short-term *and* well-publicized enforcement can produce large gains. The ten states that implemented full-scale *Click It or Ticket* campaigns increased safety belt use overall by 8.6 percentage points, to 77.1 percent. The states used paid and earned media and statewide law enforcement for four weeks. But in states that increased enforcement without publicizing the effort through paid media, belt use rose an average of only half a percentage point.[13]

And states employing the model are being rewarded. In 2005, the Bush administration endorsed a bill that would give additional highway funding to states that have primary seat belt laws and who have usage rates of 90 percent or higher. If the bill passes, a state like Michigan, for example, could gain an additional $14.3 million.[14]

Price: The Second "P"

Price is one of the key marketing tools that an organization uses to achieve its marketing objectives. It is a powerful one, often the major factor influencing a buyer's decision. In the public sector, as you have just seen with the *Click It or Ticket* story, price isn't just related to fees for products, programs, and services. It is also reflected in monetary disincentives such as tickets and fines and monetary incentives such as discount coupons. An additional strategy you are encouraged to explore that is also described in this chapter is the use of nonmonetary incentives and disincentives. The results have surprised many— and they may surprise you.

Setting Prices for Products, Programs, and Services

Reflecting back on the public utility managers' debate regarding what to charge for the rain barrel, there are ideal sequential steps that you can take to set this price.[15]

The first step is to determine the *objective of the price*. What do you want the price that you set to do for you? Is it to just *recover your direct and possibly indirect costs*? Or are you setting the price to *maximize sales, participation, and/or usage levels*, which may mean you'll need to subsidize the offer? Perhaps instead there is a market segment that you know is eager for the product, program, or service, one that will pay "top dollar," a strategy in the commercial sector called *market skimming*. Or it may be that you want to establish a position of *quality leadership* and by pricing high create the perception that the product, service, or program is a premier one (e.g., some citizens are willing to pay a premium for personalized license plates).

> For the rain barrel scenario, assume that the utility planning to distribute the rain barrels is doing this for the first time. The driver for the effort is not as much to conserve water as it is intended to help avoid runoff into storm drains, causing problems with water quality and fish and wildlife habitats. With some in the utility skeptical of household interest, the management team wants to demonstrate that households in the service area are in fact interested in capturing rainwater from the roof and will be willing to purchase the product and make the effort to install and maintain it. By proving demand for the product, a case can then be made for ongoing distribution by the utility or

support for contractors to sell and distribute the rain barrel. Given this, it is likely that the team will be interested in establishing a price for this first offering that will maximize sales, knowing this may mean selling the barrels at cost or less than cost (subsidizing). Let's assume that the utility had decided that if they could get 2 percent of households to purchase a barrel, or about 3000 barrels, administrators have said they would consider it a success.

After the objective is established, the next step is to *assess market demand*, what you would call citizen interest in the public sector. And you will want to know how this demand varies, if at all, by alternative prices. If a particular product is price sensitive, probable sales will vary depending on the price. When demand varies significantly, it is said to be price sensitive or "elastic." If, on the other hand, demand doesn't vary significantly by price, it is said to be price insensitive or "inelastic."

Returning to the rain barrel project, managers could turn to other cities that had offered rain barrels to their citizens to learn what response rates they experienced and prices they charged. They could also refer to similar efforts, such as a program promoting low-flow toilets. Assume they discussed lessons learned with other cities and that they also participated in an omnibus survey offered by a research firm, a survey that has multiple clients who pay only for the questions and results for those questions that they submit for the survey. Furthermore, let's assume that results of this survey showed that overall, 25 percent of households indicated they were very interested in having a rain barrel and that at $80, 5 percent would be very likely to purchase one from the city, but at $30, 15 percent would be very likely. They would have established that citizen interest seemed strong relative to their goal and that there was apparent price elasticity.

Your next important consideration is the *cost* of the product: direct costs as well as indirect (overhead). Demand estimates help set a ceiling for a price, and the cost could be considered the floor.

Assume direct costs for the rain barrels were estimated by the team to be $35, with an additional $15 per barrel for overhead costs including staff time and estimated promotional expenses. The total cost then is estimated at $50 per barrel.

Before moving on to actually setting a price, now make an effort to *analyze the competition* for the product being offered. In the public sector arena, you will often need to interpret broadly the definition of competition, considering also what citizens are using or doing instead of purchasing or utilizing your services to satisfy a similar want or need. For public transportation, for example, even though there are no other buses to take, you would consider the cost of an automobile, gas, insurance, and parking as costs associated with an alternative competing behavior.

> The competition would be fairly straightforward: the price being charged for other similar rain barrels. A search on the Web and a few calls to local nurseries and home and garden supply stores would assist in this process. Assume that the research revealed prices for a similar barrel ranged from $60 to $80.

You're getting closer now to setting a price. It is useful at this point to reach agreement with colleagues and administrators on the *overall method for price setting*. The cost of the product has set the floor. The consumer's value has set the ceiling, and the competition's pricing has provided a third parameter for consideration, one that could be thought of as the walls in the room.

> Taking into consideration the desire the team has to prove there is citizen interest in harvesting rainwater, it is likely that they will decide to base their final price primarily relative to their costs, estimated at $50 per barrel. They will also take into consideration the going retail price of $60 to $80, with an interest in stimulating demand for the utility's offering.

The decision on pricing method has helped to narrow the range for *selecting the final price*. You will now consider several additional factors. Does the organization want to subsidize the effort? If so, will you subsidize this for all or for only some market segments (e.g., low-income households)? Is this price one that you can "live with" in the future, or will funding be tighter and subsidies less likely? How will it look to citizens if your launch price is lower than the price in subsequent years? Will they remember and complain? Are there any policies or legislative mandates that need to be considered? Are you going to provide bulk discounts or rebates to increase short-term sales?

By setting the final price at $55 per barrel and limiting purchases to one per household, managers believed they would be able to cover their costs, including any unanticipated ones. This would also help manage the demand. After all, they only had 3000 barrels to sell this first year, representing 2 percent of households. Even though 15 percent of households had said they would be very likely to buy at $30, the plan was to sell these at a single community event, and the expectation (hope) was that only a portion of those interested would actually show up, especially given the final price of $55.

Going forward, it is important to recognize that the pricing task is probably not over. Adjustments to basic prices are likely to be needed to account for various customer differences and changing situations on an ongoing basis. Table 4.1 summarizes five price adjustment strategies often used in the private sector, with application in the public sector as well: *discount and allowance pricing, segmented pricing, psychological pricing, promotional pricing,* and *geographical pricing.*[16]

TABLE 4.1 Price-Adjustment Strategies

Strategy	Description	Example
Discount and allowance pricing	Reducing prices through use of discount coupons, bulk rates, rebates, or others	A city offering lower parking prices for hybrid cars
Segmented pricing	Adjusting prices to allow for differences in customers, products, or locations	A city utility charging low-income seniors less for utility services
Psychological pricing	Adjusting prices for psychological effect	A state agency setting the fine for tossing a lit cigarette butt on state highways at $1025
Promotional pricing	Temporarily reducing prices to increase short-run sales	Pricing the rain barrels below competitive offerings and cost for the first 3000 customers
Geographical pricing	Adjusting prices to account for the geographic location of customers	Fines for littering vary based on state or local roadways and by county within the state

Monetary and Nonmonetary Incentives and Disincentives

As noted earlier, setting prices for products, programs, and services is only one of the pricing decisions and options that you will consider. Four additional pricing tools can be used to influence citizen participation and behavior: *monetary incentives* (e.g., discount coupons for bike helmets), *monetary disincentives* (e.g., fines for littering), *nonmonetary incentives* (e.g., public recognition as an environmentally-friendly business), and *nonmonetary disincentives* (e.g., public exposure for owing back taxes).

Monetary Incentives

Four examples of the use of monetary incentives follow. You will consider how this strategy is being used to encourage children in India to attend school, entice young people in the United States to sign up for military duty, increase the likelihood that postal workers show up for work in Britain, and persuade families to move to a small rural town in Kansas.

Incentives to Encourage School Attendance

In many parts of India, persuading parents to send their children to school takes more than words of encouragement. An article in *The Washington Post* in April 2005 describes a different incentive, one that addresses a more urgent citizen want and need—hunger. One such citizen was a nine-year-old girl named Munni who lived in Dataan, India. Munni's parents had pulled her out of school when she was six. Like many other children in India, she was needed at home to take care of her three siblings while her parents worked ten-hour days to earn less than $2 to support the family. Her mother said the new midday free lunch the school started offering was the reason she sent her back. "They only gave free food to the children who went to school, not those who were at home. So I sent her back to school last year."[17] She also sends her younger children with her, who then also get a free meal. Dataan's school records show a 23 percent increase in girls' enrollment and attendance since the program began in 2002. The program became mandatory across the country in January 2005. An earlier effort to assist poor families and improve education provided six pounds of wheat monthly to children who attended school. It was abandoned because students were attending class only on the day the free food was distributed. A member of the government's National Advisory Council said "When schools provide midday meals, children often rush to the schools on their own."[18]

Incentives for Military Recruiting

For 20 years, the all-volunteer U.S. Army succeeded in filling its manpower and leadership needs with its enlistment bonuses and generous scholarships. Recruits signed up in such numbers that there were annual surpluses that could be held over to succeeding years. But when the Iraq war began to stretch from months into years, the view of the military as an attractive option for young Americans gradually began to change. As of June 2005, the Army and other military services failed to meet recruiting goals for four months straight. For the Army, enlistment bonuses had increased from $6,000 for most recruits to $20,000. Officials were confident that by midyear they would reach their target for increasing enlistment among riflemen.[19] Most blame the disappointing numbers realized in subsequent months on tough realities such as longer deployments, from months to years; constant news of casualties from Iraq and Afghanistan; opportunities in a sounder job market at home; and parental fears, even threats. The military tried other strategies: increased advertising targeting patriotism, more recruiters, raising the eligible age for the Army National Guard or the Reserve from 35 to 39, accepting more recruits who are not high school graduates, shortening the enlistment commitment to 15 months, and decreasing the amount of time traditionally required for team and unit training. As of June 2005, the Pentagon was also considering asking Congress to double the enlistment bonus it can offer to the most-prized recruits—from $20,000 to $40,000.[20] Only time will tell if these increased incentives and promotional strategies worked. The question is how high will the incentives need to go to equal perceived costs? And will there be enough potential recruits who value this benefit/cost exchange to meet aggressive goals?

A Chance to Win a Car Decreases Absenteeism

On a lighter and more encouraging note for monetary incentive strategies, in Britain the postal service feels they have discovered a cure for what they consider "rampant absenteeism" among its staff. According to an article in *The Week*, all Royal Mail employees who come to work as scheduled for a period of six full months are entered in a drawing to win a car. The report indicates that since this single program began six months ago, the postal service has seen a 10 percent increase in attendance. "We have 1,000 more people every day than we would otherwise have if nothing had changed,'" said a Royal Mail spokesman.[21] Go figure that one!

Incentives Luring People to Move to Rural Towns

For one final example to represent the range of monetary incentives and agencies' use of them, consider what is happening in a few rural communities in Kansas who share a Web site, www.KansasFreeLand.Com, that hints of their incentive strategy (see Figure 4.3). According to an article in *USA Today* in February 2005, one of those communities, Ellsworth, is a town of about 2,900 with "one grocery store, one stoplight and no mall, no fast food restaurant and no movie theater."[22] Their goal is to reverse decades of population loss as a result of the decline of small family farms and businesses. They also seek to expand the tax base and keep schools from closing. For years, they tried "elephant hunting"—going after the big companies who would bring a big workforce. For the most part, it didn't work. Now they have a new mantra they call "economic gardening"—building one family at a time—and their incentives seem up to the challenge. In Ellsworth, for example, if you agree to build a house there, you pay nothing for the lot that it is on. If you enroll a child in school, you receive $1,500 towards the down payment on your home and $750 for the second and third child. The lenders and bankers of Ellsworth County have agreed to apply the value of the free lot received towards the down payment on the home, and all fees normally charged by the bank associated with financing the construction of a new home or purchase of an existing home are waived. They will also waive the water hook-up fee, sewer tap fee, and building permit fee, and takers can also have their choice of a family golf pass for one year, annual family swimming pool pass, or waiver of monthly recreation fees for one year.[23] Promotions include daily two-hour bus tours around the county, visiting several cities participating in the program. Initial results for Ellsworth's "Welcome Home Plan" have been encouraging: 88 new residents, 24 families, and 33 new schoolchildren, drawing $6,000 each in additional state education aid.

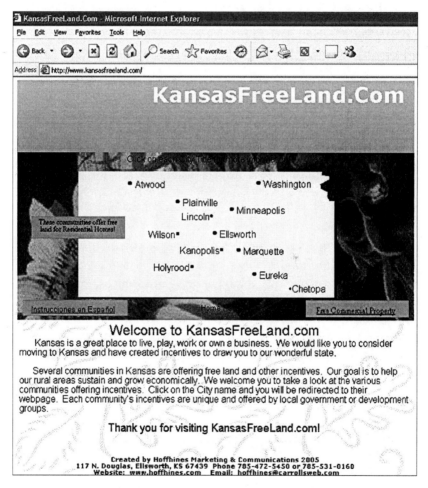

FIGURE 4.3   Using monetary incentives to lure people to move to Kansas

Monetary Disincentives

A monetary disincentive is just as it sounds. It is a strategy used to influence citizens *not* to do something. In the following examples, you explore how it is used to persuade citizens in Ireland to bring reusable bags to stores for their purchases, to convince pet owners in a small town in Italy that they should take better care of their pets, and to keep cigarette butts and jugs of urine off the highways in Washington State.

Discouraging Purchase and Littering of Plastic Bags

In Ireland in the spring of 2002, a tax of 15 euro cents for a plastic bag was introduced in an attempt to curb litter and to encourage shoppers to use tougher, reusable bags. Littering of bags had become so visible that some had even resorted to calling the plastic bags Ireland's "national flag" because they were such a common sight in trees and shrubs, on streets and shorelines, and around the countryside. There was concern for the country's beauty, as well as the health of wildlife and habitats. The 15-euro-cent charge per bag was applied at the point of sale in shops, supermarkets, service stations, and other retail outlets. Of noteworthy interest is that revenue generated from the Plastic Bag Environmental Levy was designated for a new Environmental Fund that would be used to support waste management, litter, and other environmental initiatives. Evidently, some Irish citizens were irate about the new tax. According to one article, words like "terrible" and "disgraceful" were used to describe the tax, with one person saying, "They are putting the price of food up without telling us."[24] Less than six months later, however, it appears the disincentive was working. The Environment Minister reported a 90 percent reduction in the use of bags and that 3.5 million euros had been raised so far that would be spent on environmental projects. The estimate is that in the first three months, shops handed out 277 million fewer bags than normal.[25]

Discouraging Animal Harm

Pet protection was the focus of stiff fines in the city of Turin, Italy, in April 2005 where a 20-page rulebook was adopted by the city to protect the rights of pets. Don't walk your dog at least three times a day, and you will be fined up to 500 euros ($844). Dye your pets' fur, trim their ears, or dock your dog's tail, another 500 euros. Feral cat colonies are now officially protected and cannot be disturbed. Even tiny goldfish in Turin's main park now have rights too. They can no longer be scooped up, put in plastic bags, and awarded as prizes in street fairs. And oh, by the way, dogs may be led for walks by people on bicycles, the rules say, "but not in a way that would tire the animal too much."[26] To enforce the law, Turin police will be relying heavily on citizens to report these unlawful behaviors.

It will be most interesting to revisit this initiative in a few years and discover whether the monetary disincentives were making the intended difference or whether they became targets of citizen jokes or cries for personal responsibility.

Discouraging Littering

A news release in May 2005 regarding the results of Washington State's litter prevention campaign touted the headline "Ounce of prevention is worth 4 million pounds of litter." The results from a litter survey in 2004 found a decline from 8,322 tons to 6,315 tons (24 percent) compared to a similar survey conducted in 1999. This reduction of more than 2,000 tons represented 4 million fewer pounds of litter on Washington's roadways. In the years between the two surveys, the Department of Ecology launched an aggressive anti-litter advertising and enforcement campaign, using a "Litter and It Will Hurt" theme. The prevention campaign includes "Litter and It Will Hurt "advertisements, road signs, posters, the toll-free citizen-reporting line, litter-bag distribution, and increased ticketing for littering (see Figures 4.4 and 4.5). The toll-free litter hotline (866-LITTER-1) received more than 40,000 calls since its launch in April 2002, averaging more than 1,000 per month. Calls come in from motorists who witness people throwing trash from vehicles or losing materials from unsecured loads. When a citizen notices someone throwing something out the window (most often a lit cigarette butt), they call the hotline and are asked to report the license number, description of the vehicle, time of day, type of litter, whether it was thrown from the passenger or driver's side of the car, and approximate location. Within a couple days, the registered owner of the car receives an envelope from the state patrol. The letter inside alerts the owner, for example, that a citizen noticed a lit cigarette butt being tossed out the driver's side of your car at 3 p.m. on Interstate 5, near the University District. This is to inform you that if we had seen you, we would have pulled you over and issued a ticket for $1,025. Now that's one-on-one marketing!

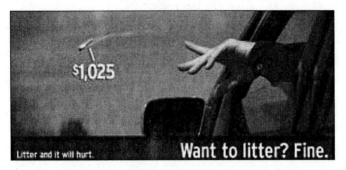

FIGURE 4.4   Washington State's litter campaign focused on a hotline and stiff fines. (Courtesy of Washington State Department of Ecology)

FIGURE 4.5   Washington State's litter poster at truck weigh stations (Courtesy of Washington State Department of Ecology)

Nonmonetary Incentives

There are also ways to encourage participation or changes in behavior that don't involve money. As you will read, Singapore has a creative way to motivate taxi drivers to obey speed limits, countries around the world are influencing preferences for and purchasing of environmentally friendly products, and one county in the U.S. added value to pet licensing without raising the fee or increasing agency costs.

Encouraging Romance

Singapore is so well known for strict laws defining appropriate public behavior that some call it the "Fine City." In fact, t-shirts sold as souvenirs flaunt the image, as did one with the following imprints: "No Smoking (Fine $1000); No Urinating in Lifts (Fine $500); No Feeding the Birds (Fine $1000); No Eating or Drinking in the MRT (Fine $500); No Littering (Fine $1000); Not Flushing (Fine $150); Possession of Fire-Crackers (Cane); Possession of Drug 20 Grams (Death Sentence); Vandalism (Jail and Cane)." And these don't include others that you may have heard about, including heavy fines associated with spitting (even before the SARS outbreak) and chewing gum. Singapore may not be as well known, however, for their creative and innovative use of nonmonetary incentives as well. To encourage taxis, for example, to drive within the speed limits and thus avoid accidents, electronic scanners that sense that a taxi equipped with a special chip is driving over the limit will set off a loud "ding-ding-ding" in the vehicle, warning the driver to slow down and prompting the passenger to ask, "What's wrong?" To increase safety at crosswalks in the city, pedestrians are flashed the number of seconds they have to get across the street before the green light changes, in addition to a standard flashing hand. Restaurants that offer healthy choices are publicly recognized, as in the Healthier Chinese Cuisine initiative where chefs are featured and recognized who have dishes that contain less fat, salt, or sugar and have added vegetables or fruit. As a final and more unusual example, the government, who is concerned with a declining birthrate, has offered unmarried university graduates (a targeted market for procreation) matchmaking services and a Web site creating a "Friends"-like cyber lounge that it calls the LoveByte Cafe, which includes dating advice. The government has also created an annual Romancing Singapore Festival held in February to celebrate love, romance, and relationships. In 2004, the festival even included cologne created by students from Singapore Polytechnic's School of Chemical and Life Sciences formulated to create "a mood for love and romance."[27]

Encouraging Environmentally Friendly Purchasing

The worlds' first eco-labeling program was created in Germany in 1977 to influence consumers to purchase environmentally friendly products over others in the same category. Many claim it's working. The German Blue Eco Angel now covers over 4,000 products (its only exclusion is food and pharmaceuticals) that have positive environmental features. Products are approved by the German Environmental Protection Agency based on an evaluation by an Eco-Label Jury composed of industry members, environmental associations, trade unions, churches, and public authorities. Criteria include efficient use of fossil fuels, use of alternative products with less impact on the climate, reduction of greenhouse gas emissions, and conservation of resources. When approved, they are reviewed every two or three years[28] (see Figure 4.6).

FIGURE 4.6   Germany's Blue Angel eco-label recognizing environmentally friendly products[29]

Encouraging Pet Licensing

One final example underscores the point that codes, potential fines, and laws (disincentives) may not be enough to motivate citizens to act—that providing something "in it for them" can be, and often is, the key. In King County, Washington, getting and paying for a pet license is positioned as "a gift of love" rather than a law. A promotional brochure highlights fringe benefits. When your pet is wearing a county license, you are assured that you will *be notified if the pet is found* by King County Animal Control or a concerned neighbor who accesses the found pet information line. Your pet will get a *free ride home* on the first impound. Officers will attempt to return your pet home immediately, skipping a visit to the animal shelter, thus *avoiding an impound fee*. Your licensed pet will be *cared for at the King County Animal Shelter* for at least five days after phone contact with you and up to two weeks after mailed notice before it is adopted or euthanized. A license also includes participation in the *Vacation Pet Alert Program*, which lets the county know who will be responsible for your pets' care and where you can be reached if necessary. If your pet gets loose during your vacation, the county will call the number you have given them. Readers are now potentially left with the idea that the average $20 fee is worth more than compliance.[30]

Nonmonetary Disincentives

Nonmonetary disincentives have the same job to do as monetary disincentives. They are used to persuade a target audience *not* to do something, but in this case without the threat of fines or tickets. It is instead the use of threats such as mandatory community service (e.g., a litterer having to pick up litter on roadways), public embarrassment (e.g., having to register as a sex offender when moving into a new neighborhood), or even being sued (e.g., a vacated property posing a safety risk). In the following example, many in this town were surprised how fast things moved when they tried this approach.

Motivating Property Owners to Clean It Up

The *Filthy 15* is a Web site that features 15 boarded up homes, empty apartment buildings, and other structures considered the worst violators of city codes for Tacoma, Washington. It's working as an incentive to get property owners to "get moving." Visitors to the site see photographs of each of the *Filthy 15,* and when they click on a photo, they can read detailed descriptions of what city officials are doing and what property owners have agreed to do. The focus is on properties the city has been working on that haven't had substantial movement. City officials hope that the community will then know the city is working on it and, more importantly, that the public display will inspire owners to take action. After the *Filthy 15* Web site had been up and running for only a few days, the city reported that they started seeing some action,

perhaps stimulated by local television news coverage and a story in the
local newspaper about the Web site. Some homeowners claimed they
planned to clean them up all along, and others had already summoned
their contractors to the site. And when they've succeeded in motivating
owners of these properties, the city said they have another 300 that
could one day end up on the *Filthy 15* list.[31]

Decisions Regarding Incentives

How do you decide when to use an incentive and whether it should
be monetary or nonmonetary in nature? It helps to return once more
to the Exchange Theory and examine the potential role that each
of these tactics can play in increasing value and decreasing costs,
making the desired exchange more likely.

As a marketing tactic, incentives are most often used to increase
sales (in the public sector we refer to these more often as purchases,
participation, and compliance) beyond what we are getting with current strategies or anticipate we are likely to get. Stated informally,
they are used to sweeten the pot. Described more formally, they are
used to increase perceived value or decrease perceived costs.

Our four incentive tactics work in different directions, illustrated
in Table 4.2 and summarized as follows:

- A monetary incentive reduces the monetary price of the
  desired behavior.
- A monetary disincentive increases the cost of the competing
  behavior.
- A nonmonetary incentive increases the perceived value of the
  desired behavior.
- A nonmonetary disincentive decreases the perceived value of
  the competitive offering.

Managers choose from among these tactics based on a variety of factors, including resources (e.g., for subsidizing coupons), feasibility
(e.g., to inspect dry cleaners for environmentally friendly practices),
potential general public response (e.g., placing a tax on plastic bags),
potential target audience reaction (e.g., to being forced to use a hands-
free cell phone when driving), and potential competitive reaction

(e.g., FedEx response if the U.S. Postal Service lowers prices for overnight delivery).

TABLE 4.2   Incentives to Decrease Costs and/or Increase Value

	Supporting the Desired Behavior	**Attacking the Competing Behavior**
Behaviors	• Purchasing products or services • Complying with laws • Participating voluntarily in desired behaviors	• Purchasing competing products • Ignoring laws • Participating in legal but undesirable behaviors
Cost-Related Tactics	**Monetary incentives** decrease costs of the desired behavior. *Offering discount coupons for lockboxes for guns at a variety of retail outlets.*	**Monetary disincentives** increase the costs of the competing (or undesirable) behaviors. *Raising the fine for discarding a lit cigarette butt to $1,025.*
Value-Related Tactics	**Nonmonetary incentives** increase the perceived value of the desired behavior. *Rewarding a dry cleaner for being an EnviroStar, including publicity in newspapers as well as a banner to display on their building.*	**Nonmonetary disincentives** decrease the value of the competing behavior. *Restricting smoking to areas around the building that are not covered or sheltered.*

Summary

As these examples have demonstrated, pricing strategies and tactics (both monetary and nonmonetary) are essential and instrumental tools in the marketing mix. You saw how they helped to increase seat belt usage, attendance at school, use of reusable grocery bags, licensing of pets, purchase of environmentally friendly products, the number of residents in small, rural towns on the brink of extinction, and the cleanup of dangerous and dilapidated buildings. You saw how they are being used to decrease employee absenteeism, litter, and automobile and pedestrian accidents. Although marketers or those with a marketing mindset are not always, even often, responsible for developing policies such as fines for littering or prices for personalized license plates, they can be instrumental in helping make these decisions. They are the ones the agency should depend on to know the value that the target audience places on the potential exchange. They know the target audience and what will persuade them and what won't. If they don't, they will know where and how to find out. They can be used as experts on what barriers and benefits citizens see to compliance and what incentives and disincentives will tip the scales, making the desired exchange more likely. They should definitely be at the pricing table and if not in person, at least in the mindset of those who are.

5

OPTIMIZING DISTRIBUTION CHANNELS

"When I first arrived in Nepal just over three years ago, I was told by everyone I met that condoms were available everywhere. I wondered why I had been asked to come to Nepal and expand the depth and reach of condom availability for HIV/AIDS prevention and family planning purposes. However, when I myself went to try and find condoms in the marketplace I found that outlets carrying condoms were few and far between and that there were even fewer condoms available in late night establishments that are often linked with risky sexual behavior. Even though condoms had been promoted and distributed by His Majesty's Government and social distribution companies for over 25 years, we decided to commission a national condom retail outlet audit to find out if the perceptions of condom availability matched the actual availability of condoms in the private sector. The results of the national survey stunned everyone. Out of all potential condom outlets surveyed that could carry condoms, 77% had never sold a condom. This finding shouted 'opportunity.'"

Steven W. Honeyman, Country Representative
Population Services International

For a moment, if you will, put on your citizen hat, assume you have a need or desire for the services listed here, and then answer freely these related questions:

- Where would you like to get your passport? Renew it?
- How would you like to return a library book?
- When would you like to be able to talk with your child's teacher?
- What would you really like the lobby of the post office to look like?
- How long is it reasonable to wait on hold when you call the IRS?

Now, return to the role of a public sector manager. Do you believe you should strive to provide the level of access that citizens want, levels that have been raised by our everyday experiences when shopping, dining, banking, and traveling? Or do you believe instead that the public sector is different, that citizens don't really expect the same levels of convenience from you, and that they might even think you were being frivolous if you mimicked the commercial sector?

We think the answer is that it depends on your agency's objectives and goals. What is certain, and a given, is that convenience of access does influence behaviors, and related decisions require a rigorous analysis of anticipated gains from increases in targeted citizen behaviors stacked against your costs for increasing convenience. We further suggest, as illustrated in the following story, that the rigor is worthwhile.

Opening Story: HIV/AIDS in Nepal— Sarita is Empowered to Buy Condoms When and Where She Needs Them

Challenges

The challenges facing condom distribution activities in Nepal in 2002 were many: an estimated 60,000 individuals had already contracted HIV/AIDS; there were large unmet needs for modern family planning methods, including use of condoms; and nearly eight years of civil war had racked the countryside.

Condom promotion and distribution, which started 25 years earlier, had seen only limited growth and was primarily aimed at family planning. Little was being done to promote condom use as a barrier against HIV and sexually transmitted infections. Because of this primary emphasis on condom use for contraception, condoms were not easily available at "hotspot" locations where high-risk sexual activity was known to take place.

Putting a face to the problem, Sarita tells her story, one that is not unique—thousands of women throughout Nepal have very similar stories to share. After the death of her husband and the loss of two brothers in the ongoing civil conflict, she decided to take a risk and move with her young son from their village to Kathmandu in search of a better life. She soon found work in a dance restaurant, and although she had several customers who gave her cash and gifts in exchange for sex, she did not consider herself to be a sex worker. "I only have sex with good men that become my friends," she explains.

She and women like her face enormous challenges: "When I first arrived in Kathmandu, it was difficult to buy condoms late at night or around the dance restaurant where I work. I was afraid to buy condoms at the local pharmacy because I knew the man who worked there and I was embarrassed. If I was caught by either the authorities or my boyfriends carrying condoms, they would assume I was a prostitute and this would create a lot of problems."

Strategies

For women like Sarita, increased availability of and accessibility to condoms was literally a matter of life and death. It became imperative to develop new channels of distribution, focused not just on "supplying" condoms but also on improving access in relevant locations and at convenient times. In order to do this, the central government, in collaboration with Population Services International (PSI)/Nepal, turned to the private sector as a vibrant, exciting, and newly revitalized partner in the overall delivery of condoms to consumers. As in many countries, condoms in Nepal were already available from government health units free of charge—the problem lay instead with accessibility. After examining weaknesses in the current distribution system, PSI/Nepal helped develop new and innovative strategies for the government to reach high-risk target groups.

New partnerships were formed with private sector trade associations, trade unions, non-governmental organizations (NGOs), and companies that began directly marketing condoms to their members. This generated income for the associations while also keeping their members free of sexually transmitted diseases and allowing them to better plan their families.

New distribution channels were created, ones linked to target groups like the fast-moving consumer goods company, which normally sold sweets and dried noodles, that was contracted to make condoms much more widely available across the country by opening convenient new condom outlets. NGOs with links to late-night establishments (dance and cabin restaurants, pubs, singing bars, and massage parlors) were contracted to open HIV/AIDS-focused condom outlets near high-risk meeting places, and mass media let the market know about it (see Figure 5.1).

To expand into new territories, private sector companies with networks across the country began to supplement the limited existing

FIGURE 5.1   Number One condoms on sale in a bar known to be frequented by sex workers late at night (Note the promotional sign on the wall between the liquor cabinets.)

family planning distribution and added over 30,000 new outlets to the existing network. Using companies that normally handled only fast food to distribute condoms for the first time resulted in sharp increases in efficiency, more effective targeting of distribution activities, and greatly reduced costs (see Figure 5.2).

FIGURE 5.2   A neighborhood convenience store where Number One condoms are sold on the front counter and promotional banners are prominently displayed across the front of the store and in each display case

Rewards

There has been a dramatic improvement in condom distribution over the past few years (since 2003). The number of socially marketed condoms (that is, condoms sold to distributors at a subsidized price for public health benefit) increased 43 percent the first year and 34 percent in the second year, compared with an 8 percent average growth over the prior three years. The market for subsidized condoms has now doubled in size from 11 million units to 22 million units per year.

High-risk HIV/AIDS condom consumers, such as female sex workers, have become more effectively and efficiently targeted. These days, Sarita no longer feels that she is at the same level of risk as before. "Now that condoms are available right inside the dance restaurant where I work, as well as at the cigarette stand outside, I can buy them when and where I need. I don't need to carry them in my purse all day because I can get them late at night instead." Sarita even reports that her boyfriends are increasingly bringing their own condoms with them because they are easy to buy on the spot.[1]

Place: The Third "P"

Distribution channels, simply stated, are the means you use to deliver your offerings and the means that citizens have to access them. In the marketing mix, this is the **Place "P"**, considered one of the most critical decisions facing management. Your choices profoundly affect citizen response:

- *Participation* in programs (e.g., where and when CPR trainings are offered)
- *Utilization* of services (e.g., ambiance of a community center)
- *Compliance* with rules and regulations (e.g., where trash and recycling receptacles are placed at a city park)
- *Purchase* of products (e.g., where a university's branch campuses are located)
- *Satisfaction* (e.g., how early a business traveler has to get to the airport in order to get through security lines)

Your choices will obviously also profoundly affect your costs, setting in motion the balancing act you no doubt must manage. In the next section of this chapter, you will consider the numerous channel-related decisions facing public sector managers. It is intended to broaden your perspective of channel components. Later, there is a discussion of criteria for decision-making, intended to add rigor and stability to the process.

Channel Decisions

Distribution channel decisions impact where, how, and when your offerings will be delivered and accessed. They also include the "atmospherics" surrounding the exchange process, whether it is a physical location (e.g., your gate at a flight terminal), a Web site (e.g., the site's ease of navigation), or a phone call (e.g., the amount of time you are on hold). Looking at it from the customer's perspective, your decisions impact how much time, effort, and joy the exchange will "cost" them—or not!

These decisions not only impact citizens but also often involve long-term commitments to others (e.g., a public sector partnership with the Red Cross to deliver CPR classes). Therefore, you'll want to design your channels carefully, with an eye on tomorrow's marketing environment as well as today's.

Decisions on Where and How Citizens Access Your Programs and Services

We live in a convenience-oriented world in which many of us place an extremely high value on our time, trying to save some of it for our families, friends, and favorite leisure activities. This list of components related to where and how programs and services are accessed includes of course the "brick and mortar" option that has dominated the distribution channel landscape of the past, but it also includes a mix of newer channels that are growing in stature.

Physical Location. This channel is most familiar to those agencies providing direct, face-to-face delivery of programs and services, making decisions regarding where to locate public schools, fire stations, voting booths, playgrounds, university branch campuses, community health clinics, post offices, ports, and so on. Major decisions focus on location. Consider, for example, the attention Minneapolis-St. Paul, Minnesota gives to Park and Ride locations. As of 2005, they can proudly boast on their Web site that there are "free parking lots all over the metro area." In fact, they list over 130, including ones that appear to be standalones as well as ones located in a variety of familiar locations such as shopping malls, city halls, Target store parking lots, and, of course, Lutheran churches. In addition to street address, they note for each location the numbers for bus routes serving the lot, any tips on parking instructions, and even whether the location includes a bike locker.[2]

Phone. Of most interest to the marketer when choosing and managing this distribution channel is its potential use by citizens for *placing orders* (e.g., signing up for an exercise class offered at a community center), *performing transactions* (e.g., participating in a citizen survey), and actually *receiving services* (e.g., calling 911). Putting back on your citizen hat, you know this customer contact point can "make or break" your image of a governmental agency as well as the deal. Although the phone is a convenient option in the mix, decisions to develop and utilize this option need to be made with assurance that the customer's experience will be a pleasant one. Tobacco quitlines are widespread because of their proven ability to offer universal access; address ethnic, gender, and age disparities; meet smokers' strong preference to be counseled on the phone instead of face-to-face; and most importantly, help smokers quit. Convenience features offered by many include toll-free numbers, "live" counselors answering the phone, and availability seven days a week, early in the morning (when having that first cigarette with a cup of coffee) to late at night (when a long, hard day creates a new resolve).

Fax. Before we unplug this option and store it in the closet, consider this unique potential role for a fax machine. In Wisconsin, an innovative, effective, evidence-based tobacco cessation program has added an additional component to their mix, "The Fax to Quit Program." When a smoker is identified in a healthcare setting and indicates that he or she wants to make a quit attempt, the patient is asked to agree to have his or her name and number faxed to the Quitline and then signs a consent form. The state-sponsored Quitline then makes the initial call to the patient to begin the counseling program. Smokers who speak little or no English can request an interpreter on the enrollment form. In the end, the burden and barrier of making the initial call has been shifted from the smoker to the Quitline counselor.[3]

Mail. As with the phone, it is clear this option is also still regarded as highly convenient by many citizens and is one that can be cost effective for the government. In 1998, to attest, voters in Oregon passed a ballot measure directing all elections to be conducted by mail. A ballot is mailed to each registered voter and then returned to the county elections office. Statistics show that this convenience angle can make a difference, with voter turnout in Oregon for the 2004 general election at 74 percent of eligible citizens, compared with 64 percent nationwide.[4] Consider as well the cost savings for the government, discussed in the Federal Election Commission book "Innovations in Election Administration 11: All-Mail Ballot Elections"—"No poll workers includes: no recruitment; no notices to be sent; no classes to conduct; no distribution and retrieval of election day supplies; no last-minute cancellations from workers who had agreed to serve; no paychecks to cut and mail; no W-2's to send; no pre-dawn election-day hours to line up replacement workers. No polling places includes no polling place leases, telephones, utilities; no searching for or preparation of accessible locations; no frantic phone calls about locked doors; no preparation, set-up, tear-down, or emergency repairs of voting machines or devices; no confusion about where people must go to vote."[5]

Mobile Units. It is probably obvious that this distribution channel is usually more convenient for citizens, typically arriving closer to their homes, work, school, and shopping. Less obvious is that it can also be a winning economic strategy for the government as well. In New Zealand, the MidCentral District Health Board figured out a way to use mobile dental clinics to improve access to services as well as to reduce onsite clinics and related costs. When clinics were closed at 15 schools, children had to overcome barriers of making appointments and arranging for a parent or guardian to transport them. The purchase of two new mobile units in 2004 meant services could again be provided onsite to those 15 schools. Mobile units painted with oral health messages were expected to be a highly visible focal point when visiting schools and traveling through communities. It is estimated that up to 4,000 children will receive services in the two new mobile units each year.[6]

Drive-thrus. Although you can order a hamburger, make a bank deposit, pick up prescriptions, pay your respects at a funeral parlor— even get married—all from the front seat of your car, this is a fairly new option in the public sector. Libraries, however, are apparently hot on the trail. In Harford County, Maryland, for example, the Bel Air Branch Library drive-thru lanes resemble those at fast food restaurants. At 8 a.m., customers can return books, pay late fees, and pick up items they requested in advance, all before the building's doors open at 10 a.m. It is reported that when the service was first offered in 1998, 670 people drove through the first month. Two years later, that number had risen to 4,300 users per month and the window stays open until 8 p.m.[7]

Internet. Gaining information about governmental programs and services through the Internet is of course commonplace today. In marketing terminology, however, this is using the Web as a communication channel. Of interest in this chapter is the utilization of the Web as a distribution channel—a way for citizens to actually receive services, order products, or perform transactions. Some call this movement e-governance, and it is having a positive impact on the productivity and performance of the public sector. Examples appear to be emerging like crocuses in the spring: going "online" instead of "in line" to purchase or renew a license for your pet; joining government sponsored chat rooms for support for quitting smoking; filing tax returns; making campground reservations; getting a replacement Medicare card; ordering vital records, publications, or materials; and finding a carpool or vanpool partner. In August 2005, the North Carolina Triangle Transit Authority announced an online "store" for riders to purchase passes for bus and shuttle services, available of course 24 hours a day, 7 days a week.[8] This online purchase system accepts American Express, Discover, MasterCard, and Visa, charging a $1.00 shipping and handling fee per transaction.

Videos. This distribution mechanism can extend the reach of efforts (e.g., connect town hall meetings at various locations being held across a state for citizen input) as well as potentially cut costs and improve citizen satisfaction. In California, the Orange County Corrections Department installed a video for visitations at its jail that houses an average of 3,800 inmates, the fifteenth largest in the country (2003). According to officials, the reasoning behind the video visitation center was straightforward. They wanted to reduce opportunities for contraband to enter the jail. Even though video visitation can't provide a human touch, the reality was that they had to put a stop to all touching anyway in 1999 in an effort to stop contraband. The atmosphere in the visitation center is considered far more user friendly and has actually increased visitation because of its convenience. It's not far from the actual jail, and the freestanding structure provides a more comfortable environment for visitors than any area that the compound facilities had offered. In 2003, the center was averaging 600 visitors a day during the week and 1,000 per day on weekends.[9]

Home Delivery/House Calls. Bringing services to citizens' doorsteps may not be applicable to a majority of public sector agencies. But for a few, it can make all the difference. Public health and foster care outreach workers, for example, often need to see the home environment. Some utilities offer home energy audits or landscaping consultations and services that can only be performed onsite. Although of course the United States Postal Service has picked up outgoing mail for decades, their Pickup On Demand service is relatively new, targeting especially business owners and those with home offices in ZIP codes with a designated post office for city delivery. For a fee of $12.50 (2005), regardless of the number of packages, outgoing mail can be picked up in most cases within two hours of an online request or can be scheduled up to six days in advance.

Where Customers Shop, Dine, and Hang Out. In keeping with the spirit of bringing programs and services to customers (instead of asking them to come to you), it may be advantageous to consider locations that your target audience already frequents, such as grocery stores for flu shots, street corners for needle exchange programs, and gas stations for litter bags. In this case, we are considering these channels as more than an option for communications. They become distribution channels for programs, products, and services. Consider this headline in the *Chicago Tribune* on January 2, 2004: "Rapid HIV tests offered where those at risk gather: Seattle health officials get aggressive in AIDS battle by heading into gay clubs, taking a drop of blood and providing answers in 20 minutes." The article reported that Public Health-Seattle & King County had begun administering rapid-result HIV tests in bathhouses and gay sex clubs. It was seen at the time as one of the most aggressive efforts in the nation. Sending health counselors to bathhouses for standard HIV testing was fairly common. But this meant that the client would then need to make an appointment at a medical clinic and typically wait at least a week to get results, a critical step in the prevention process that was not always taken. With this new solution, questions were raised about whether people carousing in a nightclub could handle the sudden news if it turned out they were HIV-positive. But health officials seemed prepared with answers. Counselors were to meet with clients to present results. They would refuse to test people who were drunk or high or who appeared emotionally unstable. Initially, sex club and bathhouse owners seemed concerned about whether this effort would drive away customers. Perhaps the fact that one of the clubs—a year and a half later (August 2005)—touts the availability of rapid tests every Friday night from 10 p.m. to 2 a.m. on their Web site reflects how things actually turned out.[10]

Kiosks/Vending Machines. As financial institutions discovered in the '80s, standalone ATM machines can substitute for some "brick and mortar" facilities and face-to-face services and at the same time increase customer satisfaction and perceived value. After all, they provide banking customers with added convenience of location, extended (24/7) hours, and typically less processing time. Governmental agencies have discovered the same benefits for their organizations as well as their customers. Travelers on Washington D.C.'s Metro can use automated systems to purchase a computerized fare card based on the anticipated number of trips and destinations, similar to the purchase of a phone card. The machine takes nickels, dimes, quarters, and bills from $1 to $20 and returns up to $4.95 in change. It also accepts credit cards. When the card is inserted in the entrance gate, the time and location are recorded on its magnetic tape, and the card is returned. When exiting, the fare is automatically deducted based on the destination and returned if any value is left on it. Should you arrive at a destination and find that your fare card doesn't have value, you can add the necessary amount at the Exitfare machines near the gate.

Decisions on When Citizens Can Access

Distribution planning also includes consideration of the impact of hours and days of the week you are "open for business" (or not) on both your agency's costs as well as your citizens' participation and satisfaction.

The state of Utah found a way to provide 24/7 service without buildings or phone centers. They call it their "24/7 Live Help" and tout the ability to "chat live" with a customer service representative with a simple click on the Live Help button. Customer service representatives in the "chat room" can address a variety of citizen questions ranging from how to start a business in Utah to finding employment or checking on weather conditions or the status of construction projects on specific roads. Should the representative be "assisting other customers," a dialog box for sending an email is offered as a substitute.[11]

Availability seven days a week may be a serious consideration for some agencies. In September 2005, Washington State launched a two-year pilot program to determine whether opening state-managed liquor stores on Sunday from noon to 5 p.m. was economically feasible. Twenty state liquor stores were chosen for the pilot, ones with the greatest projected Sunday revenue potential based on current retail sales levels, population density, proximity to shopping centers, and proximity to other businesses open on Sundays. It was estimated at the time that the pilot would generate an additional $9.55 million in gross revenue and about $3.7 million in net revenue with about 25 percent of this to be sent directly to health and prevention programs. In determining whether to open additional stores, managers will compare the expenses to the amount of additional sales generated. It also will measure whether Sunday sales negatively impact sales in state and contract stores near the 20 pilot stores.[12]

Decisions on Wait Times

An additional convenience variable to manage is wait time, experienced by your customer in a variety of ways. It can be the amount of time between their arrival at a facility and actual receipt of services (e.g., time waiting in line at a customs clearance station). It also includes the amount of time elapsed between applying for or requesting services and actual receiving them (e.g., a callback in response to a request for back tax information). It applies to time spent on hold waiting for assistance on a phone line (e.g., an information line providing detailed restrictions and guidelines on goods that can be brought into a country and will need to be inspected at a border crossing), and it is compounded when callers need to be transferred to a different person or department.

Consider the following service improvements undertaken by Hong Kong's Immigration Department with an objective to reduce time customers need to spend waiting for department services. You can imagine that these improvements probably met additional agency objectives as well, including decreasing costs and increasing service usage levels.[13]

- To decrease wait time at the Lok Ma Chau boundary-crossing point, the number of immigration clearance counters was increased in 2003 from 28 to 50, and passenger queuing areas were enlarged.

- To develop and promote Hong Kong's position as a preferred international and regional transportation and logistics hub and to remain competitive in the shipping industry, a "one-stop" office was set up to handle a variety of formalities for vessels arriving in and departing from Hong Kong. As a part of this effort, one initiative, which was launched in 2000, included acceptance of pre-arrival clearance applications for ocean-going vessels through electronic mail and the use of electronic digital signatures. Furthermore, those with prearrival clearance were able to proceed directly to a berth or terminal without the need to wait for immigration clearance while anchored.

- A Queuing Information System was installed at major immigration offices to assist customers by letting them know when they could expect to be interviewed. Tags are issued to visitors from a computer, which also prints out the estimated time for their interview. Updated information on the queuing situation can also be monitored on an electronic digital display board in the public waiting halls.

One final recommendation on wait times is to explore ways to manage perceived, as well as actual, wait times. If you've been to Disneyland, you have no doubt experienced the masters of perception at work, with lines that look shorter because they are queued in zigzags rather than straight and offer entertainment while you wait, distracting you and making the time standing seem shorter. In a similar vein, it may be beneficial to give your clients an expected amount of time they will need to be on hold or stand in line. In many cases, it may not be as long as they may be imagining, making it more likely they will wait instead of hanging up or leaving because they did not know how long (or short) the wait would be. (An obvious, but important, caveat for providing an anticipated wait time is ensuring that it is accurate as customer satisfaction is highly correlated with expectations, and you have just created one you'll need to meet.)

Decisions on Ambiance

Decisions regarding the "look and feel" of distribution channels should also have marketing input. Remember, marketing consists of influencing behaviors, and factors such as cleanliness, comfort, and aesthetic pleasure (or the absence thereof) have an impact on customer decisions. A couple conditions make it more likely you should give this facet your attention.

It is probably safe to assume that if your customers are going to spend a significant amount of time at your place, it matters more than when they just go in and out, with implications for those managing buses, subways, ferry terminals, airports, streets, parks, schools, libraries, community centers, museums, and the like. By comparison, it is probably less important at utility customer service windows, the post office, license renewal offices, and police departments, to name a few.

It is also more important as an area of focus when your customers have competitive alternatives, as commuters do to take their own (clean) car to work, as readers do to go to Barnes & Noble and sit in a cushy chair with a latte, and as exercisers do to join a hip athletic club rather than a community center aerobic class.

Channel Decision Criteria

The vast array of distribution channel options and components that you can and often should influence are out on the table for you now, waiting for your consideration. You are ready to judge serious options for their potential to impact two sides of the scale: the economic value to your agency and the convenience value for your customers. It is a balancing act, with the name of the game being to find the optimal convenience level, one where to go any further would have a diminishing rate of return on your investment or to stop short would be a missed opportunity.

Assessing Economic Value to the Governmental Agency

Answers to a few basic business questions will assist you in sorting through ideas for choosing distribution channels for new programs or making improvements to current ones, creating a short list to take to the next analytical platform.

Does the idea being considered have the potential to *decrease delivery costs* for your agency? Decreased costs might be realized through savings from reduced staffing levels, facility requirements, or other operational costs. Kiosks in post office lobbies and renewal of driver's licenses online are fair representations of this potential.

Does the idea have potential for *reducing other costs*, ones not directly associated with service delivery, but ones with significant budget implications for your agency or a "sister" agency?

Assume, for example, that you are a manager of a state tobacco prevention and control program, and you have been asked by a legislative committee whether you should consider extending the hours of your tobacco Quitline from 8 p.m. until midnight. Assume as well that you have a counterpart in another state that extended the hours of their Quitline to midnight a year ago. You would probably be interested in knowing the answers to several questions to help fill in the first blanks in Table 5.1. How many more calls did they get? What percent increase did this represent for them? What do they know about the age and other demographics of those who called during those hours?

Based on this, you would then estimate how many more citizens in your state you could expect (roughly) to call. And based on experience with your own Quitline, what percent of those callers are likely to quit successfully—for good? After that number is estimated, you would want to know the costs savings "per quit." What does your agency consider to be the state's medical-related costs for a tobacco user per year, averaged over a lifetime? You would then project a gross potential savings, an amount that would then be reduced by the annual costs for those four additional hours per day, including staff, phones, promotions, and other incremental costs. In Table 5.1, a hypothetical scenario is presented. In reality, a more sophisticated financial model would most likely be employed, one projecting cost savings based on a variety of scenarios, variables, and assumptions.

TABLE 5.1   Hypothetical Estimate of Projected Savings from Extended Hours to a Tobacco Quitline

Number of current calls to the Quitline annually	20,000
Percent increase assumed by extending from 8 p.m. to midnight	10%
Number of new callers	2,000
Percent of those callers expected to quit "for good"	20%
Number of additional citizens who quit	400
Average state-related cost savings "per quit" per year	$3,000
Annual gross cost savings (400 × $3,000)	$1.2 million
Annual costs associated with extended hours	$200,000
Net cost savings	$1 million
Return on investment ($200,000 to $1 million)	500%

Does the idea instead (or even better yet, in addition) have the potential for *increasing revenues* as a result of increases in purchases or participation? And will these additional revenues recover the costs, and maybe then some, for the new or improved distribution channel? A more conveniently located park and ride or bus stop or an improved bus schedule, for example, has the potential to increase ridership, likely just filling excess capacity. Improved atmospherics and parking availability for a community center might win the business of some organizations that are shopping around and interested in renting your facility for a management retreat. Removing graffiti from walls in a subway may increase feelings of safety and convenience, making a taxi ride seem less justifiable.

Assessing Convenience Value for Citizens

Now you move to the other side of the equation, the customer's likely response to the idea. Notice in each of the business considerations just mentioned, the consistent use of the word potential. Potential economic gains (decreased costs, increased revenues) for the most part will rely on a positive citizen response. That response must now be assessed.

Will the increased convenience or improvement to the distribution channel actually *increase purchases and/or participation?* Enough to cover your costs? How do you know? Several measurement techniques can assist you, ones that will be discussed more fully in Chapter 11, "Gathering Citizen Inputs and Feedback," but that are worthy of brief mention here. First, find out what other agencies (even ones around the world) have experienced when they introduced this or a similar idea. One of the benefits you have when working in the public sector is that you can ask this question of other similar agencies. This doesn't happen in the private sector. A bank marketing director, for example, can't call their counterpart at a competing bank and ask how their new online banking is working for them. If it's a new idea that has never been tried before as far as you know, you could do a pilot, measure results, and then conduct the cost benefit analysis. In the library example mentioned earlier, the drive-thru lane was tried in one branch first, prior to expansion to other branches in the state. One additional strategy to project citizen response would be to conduct survey research, testing the potential idea with citizens, measuring their interest levels and likelihood of purchase and/or participation.

Will it *increase citizen compliance*? What if you put "drive-by" litter receptacles at weigh stations for truck drivers? Would you be able to recover your costs for this effort through savings in costs for litter pickup or related environmental cleanup? Will more homeowners get a building permit if they can apply and submit applications online and if inspectors make "house calls" on weekends rather than during business hours only?

Does the idea have the potential for *increasing citizen satisfaction*? Will parents be more likely to vote "yes" on the next school levy if they have convenient and easy access to teachers through email and to homework assignments posted online?

Prioritizing Distribution Channel Options

As stated in the title of this chapter, the goal is for you to optimize distribution channels. Figure 5.3 puts this balancing act in motion, assisting you in sorting options you have into one of four corners.

In the upper right (*Top-Priority Ideas*), there are those that are the most attractive, ones that have the greatest potential for increased economic gains for your agency as well as added convenience value

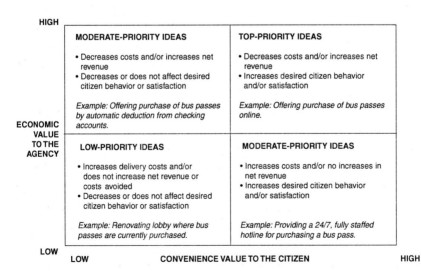

FIGURE 5.3   Prioritizing Channel Selection and Improvement Ideas

for citizens. In the opposite corner there are those that should fall off the consideration list because they are projected to have minimal economic and convenience gains (*Low-Priority Ideas*). You are then left with ones you might consider at some future point (*Moderate-Priority Ideas*), ones that seem attractive either because of their economic promise or their potential for influencing citizen behavior or satisfaction. The problem is, it doesn't look now like they will do both, and so they should be put in their appropriate place—the back burner.

Summary

Distribution channels are the means you have chosen, or could choose, to deliver your offerings to citizens. It was pointed out in your readings that this is not about delivering messages or information; this is about delivering your product. In managing these channels, you are faced with multiple decisions regarding where, how, and when citizens will access your offer and whether the experience will be pleasant—or not. Options for delivery include physical locations, phone, fax, mail, mobile units, drive-thrus, the Internet, e-governance, videos, home delivery/house calls, where citizens currently shop, dine, or hang out, and kiosks or vending machines. A typical channel manager also has an impact on hours and days of the week you are open for business, how long citizens need to wait, and the atmospherics surrounding the exchange, decisions that are especially important when customers spend time at your place and when they have option to go somewhere else.

These are decisions that warrant marketing input as the marketer can provide insight on what is needed (or not) to achieve desired citizen response levels. The marketing perspective can help the agency monitor and manage the exchange to gauge and meet established agency objectives for desired participation rates, purchase levels, compliance, and/or satisfaction.

This market analysis can then be combined with the financial implications of a new or improved distribution channel idea to assist in prioritizing and focusing on those with the most promise for increased economic benefits as well as citizen value.

6

CREATING AND MAINTAINING A DESIRED BRAND IDENTITY

"Energy efficiency has finally come of age. Today, with energy prices at an all-time high, and the era of cheap energy most likely over, consumers and businesses are increasingly investing in energy efficiency for a variety of benefits: to save energy, save money, help the environment, provide a better future for their families, and reflect commitment to social responsibility. ENERGY STAR® has succeeded as a brand because of our common sense approach to promoting better, more efficient technologies and practices, and because we've been able to translate the value of these practices to consumers and industry. Building awareness and demand did not happen overnight. It took patient, steady work with our industry partners, careful program design, and a brand communications strategy that has evolved with the times."

Jill Abelson
Communications Manager
ENERGY STAR®

The following question isn't a test. It's an exercise. Be sure to take your time. When you read each of the following names, write down the words, images, and feelings that come to your mind ... first.

- IRS
- The National Archives
- Department of Labor and Industry
- The U.S. Presidential Elections
- Smokey Bear
- Singapore
- Canada
- Las Vegas
- Paris
- Harlem
- Your City's Police Department
- Your City's Library
- Your District's School Superintendent

Now, a second question. Who is responsible for what came to your mind, for whether you had rich positive associations or vague, even negative ones? If you interpret the word "responsible" to mean "able to respond," it suggests that managers and directors of these agencies, program, cities, and nations can and should be the ones looked to—for maintaining a strong brand, strengthening a weak one, or changing an undesirable one. In this opening story on creating and maintaining a desired brand image for a governmental program, the role that marketing plays to fulfill this responsibility will become clearer.

Opening Story: ENERGY STAR®—A Brand Positioned to Help Protect the Planet

 The U.S. Environmental Protection Agency (EPA) established the voluntary ENERGY STAR program in 1992, and it has partnered with the Department of Energy (DOE) since 1996 to increase the nationwide use of energy-efficient products and practices. Computers and monitors were the first labeled products, integrating the power-saving features initially used in laptop technology. Today, the program encompasses more than 40 product categories for the home and workplace, as well as complementary programs for new homes, existing homes, and commercial and industrial buildings. This story focuses on ENERGY STAR's efforts in the residential market. A strong brand strategy played a key part in building one of the most successful government-industry partnerships.

Challenges

At the early stages, before consumer demand could be created for ENERGY STAR, EPA needed to encourage the marketplace to manufacture more energy-efficient products and to use the label. Manufacturers that met the voluntary specifications were encouraged to label the qualified products with the ENERGY STAR logo. After the label for computers was established, EPA used this success to work with other manufacturers to expand the program to a wider array of labeled products, moving first to other types of office equipment and then to heating and cooling equipment, appliances, light fixtures, new homes, and electronics.

The next challenge facing ENERGY STAR was how to get consumers interested in purchasing energy-efficient products. Research showed that consumers had little knowledge about the energy use of products—and almost no awareness that the energy they used at home contributed to air pollution and greenhouse gas emissions. Using this research as a foundation for brand education and messaging, EPA set off on a brand communications campaign, this time directed at consumers.

Strategies

Planning began in 1996 with identifying the primary target audience as environmentally concerned consumers who wanted to save money on utility bills. The target consisted of college-educated consumers ages 25 to 54 with above-average incomes who were living in regions with high energy costs (due to extreme heating or cooling seasons).

Key messages addressed the insight that most people didn't understand the link between home energy use and air pollution.

Given the fact that the target audience wanted to do things to help protect the environment, the brand promise was born:

"By purchasing ENERGY STAR products you can save money and help protect the environment at the same time."

The brand personality was intended as "smart, credible, easy, important, and approachable." Building brand credibility was also a key aspect of the launch. For consumers to trust the ENERGY STAR label, they needed to know that it was coming from a reliable source—the U.S. EPA.

The launch of the brand focused on media tours in each market where spokespeople delivered "did you know" factoids (Did you know your house pollutes more than your car?) with local consumers offering testimonials about cost savings with ENERGY STAR labeled products. EPA developed television and print public service announcements (PSAs) to help maximize message impact. Local utilities, retailers, and manufacturers helped promote the program through education, rebates, and in-store promotion. Other private companies carried brand messaging, including in-store video at Blockbuster, cups and bags at McDonald's, and online messages through Yahoo! In eighteen months, national recognition of the ENERGY STAR label grew from zero to 27 percent.

Over the years, EPA continued umbrella brand communications through new PSA campaigns, media relations activities, educational materials, national retail promotions, and a consumer Web site (www.energystar.gov) and toll-free hotline (see Figure 6.1).

National product promotions, such as the *Change a Light, Change the World* campaign helped build and support the ENERGY STAR brand. The *Change a Light* campaign pairs up EPA/DOE, utility partners, and national retailers in a unified educational effort about efficient lighting. This promotion uses a social marketing model to encourage consumers to make a pledge to do their part while also offering consumers a low-risk way to try the ENERGY STAR brand (see Figure 6.2).

The future brand strategy will evolve by continuing to increase brand awareness while also increasing the depth of understanding of both the environmental benefits of the brand and breadth of ENERGY STAR product and service offerings. In addition, the brand

FIGURE 6.1   Print PSA for ENERGY STAR

will focus on strategies to engage the loyal consumers of ENERGY STAR to help advocate for the brand to their friends and families.

Rewards

ENERGY STAR achievements to date include the following:

- The ENERGY STAR label is now recognized by more than 64 percent of the American public—awareness is higher in areas with active utility partners.

- 30 percent of U.S. households report knowingly purchasing an ENERGY STAR qualified product in the past year.

- Consumers have purchased more than 1.5 billion ENERGY STAR qualified products.

FIGURE 6.2   A campaign pairing up the U.S. Environmental Protection Agency with the Department of Energy

- There are more than 1,400 manufacturing partners in 40 ENERGY STAR product categories representing 32,000 models.

- The program has more than 800 retail partners representing 21,000 storefronts.

- Many local builders are constructing 20 percent or more of their new homes to meet ENERGY STAR criteria.

- There are more than 2,000 ENERGY STAR labeled commercial buildings.

- In 2004 alone, Americans with the help of ENERGY STAR saved enough energy to power 24 million homes and avoid greenhouse gas emissions equivalent to those from 20 million cars—all while saving $10 billion.

Branding in the Public Sector

Brand and branding conversations are familiar, even old, in the private sector. They got really fired up in the '70s by articles on positioning, especially those of Al Ries and Jack Trout who ignited the advertising world with bold contentions that positioning starts with a product, but it isn't what you do to a product. "Positioning is what you do to the mind of the prospect. That is, you position the product in the mind of the prospect."[1] We would add, "where you want it to be."

Branding is one strategy you and your agency can use to secure a desired position in the prospect's mind. (Decisions you will make regarding the first 3Ps and how they are eventually executed contribute to this positioning as well.) The process begins with decisions regarding a desired brand identity (how you want to be seen) and is then managed to ensure that your brand image (how you are actually seen) is on target.

No doubt you have been witness to conversations in the public sector where a colleague mentioned something related to branding, started by a comment like "We need a better brand image." Some responded with big smiles on their faces, eager to carry the conversation forward and glad someone brought it up. There were also, no doubt, those in the room who responded with a skeptical eyebrow, probably thinking to themselves, "Here we go again. Playing like we're a big business. Branditis strikes again!"[2] And then there were a few souls with blank stares and the courageous among them who proclaimed, "I thought branding was something we did for cattle."

To help develop your response to conversations such as these in the future, this chapter begins with definitions, associated branding terminology, and a description of elements typically included in decisions regarding brand identity.

Branding Defined

Branding terminology is bantered around a lot among academics, as well as advertising and marketing professionals. Although labels are not as important as the distinctions themselves, it helps to have some familiarity with them. The presentation in Figure 6.3 is intended as a

---

A Branding Primer

Brand is a name, term, sign, symbol, or design (or a combination of these) that identifies the maker or seller of a product, which can be a tangible good, service, organization, place, person, or idea.[3]

Brand Identity is how you (the maker) want consumers to think, feel, and act with respect to your brand.

Brand Image is how consumers actually do think, feel, and act with respect to the brand.

Brand Essence is the core idea that you want the brand to evoke in the target audience.

Branding is the process of developing an intended brand identity.

Brand Awareness is the extent to which consumers recognize a brand.

Brand Promise is the marketer's vision of what the brand will do for consumers.[4]

Brand Loyalty refers to the degree to which a consumer prefers and consistently chooses to purchase the same brand within a product class.

Brand Equity is the value of a brand, based on the extent to which it has high brand loyalty, name awareness, perceived quality, strong brand associations, and other assets such as patents, trademarks, and channel relationships. It is an important although intangible asset that has psychological and financial value to a firm.[5]

Brand Elements are those trademarkable devices that serve to identify and differentiate the brand.[6]

Brand Mix or Portfolio is the set of all brands and brand lines a particular firm offers for sale to buyers in a select category.[7]

Brand Contact can be defined as any information-bearing experience a customer or prospect has with the brand.[8]

Brand Performance relates to how well the product or service meets customers' functional needs.[9]

Brand Extension is using a successful brand name to launch a new or modified product in a new category.

Co-Branding is the practice of using the established brand names of more than one company on the same product or are marketed together in the same fashion.[10]

FIGURE 6.3   A Branding Primer

quick reference, providing you with a listing of terms used most frequently and a concise, albeit simple, description of each.

Brand Elements

Elements of the brand are those devices that serve to identify and differentiate the brand. Most are trademarkable and include the *name* and any *slogan*, *logo* (graphic elements), *characters, music, signage, packaging,* even *colors* used consistently. When they're really good, as portrayed in the following example, you'll want to control their use by others and leverage their perceived value as they become vital to your success.

> The guardian of forests in the U.S., and one of the world's most recognizable fictional characters, has been a part of the American scene for more than sixty years. Smokey Bear, dressed in a ranger's hat and belted blue jeans and carrying a shovel, has been the recognized wildfire prevention symbol since 1944 (see Figure 6.4). The slogan "Only YOU Can Prevent Forest Fires" was first used in 1947 and was only changed slightly in 2001 when his message was updated to "Only YOU Can Prevent Wildfires" to address the increasing number of wildfires in the nation's wildlands (see Figure 6.5).

FIGURE 6.4   Poster used in 1948

FIGURE 6.5   Image and slogan used in 2005

By 1952, the Smokey Bear symbol began to attract commercial interest, enough so that legislation was passed to take Smokey out of public domain and place him under the control of the Secretary of Agriculture. An amendment in 1973 offered commercial licensing and directed that fees and royalties were to be used to promote forest fire prevention. Hundreds of items have been licensed under this authority over the years, several featured in Smokey's "Museum" on his official Web site SmokeyBear.com.

In 1984, Smokey's 40th birthday was commemorated, and Smokey became the first individual animal ever to be honored on a postage stamp. In 1987, Smokey Sports was launched with a "National Smokey Bear Day" conducted with all major league baseball teams in the United States and Canada. The decade of the '90s opened the door for Smokey's revitalization and revival by celebrating his 50th birthday nationwide with high visibility activities and events, and in 2004, he celebrated yet another milestone with a "Sixty Years of Vigilance" theme.

Has all this effort to prevent wildfires had an effect? Well, according to the USDA Forest Service, in 1941 over 30 million acres of wildlands were burned by carelessness; in the 1990s, less than 1 million acres were burned.[11]

Brand Function

By definition, the primary practical function of a brand is to identify the maker or seller of a product, with product interpreted broadly here to include tangible goods, services, organizations, people, places, and ideas. Of most interest is what good this can do ... for you as well as your key publics.

For your agency and its programs, a strong brand image can serve you well in helping meet several marketing objectives. Heightened awareness and understanding of the features, spirit, and personality of your brand may make all the difference in *usages levels* (e.g., seeing your city as a great travel destination spot). A recognizable and trusted brand image may make it more likely that a citizen will *participate* in one of your programs (e.g., joining a Neighborhood Watch group). It might even persuade someone to *comply* with guidelines and laws (e.g., properly disposing of litter).

In the spirit of a win-win situation, strong brands meet the needs of citizens as well, assisting them in finding what they are looking for, helping them make their decisions quickly and with confidence. It may even satisfy a less tangible need as a form of self-expression. The following example brings this to life.

> The U.S. Department of Agriculture has established a set of national standards that food labeled "organic" must meet, whether it is grown in the United States or imported from other countries. Consumers interested in purchasing organic produce, meat, eggs, dairy products, and foods made with organic ingredients can look for the official USDA organic seal, often signified with a sticker on vegetables and fruit, organic produce displays, or on packaging labels, as illustrated in Figure 6.6.

Creating a Desired Brand Identity

Six steps are proposed to create a strong brand image, with simple questions that will assist you in completing each step. The first five steps are illustrated with an example to increase physical activity among youth. To provide a range of branding examples, the sixth step is described with a different example, one with an intention to decrease littering.

FIGURE 6.6 Sample cereal boxes illustrating four labeling categories. From the left: cereal with 100 percent organic ingredients, cereal with 95 to 100 percent organic ingredients, and cereal with 70 to 95 percent organic ingredients. Makers of the cereal with less than 70 percent organic ingredients may list specific organically produced ingredients on the information panel of the box but may not make organic claims on the front of the box[12]

Step 1: Establish Brand Purpose

What marketing objectives do you want the brand to support? As noted earlier, most commonly these will be objectives related to influencing citizens to support your organization, participate in your programs, utilize your services, and/or comply with guidelines and laws.

"VERB™ It's what you do" is a national, multicultural social marketing campaign coordinated by the U.S. Department of Health and Human Services' Centers for Disease Control and Prevention (CDC) with a purpose to influence young people ages 9 to 13 (tweens) to be physically active every day.[13]

Step 2: Identify Target Audiences for the Brand

Who are primary target audiences that will be exposed to the brand that you want to influence? Although in reality many citizens in the general public will be exposed to your brand, it should be designed with specific groups of people in mind, those you want to be most influenced.

Although the primary target audience for the VERB effort is tweens, additional important audiences include other school-aged kids—who no doubt will be exposed to the campaign—parents, and adult influencers (e.g., teachers, youth leaders, physical education and health professionals, pediatricians, health care providers, and coaches).

Step 3: Articulate Your Desired Brand Identity

What do you want target audiences to think and feel when they are exposed to your brand? In the beginning of the chapter, you were encouraged to note the images, words, and feelings that came to your mind for a variety of agencies, cities, and nations. This is your chance to envision how you hope target audiences will respond. This step can be as simple as filling in the blanks to the following sentence: "I want my target audience to see (MY BRAND) as _____."

Based on formative research and pretesting, VERB's program planners determined they want tweens to see regular physical activity as something that is cool and fun. Words like "exercise" rarely appear in campaign materials, with references to activities, games, play, and sports more the norm.

Step 4: Craft the Brand Promise

What benefits for the target audience will you highlight? The trick in this step is to focus on benefits for your target audience, not your agency, ones the target audience is likely to experience if they engage in the desired behavior.

Tweens are promised that they will receive what formative research indicated they wanted—that by choosing and engaging their VERB, fun will follow, including in many cases great prizes and great deals (see Figure 6.7). Primary benefits articulated for parents and adult influencers emphasize that increased physical activity will help reduce childhood obesity, citing that children today spend less time being physically active and more time doing sedentary activities. As a result, there has been an increase in the number of overweight youth in the United States, and research shows that being overweight can increase one's risk for type 2 diabetes, high blood pressure, sleep apnea, and gall bladder disease.

FIGURE 6.7   Campaign material used in Lexington, Kentucky highlighting the brand promise

Step 5: Determine the Brand's Position Relative to the Competition

What makes your brand a good choice, one better than the competition? Challenge yourself here to first identify the competition, direct as well as indirect. In the public sector, this often relates more to alternatives that citizens have to programs and services that you offer (e.g., UPS for the Postal Service and french fries for the "5 A Day" campaign that promotes fruits and vegetables). Then dig deep for your brand's unique points of difference. What do you offer that the competition doesn't? What can you do better?

VERB clearly distinguishes itself from a generic exercise brand. As the slogan "It's What You Do" implies, tweens have different interests and skill levels, and there are many verbs that can get them into action. Tweens are encouraged to use their imagination. Materials suggest they can decide to walk, leap, run, dive, play, twist, bounce, tumble, spin, swing, tag, jog, flip, dash, catch, dance, run, swim, hop, kick, dribble, climb, skate, bowl, bike, stretch, or pitch ... or any combination of these. You decide (see Figure 6.8).

Step 6: Select Brand Elements

What name, slogan, logo, and colors will be associated with the brand? Will there be any consistent use of characters, music, signage, or packaging that will be a core element of the brand? In choosing brand elements, a judicious approach will be most rewarding, one that will support decisions you have already made regarding brand purpose, target audience, brand identity, brand promise, and brand

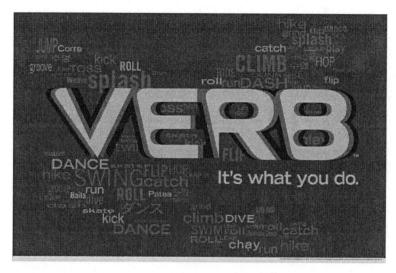

FIGURE 6.8   Tweens are encouraged to "pick their verb"

positioning. Kotler and Keller have identified six major factors to guide these selections, ones that can be used to evaluate a pool of options, testing them with target audiences relative to these ideals:[14]

> **Memorable**—How easily will this brand element be recalled and recognized? Short and catchy names and phrases such as Click It or Ticket and AMBER Alert can help, as can symbols such as ones used for recycling (see Figure 6.9).
>
> **Meaningful**—Ideally, the brand element suggests something informative and relevant to the target audience, something that helps them decide whether to "participate." Consider the inherent and rich meaning in names such as "Neighborhood Watch" and "Parents: The Anti-Drug."

FIGURE 6.9   Recycling symbol

Likeable—How aesthetically appealing are the proposed brand elements, both visually as well as verbally? Is it something citizens might even want to put on their clothing, cars, or perhaps in their homes, images such as ones of the Great Wall of China or the Eiffel Tower? Or how about your state's litter prevention slogan?

Transferable—Will you be able to use the brand element under consideration to introduce new products in the same or different categories? A different version of the recycle symbol, for example has been used for glass and corrugated packaging. (See Figure 6.10.)

Adaptable—Consider how adaptable and updatable the brand element will be in the future. This is especially true when using characters as a core element of the brand, ones like Smokey Bear.

Protectable—Will you be able to legally protect the brand element, or is it so generic that "anyone" could use it? Can it be too easily copied or used inappropriately? Although it might at first seem flattering, it is important that names retain their trademark rights and not become generic, as Kleenex, Xerox, and Jell-O did in the private sector.

One campaign that has made great choices regarding brand elements to achieve these ideals is the tough-talking litter prevention campaign

FIGURE 6.10   Extending the recycle symbol to specific materials

sponsored by the Texas Department of Transportation—Don't Mess with Texas®.

As you read the following quote from the official Web site for Don't Mess with Texas, you'll get a sense of a desired brand image: "You may wonder how a little saying aimed at educating folks about not dropping candy wrappers and soda cans took on a life of its own— catching on like wildfire and quickly becoming an internationally recognized rallying cry. It's because the slogan and the campaign advertisements have managed to capture the spirit of Texans them- selves. Don't Mess with Texas says it all. It's bold. It cuts to the point. It's full of pride. What others have called braggadocio we Texans call pride ... after all, it ain't braggin' if it's true. We're crazy about our home state and we want the world to know it."[15]

Clearly some of the success in achieving 95 percent name recogni- tion among Texans is due to the selection of campaign elements that reflect this spirit, starting with the selection of the campaign's name.[16] Colors in the campaign logo match those of the state flag (red, white, and blue), and the use of the star symbol with a highway graphic con- nects it to the flag as well (see Figure 6.11).

FIGURE 6.11   Litter prevention slogan on the left and the Texas State flag on the right

The campaign uses a variety of ways to make the brand visible, including traditional channels such as television, radio, outdoor bill- boards, road signs, and special events such as the annual statewide Don't Mess with Texas Trash-Off. The brand is also supported through more nontraditional strategies, with celebrities including Willie Nelson singing songs for the cause and a Web site that offers bumper stickers and merchandise such as coffee mugs and baseball caps (see Figures 6.12 and 6.13).

FIGURE 6.12   Don't Mess with Texas bumper sticker offered free to residents

FIGURE 6.13   A portion of Don't Mess with Texas merchandise sales help fund the "Don't Mess with Texas" litter prevention campaign

Most importantly, the brand supports the state's objectives to reduce littering. In less than ten years following the launch of the campaign, litter on Texas roadways was reduced by 52 percent. Perhaps the fact that in 2005 the Texas Department of Transportation began cracking down on unauthorized use of the slogan and logo is one additional indicator of the brand's evolution.

Maintaining a Desired Brand Image

After selecting and designing brand elements, your branding tasks now enter a second phase, that of launching and managing this identity to ensure its intended outcome—a desired brand image. You will need passion for your brand in order to encourage its use and perseverance to take good care of it.

Develop Guidelines for Usage of Brand Elements

The good news for you when you've developed a strong brand for your agency or one of its programs is that your fellow colleagues and marketing partners will want to use it. The bad news is they will, and unless told otherwise, they may enjoy taking a little creative license. (Just imagine members of a state's drowning coalition dressing Smokey Bear up in a swimming suit wearing a life vest and a slogan "Only This Can Help Prevent Drownings!") You have an internal branding job ahead of you. One effective technique to help ensure a consistent use of all brand elements is to develop (and it can be simple) a style manual, sometimes also referred to as a graphics standards manual or brand identity guidelines. It should inform and assist others in reproducing and displaying the brand. It should inspire them as well.

Smokey Bear is protected with such a guide, providing uniform standards for all aspects of Smokey's image, from drawings to placements of logos to the manufacture of the costume to public appearances (e.g., the person wearing the costume is not to speak during appearances and should refrain from using alcohol or drugs prior to and during the Smokey Bear appearance). It includes details on acceptable colors, specifying specific numbers within the universal Pantone Matching System (PMS); placement of logos and taglines, including types and sizes of fonts to be used; and the importance of not using Smokey for non-fire prevention messages. The guide also attempts to inspire readers to want to conform to the guidelines, articulating that one of the reasons Smokey continues to be such a powerful icon is because he is carefully managed by those authorized to use his likeness. The standards keep him strong.[17]

Audit and Manage Brand Contact Points

You'll have additional internal branding tasks as well because brands are not built (or brought down) by promotions alone. Customers come to know a brand through a range of contact and touch points: interactions with agency personnel and your partners; experiences when online, on the telephone, or performing transactions at your facility; and personal observation and associations when utilizing programs and services.

Consider contact points that Hong Kong International Airport, the world's fifth busiest international passenger airport, must manage in order to reinforce their official branding as a "dynamic physical and cultural hub with world-class infrastructure." Experiences that need to be managed to achieve this desired image are expansive and include ease of *checking flight arrival and departure information* on their Web site; access to *transportation* by land and sea to and from the airport, requiring coordination and assurance of user-friendly connectivity for arriving passengers as well the 48 million residents of the Pearl River Delta region; time required for *checking in for flights*; services available while *waiting for flights* with implications for retail shops, food service, Internet lounges, and children's play areas; even options for *passing the time* for longer waits. It doesn't seem surprising, given this brand promise, that future development adjacent to the airport includes construction of an Asia-World Expo exhibition center, a second hotel project, and even a nine-hole golf course![18]

Ensure Adequate Visibility

When launching a new brand or even a revitalized one, adequate exposure of brand elements will be crucial to its eventual orbit and landing in a desired position in the minds of key publics.

The City of Atlanta understands this concept. In February of 2005, an initiative called the Brand Atlanta Campaign was launched, charged with creating a new branding strategy and marketing plan for Atlanta. The Brand Atlanta Group, headed by the city's mayor, is hoping to put together $4.5 million for the campaign and has raised $1.9 million as of August 2005. Some think it will need more like $10 million. While Atlanta spent $3.2 million on branding in 2003, it is estimated that those considered its peers—Orlando, New Orleans, New York, Chicago—spent an average of $9 million. Las Vegas, a branding leader, spent $51 million.[19] Major events are planned to create enthusiasm as well as to raise funds for the campaign, beginning with a "block party" concert where the slogan and new logo will be unveiled and a three-day open house at about 90 museums, art galleries, theaters, and other cultural venues.[20]

Track and Monitor Your Brand's Position

To ensure that the brand has landed in the desired position and remains there, you'll want to keep an eye on it. This may involve a variety of research techniques, ones that will be described in more detail in Chapter 12, "Monitoring and Evaluating Performance." It will involve research that ideally measures your brand image prior to your efforts and then compares this baseline to results after your launch or repositioning. It will count on your having clearly identified your desired image, giving you a basis for measuring success.

According to one such public opinion survey, Greece has a new identity following the 2004 summer Olympic Games at Athens. It is now seen as a "safe destination" and "modern European country," and many Americans ranked it as the second most popular destination after Italy. These findings were reflected in the results of a random telephone survey conducted among several thousand citizens in five major countries: the U.S. (1,001 respondents), U.K. (519 respondents), Spain (502 respondents), Germany (507 respondents), and France (502 respondents).[21]

Stick with It Over Time

If you trace the history of great brands, whether in the public or private sectors, you will most likely find that the common thread is not always one of brilliance or creativity. The common thread is more likely to be that the parent organization simply stuck with something that worked—over time—and that brand trophies more often go to those who nurture and protect brand elements during storms and refurbish them as they begin to age. And the smartest of the bunch understand that just because they're "bored with it" doesn't mean it's not an "old friend" to the marketplace.

How else could a twenty-five year old dog get the privilege of ringing the NASDAQ Stock Market closing bell on Monday, September 26th, 2005? Well, this wasn't just any dog. It was McGruff the Crime Dog®, and he was celebrating his twenty-fifth birthday. This is the brand that encourages and teaches Americans how to "Take A Bite Out of Crime,"® one recognized by about four out of five adults and considered friendly, trustworthy, smart, caring, and helpful by four out of five children who know him (see Figure 6.14).[22] The idea of a national campaign to persuade citizens that they can prevent crime—and how to do so—was first conceived in 1978. The U.S. Department of Justice supported the plan, as did organizations such as the FBI, the International Association of Chiefs of Police, the National Sheriffs' Association, the AFL-CIO, and the Advertising Council who developed powerful public service advertisements with the volunteer help of Saatchi & Saatchi, an advertising agency. The

FIGURE 6.14   McGruff the Crime Dog® helping Americans "Take A Bite Out of Crime"® [23]

National Crime Prevention Council, a private nonprofit organization, serves as the day-to-day manager of the campaign, which is funded through a variety of government agencies as well as corporate and private foundations and donations from private individuals. It is one of the most successful public service campaigns in history, with a recent identity theft initiative funded by the Department of Justice to help consumers take practical steps to protect their personal information.

Revitalizing or Reinventing a Brand

Changes in citizen preferences, new competitors, new findings or new technology, or any new major development in the marketing environment could potentially affect the fortunes of your brand. Reversing a fading or floundering brand's destiny requires that you return to the brand's roots if they are strong and (pursuing the analogy) prune any dead wood, work in a lot of nutrients, and give it a good soaking. If, however, chances for revival are slim, it's probably time to find new sources of brand equity and emerge anew. Regardless of which approach is taken, brands on the comeback trail will need to make revolutionary change. Often, the first thing to do is to understand what the sources of brand equity were to begin with. Are positive associations losing their strength and uniqueness, or are they just buried too deep? Have any negative associations such as ones with product performance, service quality, partners, or any spokespersons become linked to the brand? Decisions must then be made as to whether to retain the same positioning or create a new one. There is obviously a continuum involved with pure "back to basics" and revitalization on one end and pure reinvention at the other, illustrated in the following two examples.[24]

Revitalizing a Brand

The Drug Abuse Resistance Education (D.A.R.E.) program is an extensive substance abuse prevention delivery system that operates in 75 percent of all school districts in the United States and reaches over 26 million young people worldwide by bringing police officers into the classroom. In the face of studies questioning, even criticizing, the impact of the program, and to help teachers and administrators cope with ever-evolving federal prevention program requirements, it has been recalibrated. "Gone is the old-style approach to prevention in which an officer stands behind a podium and lectures students in straight rows. New D.A.R.E. officers are trained as 'coaches' to support kids who are using research-based refusal strategies in high-stakes peer-pressure environments (see Figure 6.15). New D.A.R.E. students of 2004 are getting to see for themselves—via stunning brain imagery—tangible proof of how substances diminish mental activity, emotions, coordination and movement. Mock courtroom exercises are bringing home the social and legal consequence of drug use and violence."[25] The new brand promise, reflected in the words of their Chief Executive Officer, is to be "effective, diverse, accountable and mean more things to more people."[26]

Reinventing a Brand

Al Ries and Jack Trout, mentioned earlier in this chapter, were authors of a classic book in the '80s titled *Positioning: The Battle for*

FIGURE 6.15   Promoting the revitalized D.A.R.E. program[27]

Your Mind. One of the inspirational stories they share is of their involvement in helping to position the island of Jamaica as a premier destination for tourists.

Although the prime minister at the time was most interested in positioning the island for capitalistic investments, Ries and Trout argued they should focus first on tourism, with the rationale that many tourists work for big companies, and if they came back from Jamaica with favorable impressions, it just might encourage investments on the island. Their first exercise, as they described it, was to look in the mind of the prospect to see what mental images already exist and then select one to tie Jamaica into. They discovered the "verbal essence" of Jamaica was best characterized as "a big green island in the Caribbean that has deserted beaches, cool mountains, country pastures, open plains, rivers, rapids, waterfalls, ponds, good drinking water, and a jungly interior." They then posed what might seem like the obvious questions: "Does that sound familiar? Does it remind you of a very popular tourist destination in the Pacific?"

In the end, as you might have guessed, they recommended positioning Jamaica as "The Hawaii of the Caribbean," a position that would strongly and authentically differentiate Jamaica from the other competitive Caribbean destinations as well as provide a solid platform for steering European travelers to an option closer to home than the Pacific.[28]

Summary

You began this chapter with exposure to a variety of definitions related to branding. Most important to recall is that a brand identifies the maker or seller of a product, that brand identity is how you want consumers to see your brand, and that brand image is how they actually see it. You will have a brand image whether you intend to or not. Most important to take away from this reality is that you want your brand image to be one that you want, one that is deliberate. Six steps were recommended to accomplish this:

1. Establish the brand's purpose for your organization.
2. Identify target audiences for the brand.
3. Articulate your desired brand identity.
4. Craft the brand promise.
5. Determine the brand's position relative to the competition.
6. Select brand elements.

You also read recommendations for maintaining a desired brand image: develop guidelines for usage of brand elements, audit and manage brand contact points, ensure adequate visibility, track and monitor your progress, and stick with (a good one) over time.

If you find yourself with a fading or floundering brand, but you aren't "putting it out of business," you will need to evaluate whether to revitalize or reinvent it, both of which most likely will require revolutionary change.

7

COMMUNICATING
EFFECTIVELY WITH
KEY PUBLICS

"My experience, and the experience of the extraordinary team who led the Organ Donation Breakthrough Collaborative over the course of a two year period in 2003 through 2005, shows that it is possible to make a big difference on a major national challenge. We did it together. We did it with using communication principles that work. We did it with a modest federal investment of approximately $2 to $4 million annually. We did it fast.

Gandhi said that the key to change is 'to be the change you want to see in the world.' That pretty much sums up what we all did together."

Dennis Wagner
Social Marketing Leader & Director
Organ Donation Breakthrough Collaborative
U.S. Department of Health and Human Services,
Health Resources and Services Administration,
Division of Transplantation

By now you know that marketing is more than communications and that communications is only one of the tools that marketers have in their toolbox to inform, influence, and serve citizens. This does not minimize, however, the crucial and unique role this tool performs. Think of it as your hammer, intended to hit the nail on the head and secure your desired positioning and brand identity.

You probably have fewer challenges regarding the relevance of marketing communications in the public sector than you had with the first 3Ps. It is more accurate perhaps to say you have more questions, ones addressed in this chapter.

- How do people come up with these clever slogans like "Drive Hammered, Get Nailed" for a drunk driving prevention campaign?
- When should our agency's logo be big and prominent, and when should it just be in the fine print?
- Why do some mascots like Smokey Bear work and others are just silly?
- Our agency heads keep suggesting we need PSAs. I heard somewhere they stand for "people sound asleep." Is that true? If so, what other options do we have?
- And what do I say when the old familiar "We need a brochure" comes up, when I know people aren't reading the ones we've already got?

In this opening story, you will read how effective communications have been and continue to be critical to an agency's ambitious goal ... and to saving lives.

Opening Story: Increasing Organ Donation

Challenges

Organ donation and transplantation saves lives—lots of them. Recipients often go from being literally on the brink of death to participating fully in life—even to running marathons. In 2004, nearly 27,000 of these life-saving and life-enhancing transplants were performed.

However, the need is much greater. As of November of 2005, more than 90,000 people in the U.S. were waiting for an organ that could save their life. 17 people would die each day waiting.

It doesn't have to be this way. If every eligible deceased organ donor and their families consented to donation, there would be enough organs to stop the daily deaths and to shrink the waiting list.

Under Tommy Thompson's leadership as Secretary of the Department of Health and Human Services, an ambitious numerical goal was set in April, 2003: to save or enhance thousands of lives a year by spreading known best practices to the nation's largest hospitals to achieve organ donation rates of 75 percent or higher, with a national average of about 49 percent.

The challenge was a communications one: how to team with and persuade hospital and organ procurement organization (OPO) caregivers from several hundred organizations to rapidly learn and adapt the effective practices of those that already had high rates.

Strategies

The key strategy used was the methodology of a Collaborative. Put simply, a Collaborative is an intensive full-court press to facilitate breakthrough transformations in the performance of organizations, based on what already works. It employs an "All Teach, All Learn" approach to systematically expose the practices of high performers in clear, vivid, and compelling ways that make it easier for others to adapt and replicate these practices in their own organizations.

The Health and Human Services (HHS) Collaborative teamed with the Lewin Group, a premier national health care consulting firm, to conduct extensive reviews of large donor hospitals and their designated organ procurement organizations to codify the practices being used to generate high organ donation rates. These practices became the "Change Package" or menu of ideas for testing and adaptation that was provided to those committing to the 75 percent Aim.

Target Audiences

Because the Aim was to increase organ donation rates at the nation's largest hospitals (where most donors originate), target audiences were bedside nurses, intensivists, emergency room physicians, neurologists, hospital CEOs, nurse managers, trauma surgeons, chaplains, donation coordinators, social workers, and other key practitioners in these big hospitals and their procurement organizations who would be involved in organ donation cases. Strategies were tailored to these audiences.

Ultimately, 226 of the nation's largest hospitals and 50 of the 58 organ procurement organizations formally committed to the 75 percent Aim and fielded teams in the Collaborative.

Messages

Messages that drove the Collaborative emphasized change, action, results, and commitment. For example:

- "Every system is perfectly designed to get exactly the results that it gets. If you don't like the results you're getting, change your system." Don Berwick, MD
- "Never doubt that a small group of thoughtful committed citizens can change the world—indeed it is the only thing that ever has." Margaret Mead, Anthropologist
- "You move closer to what you focus on. If you focus on problems, you get closer to them. Instead, choose to focus on your Aims and you will get closer to them." Doug Krug, Enlightened Leadership

Some of the key messages emphasizing the need for rapid change came from organ donation recipients, donor families, and in one particularly vivid case, from the parents of a young girl who died while waiting for a lung transplant. This story, now captured on videotape and used widely throughout the entire donation and transplantation community, provides the fuel that hospital and OPO teams need to keep up an aggressive pace of learning, change, and improvement.

Messengers

The organ donation Collaborative emphasized a simultaneous top-down and bottom-up messenger strategy.

It was evident to the entire donation and transplantation community from the start that the highest levels of the government and the highest levels of the organ donation and transplantation leadership communities supported the Aim and Strategy of the Collaborative. These leaders joined with the HHS Secretary in committing to the Aim and guiding the overall effort.

Communication Channels

The most impressive channel used by the Collaborative was ongoing production of five- to seven-minute video clips that featured the people and practices of high-performing practitioners and Collaborative Teams in action.

These videos had multiple benefits, including vividly capturing the people and practices in action so that hospital and procurement teams knew *what* to adapt and replicate; rewarding and featuring those who generated results; interspersing the practices themselves with motivational and inspiring statements from national leaders, donor families, organ recipients, and those waiting; and providing every Collaborative Team member with readily transportable DVDs that could be used to educate and inspire other home-team members, ICU nurse colleagues, fellow emergency room physicians, and other donation coordinators.

Because of immediate success, demand for participation, and rapid growth in participation, HHS made a decision to begin satellite broadcasting the Learning Sessions. Other channels include the publications, events, annual meetings of Leadership Coordinating Council member organizations, a comprehensive Collaborative listserv, a Collaborative Web site, and twice-monthly All-Collaborative conference calls where participation frequently numbers 300 or more people.

Rewards

In the first 21 months, nearly 3,000 additional life-saving and life-enhancing transplants already occurred as a result of increases driven by the Collaboratives.

Organ donations have increased by an unprecedented 10.8 percent in 2004 over 2003 and are estimated to exceed that growth in 2005.

Leaders believe that new initiatives, when coupled with the continuing growth and successes of these first Collaboratives, have the potential to *double the number of annual transplants over the course of the next several years.*[1]

Promotion: The Fourth "P"

Marketing communications are used to inform, educate, and often persuade a target market about a desirable behavior. The word **Promotion** is used specifically to mean *persuasive communication* and is the fourth "**P**", the tool you count on to ensure that target audiences know about you or your offer, believe they will experience the benefits you promise, and are inspired to act. These communications represent the voice of the brand and are designed and delivered to highlight your offer, determined by decisions you have already made regarding your product, price, and place. Your marketing objectives rely on this tool for support. Your target audiences are your source for inspiration and the ones whose opinion and response matter most.

Developing these communications is a process that begins with determining your key messages, including a desired style and tone. It moves from there to considering who will deliver these messages or at least who will be perceived as delivering them. And only after this do you select communication channels as the content and format of your messages can and should drive these choices.

A brief description of each component is noted here, with more detail and illustrative examples to follow in this chapter:

- *Messages* are what you want to communicate. They are inspired by considering what your target audience needs to know and believe to be likely to act.

- *Messengers* include any spokespersons, sponsors, partners, and actors used to deliver messages, and this includes who you want your target audience to think is the "seller" or "supplier" of the product and behind the communications.

- *Communication Channels* refers to where promotional messages that you have developed will appear. These are not to be confused with distribution channels, described earlier as where and when the customer actually purchases the product, performs transactions, receives services, and/or participates in programs.

As noted, these communications decisions will be based on decisions already made regarding marketing objectives, target markets, desired brand identity, product, price, and place. They will impact decisions regarding evaluation, budget, and implementation plans. Chapter 13, "Developing a Compelling Marketing Plan," will present an outline for a typical marketing plan, one that pulls all these components together using a sequential process.

Developing Messages

Three questions are suggested as a starting point for developing key messages for your marketing communication efforts. Noting (even in bullet format) your responses to what you want your target audience to know, believe, and do as a result of your communications will assist those who actually design your communications and help ensure that the final product communicates what you intend.

What Do You Want Your Target Audience to Know?

This aspect of message development focuses primarily on information: *specifics about your offer* (e.g., changes in garbage collection due to a holiday), *facts* you want citizens to be aware of (e.g., how the proposed changes in Medicare coverage will affect them), and any important *news* they may have missed (e.g., a need to evacuate due to an impending hurricane).

Knowing about HIV/AIDS challenged many governments in the 1980s and continues to challenge most even twenty-five years later. In 2004, Tika Shrestha and his family were living in a remote village of Nepal with no access to mass media and only a few radios. Tika knew nothing about HIV/AIDS until a letter arrived from his brother in Kathmandu bearing a sticker with the message, "Protect yourself and others from HIV/AIDS." Curious to find out more, he approached a community health volunteer who explained HIV/ AIDS. He reported that now that he is fully aware of how the disease is spread and how to protect himself, he seeks opportunities to share his knowledge with others. To reach the many Nepali who live beyond the reach of mass media, the Ministry of Communication's Department of Postal Services placed this sticker on the outside of every piece of domestic and international mail for six months, ensuring that the message would reach the most remote corners of this mountainous kingdom. It is estimated that 14 million people, more than half the country's population, saw the postage stickers.[2]

What Do You Want Your Target Audience to Believe?

This is a different question. It's not about facts and information you want your target audience to have. It's about what you want them to *believe* and how you want them to *feel* about your offer, which of course includes your organization or any person, program, or efforts that are the focus for your communications. A great resource for answering this question is your brand promise—the benefits you want your target audience to believe they will experience. You can also refer to your brand identity—the images, thoughts, and feelings you want to come to mind.

It must be challenging to alter the preconceived beliefs that many businesses have about OSHA (Occupational Safety & Health Administration), the agency within the U.S. Department of Labor charged with reducing workplace injuries and illnesses, often through direct intervention. The very name for employers, especially new ones, most likely conjures up images similar to those of auditors, border patrols, customs inspectors, or even barroom bouncers. Communications on the OSHA Web site and sound bytes from agency directors make it clear, however, how they would like to be seen. Messages seem intended to reposition intervention as consultation, compliance as prevention, and enforcement as assistance. Benefits of utilizing the agency's services and complying with standards are emphasized, as reflected in a speech delivered in 2004 by the Assistant Secretary of Labor for Occupational Safety and Health in which he urged that "Focusing on human assets and strong safety and health management systems is a triple win. #1. Lives are saved. #2. Businesses save money and maximize returns on investments. #3. Safe workplaces are productive workplaces where workers with high morale and high motivation produce high quality products and services."[3]

What Do You Want Your Target Audience to Do?

Frequently, especially in the world of marketing, persuasive communications must go beyond informing and altering perceptions—they must zoom in on influencing individuals or businesses to act, to actually do something. Examples in the public sector that you have most likely been exposed to are numerous: fill out a form properly to get a building permit, call 911 for emergencies only, comply with workplace safety standards, evacuate before an impending disaster, sign up to be an organ donor, plant a tree on Earth Day, stay in school, attend public safety trainings at a fire station, sign up for the Peace Corps, talk with your children about drugs, and visit our town. Notice the focus on specific acts and behaviors. Notice how critical these actions must be to an agency's success, to supporting missions and goals for utilization of programs and services, participation rates, and compliance. Consider as well the potential benefits that motivating messages will have to citizens.

The U.S. Department of Homeland Security, for example, wants citizens to "Be Ready," not afraid. Messages on printed materials, featured in public service announcements, and reinforced on the Web site focus on persuading households and businesses to do four things: #1. Get a kit of emergency supplies. #2. Make a plan for what you will do in an emergency. #3. Be informed about what might happen. #4. Get involved in preparing your community (see Figure 7.1). Detail is provided on exactly what should be included in kits, how to create a plan that includes deciding what friend or family members to call to keep in touch, and how to get training to help others in your community. This quote on the Web site sets the tone: "While there is no way to predict what will happen, or what your personal circumstances will be, there are simple things you can do now to prepare yourself and your loved ones."[4]

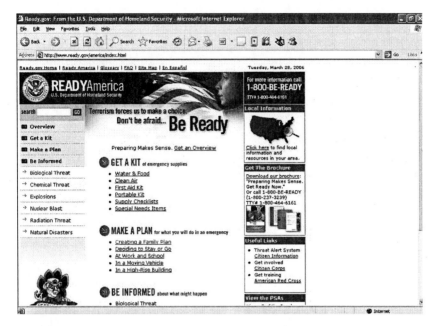

FIGURE 7.1   Web site for Ready.gov (http://www.ready.gov/index.html)

Keys to Effective Messages

Several tips are presented in this section on how to create effective messages. The foundation for your messages will be your answers to the questions just posed regarding "What do you want your target audience to know? To believe? To do?" In most cases, your most powerful options will "simply" emerge from this fertile ground. When creating specific slogans, headlines, and other key messages, your primary attention should be given to simplicity and to customer benefits. In addition, messages are more likely to be understood if they create vivid images, remembered if they are brief, and valuable if they support the style and tone of your brand personality.

Keep It Simple

Once more, Ries and Trout offer sound advice, this time focusing on the importance of brevity and clarity of messages. "In communication, more is less. Our extravagant use of communication to solve a host of business and social problems has so jammed our channels that only a tiny fraction of all messages actually gets through. And not necessarily the most important ones either ... There's a traffic jam on the turn-pikes of the mind. Engines are overheating. Tempers are rising."[5]

Evidently the U.S. Federal Trade Commission's simple message offering citizens an opportunity to sign up for the "Do Not Call" registry to cut down on unwanted telemarketing calls got through (see Figure 7.2). The list took effect on October 1, 2003, and by December of 2005, a poll conducted by New York-based Harris Interactive Inc. indicated that 76 percent of U.S. adults say they have signed up for the registry.[6]

NATIONAL
DO NOT CALL
REGISTRY

FIGURE 7.2   Logo for the Federal Trade Commission's Do Not Call Registry

Focus on Citizen Benefits

In Chapter 3, "Developing and Enhancing Popular Programs and Services," you read about the core product, one of the three levels of a product platform, the one described as the benefit consumers are seeking and expecting to receive when they purchase and consume your offer. Effective messages highlight these potential benefits. They signal your brand's promise. They frame your offer to highlight benefits (fitness) over features (exercise). Perhaps that was what officials in Canada had in mind when they created titles for their agencies such as Health Canada, Environment Canada, Public Safety and Emergency Preparedness Canada, Social Development Canada, and Status of Women Canada.

To further demonstrate this effect, compare your response as a driver in a suburban neighborhood to two alternative signs featured in Figure 7.3. Which one would you be more likely to comply with? Why?

Use Words That Create Vivid Images

Most brand names, slogans, and other key messages will conjure up some sort of image in the recipient's mind. Your job as a communicator

FIGURE 7.3   Different approaches to communicating speed limits

is for those images to be strong, memorable, and intentional. The trick is to choose words that trigger images containing meanings you want to be associated with your communications. Typically, the more vivid the image, the better.

Consider the differences in images you have for each of these two slogans: "You Drink & Drive, You Lose" and "Drive Hammered, Get Nailed." The first message, used by many states, most likely sends a "zero tolerance" message and seems targeted at social drinkers. If this is what was intended, it is probably on track. If, however, the target is a potential drunk driver, the second slogan seems more appropriate, creating a distinct and vivid image of a clear warning directed at hard-core offenders (see Figure 7.4).

FIGURE 7.4   Washington State's message for drunk drivers

Make It Easy to Remember

This seems like an obvious tip, but it is still worth a mention. You want to create slogans and key messages that people will remember when they don't have your forms, signs, brochures, posters, Web site, staff, or public service announcements with them at a point of decision making or action. This is especially important when there are desired actions with benefits and costs, both for your agency as well as the citizen.

You want citizens to remember emergency numbers such as "911" without having to find a phone book. You want drivers to remember to "Move right for sirens and lights" so that emergency vehicles can provide assistance as quickly as possible. You want taxpayers to remember to file their return by "April 15th." You want pedestrians approaching a railroad crossing to "Stop, look, and listen" and hikers to "Stay on the trail." You want travelers in security lines to "Take change and keys out of pockets" before reaching security scanners. You want pet owners to "Scoop the Poop." You want employees caught in a tall office building on fire to remember to take the stairs, form a single line, and "Put your hand on the shoulder of the person in front of you." And you want homeowners to "put yard waste out the first week of the month."

Ensure That Style and Tone Fit the Brand

An additional checkpoint for developing and selecting effective messages is that of your brand personality. By the time you get to this stage of creating messages and slogans, ideally the brand identity has been established and understood by those involved in their development. By using this identity as a resource, you make it more likely that your communications will be associated with your brand. You also make it more likely your messages will be remembered and that your desired brand image is reinforced.

Phrases describing your brand personality will help set the stage, a process that could be supported by the exercise suggested in an earlier chapter to fill in the blanks to the phrase, "I want my target audience to see my brand as _____." It would follow, then, that an agency or program that wanted to be perceived as *smart and resourceful* (a community library) would have communications that differed in style and tone from one that wanted to be seen as *warm and friendly* (a community center), and that an agency wanting to be perceived as *strong and objective* (city police) would have different messages and slogans than one who wanted to be seen as *helpful and nurturing* (a community clinic). Similarly, an agency that wanted to be seen as *responsive and reliable* (an electric utility) would highlight different features and benefits than one that wanted to be seen as *educational and full of opportunities for adventure* (a national park.). Based on the tone and style of the sign in Figure 7.5, how do you think transit managers wanted to be seen by travelers on their subway?

FIGURE 7.5   Sign in a New York subway station

Choosing Messengers

In most cases, the messenger (or source of your message) will be your organization and will be identified for your audiences by your agency's name or logo appearing on signage, printed materials, and other special promotions. However, you still face additional decisions and options regarding your messenger. Will you also include a spokesperson, and if so, who it will be? Should you consider a mascot? Will you feature additional partners in the communications, or do you want to be seen as the sole sponsor? Each decision is important to your communications' effectiveness because some messengers can achieve higher attention, recall, and influence than others, and this impact will vary by audience segment.

Three factors have been identified as most important when considering your messenger: perceived expertise, trustworthiness, and likeability.[7] This applies to your selection of a spokesperson, mascot, or partner as well as your decision to "go it alone." *Expertise* refers to the specialized knowledge the target audience thinks that the communicator possesses. *Trustworthiness* is related to how objective and honest the source is perceived to be. Friends, for example, are trusted more than strangers or salespeople, and people who are not paid to endorse a product are viewed as more trustworthy than people who are paid. *Likeability* describes the messenger's attractiveness, with qualities like candor, humor, and naturalness making a source more likeable. The most highly credible source, of course, would be one who scores high on all three dimensions, which are qualities you can consider as you explore the following messenger options.[8]

You Can Use a Spokesperson

A spokesperson could come from your agency (a state attorney general doing a radio spot warning parents of the consequences of serving alcohol to minors), from another governmental agency on your behalf (a New York police officer doing a PSA on emergency preparedness for Homeland Security), or from outside the agency (a group of children making a presentation at a community event requesting support for a new recycling center in their neighborhood).

In Japan, a nationwide campaign in 2005 to save energy by cutting down on air conditioning focused on asking workers to leave their ties and jackets home during the summer. Many people in the U.S. would have no problem with that, but in Japan, where conformity and tradition are prized, workers evidently were finding it tough to comply. Evidently to persuade them to release their inhibitions, a photo showed up in a newspaper advertisement featuring Prime Minister Junichiro Koizumi wearing a half-sleeve shirt without a tie, urging his Cabinet to follow suit. The effort seems to be having some effect. At a major Tokyo department store, it was reported that men's shirt sales were up 17 percent in May from a year earlier.[9]

You Can Be the Sole Sponsor

In this case, the most traditional of the options, the agency is the clear and sole source of the communications. Certainly when you look at the most common types of communications in the public sector (e.g., forms, brochures, applications, signs, Web sites), you'll only see one agency's name or logo. This seems appropriate in most cases, and it can be tested by referring to the three major factors presented earlier. Are you (the agency) perceived as an expert on this matter? Are you a trusted source of information? Do you have a favorable, likeable image relative to this particular communication, program, or effort?

There were mixed reactions in the news, for example, to an announcement in 2004 that the U.S. Pentagon had created its own 24-hour television channel, covering Defense Department briefings, interviews with top defense officials, and stories about the daily life and work of service members. An article in the *Christian Science Monitor* in April 2005 reflected these polar perspectives: "The anchors and reporters wear uniforms instead of neckties and suits, and the commercials promote the military, not laundry soap and cutlery sets. But otherwise, the Pentagon Channel, which is on the cusp of its first anniversary—looks and sounds a lot like CNN and C-SPAN. To the people who run the Department of Defense television network, that's exactly the point. To critics, that's exactly the problem."[10]

You Can Include Partners

For some issues, you may need support in order to achieve communication objectives—sometimes only the kind you can get from an outsider.

You may need a partner who is seen as more of an expert. Public health departments often quote the American Academy of Pediatrics as the source for childhood immunization schedules and the American Lung Association regarding the specific risk factors related to exposure to secondhand tobacco smoke.

You may want a partner to help decrease any suspicions your target audience has regarding your motives or true agenda. A local sport-fishing club might be a good partner for communications discussing homeowners as a source of water pollutants in lakes and streams, dispelling citizen perspectives that corporations are the problem, not individual citizens, and that governmental agencies are just "picking on the little guys."

You may benefit from a partner who adds likeability to your effort. Consider how the American Red Cross helps to round out the personality of a relief effort, seen by many as providing the heart as well as the hand.

You Can Create a Character or Mascot

Characters and mascots for delivering messages help create attention and recall, especially when children are one of your target audiences. They might also be a great choice for an agency or program needing a little help with the "likeability" factor.

Why has Smokey Bear been cherished and listened to for more than sixty years and McGruff the Crime Dog for more than twenty-five? Perhaps it has something to do with choosing great mascots in the first place, ones in these cases that appeal to our natural love of teddy bears and one of our best, most loyal friends. Consider as well the strategic connection that a bear has with the forest and a dog with guarding a home. Their success is also due, no doubt, to the fact that their sponsoring agencies have worked hard to keep them alive, not tiring of their costumes, names, or personalities, protecting their graphic standards, and making it easy for others to access costumes, logos, and materials for reproduction.

Selecting Communication Channels

After messages and messengers have been selected, you now face the daunting and often frustrating task of selecting communication channels—daunting because of the vast array of options and the varying advantages and disadvantages of each, and frustrating because you may not be able to afford or justify ones you would like to use. Major types of communication channels and specific media vehicles are summarized in Figure 7.6 and described briefly in the following section.

ADVERTISING

Broadcast
    Television
    Radio
    Internet: Banner Ads
Print
    Newspaper
    Magazine
 	
Ads on the Internet/Web sites
Ads on backs of tickets and receipts
Ads at theater using still shots and videos
	Outdoor/Out of Home
	    Billboards
	    Busboards
	    Bus shelter displays
	    Subways
	    Taxis
	    Vinyl wrap cars and buses
	    Sports events
	    Kiosks
	    Restroom stalls
	    Airport billboards and signage

PUBLIC RELATIONS

Stories on television and radio Articles in newspapers and magazines	OpEds Videos

SPECIAL EVENTS

Community Meetings Demonstrations/Exhibits	Fairs Tours

DIRECT MARKETING

Mail Internet/Email	Telemarketing Catalogs

PRINTED MATERIALS

Forms Brochures Newsletters Flyers Calendars	Posters Envelope messages Booklets Static stickers Door hangers

SPECIAL PROMOTIONAL ITEMS

Clothing:
    T-shirts
    Baseball hats
    Diapers
    Bibs
Items More Temporary in Nature:
    Coffee sleeves
    Bar coasters and napkins
    Buttons
    Temporary tattoos
    Balloons
    Stickers
    Fortune cookies
	Functional Items:
	    Key chains
	    Flashlights
	    Refrigerator magnets
	    Water bottles
	    Litterbags
	    Pens and Pencils
	    Bookmarks
	    Book covers
	    Notepads
	    Tote bags
	    Mascots
	    Cellphone cases

FIGURE 7.6   Typical Communication Channels and Vehicles [Adapted from: Kotler, Roberto, & Lee, *Social Marketing: Improving the Quality of Life* (Thousand Oaks, CA: Sage, 2002)]

SIGNAGE & DISPLAYS

Road signs Signs and posters on governmental property or property regulated by government

PERSONAL COMMUNICATION CHANNELS

Face-to-face meetings and presentations Workshops, seminars, training sessions	Word of mouth Word of Web

POPULAR MEDIA

Public art Songs Script in movies, television, radio programs	Comic books and comic strips Playing cards and other games

FIGURE 7.6 (Continues)   Typical Communication Channels and Vehicles [Adapted from: Kotler, Roberto, & Lee, Social Marketing: Improving the Quality of Life (Thousand Oaks, CA: Sage, 2002)]

Where Will Messages Appear?

Advertising is formally defined as "any paid form of nonpersonal presentation and promotion of ideas, goods, or services by an identified sponsor."[11] In the public sector, it is also relevant to include unpaid forms of advertising in this category, most commonly known as public service announcements (PSAs), where the space or time for the placement of the advertisement is free. A notable advantage of PSAs of course is the cost; the disadvantage is that you have very little control over where the ad will appear in the newspaper or magazine or when it will play on broadcast media, a phenomenon mentioned earlier that has led some to refer to a PSA as "people sound asleep."

Advertising can be used over the long term to build a desired image for an organization or in the shorter term to trigger a quick response. It is seen as the most pervasive of the communication tools, allowing the marketer to reach large audiences frequently (budget permitting, of course). Most advertising media vehicles provide opportunities for dramatization through sight, sound, and/or motion, as on television, radio, and the Web.

The Peace Corps introduced a new public service announcement campaign in 2003 and out-of-home PSA components eighteen months later. The campaign features a new tagline ("Life Is Calling. How Far Will You Go?") and a new logo treatment in the form of a patch.

(See Figure 7.7.) PSAs are made available to interested media outlets; they can request varying sizes of print and out-of-home media, and they can choose the length in seconds for radio and television spots.

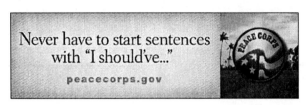

FIGURE 7.7   Peace Corps' out-of-home PSA advertising appearing on donated billboards and transit displays[12]

Public Relations is distinguishable by its outcome—free publicity. This communication channel is one of the more powerful and is often considered the most authentic and credible by receiving audiences. It provides, some believe, the ability to catch people off guard, especially those who prefer to avoid advertisements and salespersons. It has the same desirable potential for dramatization as advertising does. To get this publicity, a variety of tactics are used, including issuing and following up on news releases, press kits, and invitations to press conferences and notifying the media of opportunities for interviews and photos.

The Snohomish County Public Utility District, near Seattle, generated significant publicity in 2004—for example, when it released new financial documents and audiotapes showing that Enron had illegally obtained more than $1 billion in profits from western state ratepayers. The utility used the evidence to bolster its case related to a disputed Enron energy contract, securing hundreds of news stories, including the lead story on the CBS Evening News, countless reports on network and cable news channels, and articles in the *New York Times*, *USA Today*, and *The Wall Street Journal*. This publicity then prompted the Washington State governor, members of Congress, and attorneys general from several western states to pressure federal regulators to expedite their legal review of Enron. Ultimately, the Federal Energy Regulatory Commission expanded its Enron review, which could save the Seattle-area utility more than $100 million.[13]

Special Events include those that are parts of large public gatherings (a county fair) as well as ones organized and conducted by your agency (a tour of your facility). Activities range from those that include booths to equipment displays and showcases to community meetings to child-oriented contests and activities. There are several advantages to this channel. It can foster interaction with target audiences, allowing them to ask questions and express opinions you probably need to hear. It provides opportunities for hands-on experiences and engagement with your agency's staff, building stronger relationships.

The Chicago Police Department, for example, holds beat meetings. A beat team consists of police officers assigned to a fairly small area of the city, and every beat has a monthly public meeting, with officers from the beat and representatives from a special office such as the gang office or the youth office. As of 2004, there were an average of 250 meetings a month where police reported back to citizens on what they had done since the last meeting and new problems were discussed. Attendance from the public is seasonal, with a good meeting in the summer of about 33 citizens. On average, about 6,700 people a month come to these meetings, which importantly are best attended in high-crime areas. According to Wesley Skogan, a professor of political science at Northwestern University, these events have contributed in part to the fact that "public confidence in the police is up and crime is down. There's been an enormous decline in the crime rate, and the bulk of that has been in poor African American neighborhoods."[14]

Direct Marketing is a direct communication to specific individuals with intent to solicit some response or initiate some dialogue. Major vehicles include direct mail (a water bill insert promoting low-flow toilets), telemarketing (notifying residents of an electrical outage), catalogs (energy-saving fixtures and appliances), and Internet marketing (a listing of road repair projects and their expected completion dates). It offers the ability to customize messages and provide up-to-date information, and it is famous for its ability to elicit a response.

Consider the Web-based activities alone related to annual Earth Day celebrations. Ideas are provided for taking action in your home (how to use less water), in your classroom (games for teachers to offer their students), at work (ideas for green building), and in the community (how to find events in your state and options for volunteering). (See Figure 7.8.) You can even get the weather forecast for Earth Day

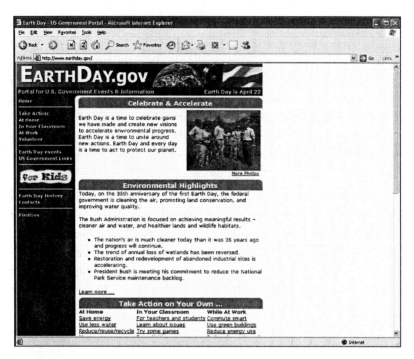

FIGURE 7.8   Earth Day events promoted on their Web site

in your community by entering your ZIP code. And partners in this effort such as Google get in the act as well, as they did in 2005 by dressing up their homepage with trees, squirrels, and birds!

Printed Materials are what most would agree is the public sector's most frequently used communication channel, so much so that when many think of marketing in the public sector, printed materials first come to mind. The array of options is familiar: forms, brochures, flyers, posters, newsletters, booklets, and calendars.

A survey of public agencies conducted by *Public Works Magazine* in April 2005, for example, found that among respondents using printed marketing materials, 73 percent distributed brochures, 60 percent issued newsletters, 48 percent developed handouts, 29 percent used door hangers, and 23 percent printed calendars. The City of Indianapolis reported use of a full spectrum of printed materials, including a brochure to promote their public works department, an electronic newsletter, water bill inserts promoting new initiatives, and topic-specific brochures covering issues related to flood control, winter weather, ozone awareness, downspout disconnection, and sump pumps.[15]

Although applications and forms are not technically promotional tools, you are encouraged to consider them as important communication vehicles, ones that can support a desired brand image or reinforce an undesirable one. An agency that wants to be seen as helpful and accessible will want forms that are clear and simple, and one that wants to encourage voluntary participation in an activity will want registration forms that take a minimal amount of time complete. Your brand identity statement will provide an excellent guide and point of reference. Your target audience will let you know how you're doing!

Special Promotional Items is a unique category and a catchall for a vast array of functional items like refrigerator magnets as well as nonfunctional ones like balloons. It is sometimes endearingly referred to in the marketing world as "trinkets and trash." At the least, these items can help launch a campaign or program message. When designed to be more strategic, sustainable, and functional, they can also serve as prompts and reminders. They can even be used as a form of recognition.

The Tennessee Valley Authority offers businesses participating in their Green Power Switch® program a window sticker, which is considered a positive public relations tactic because it signals to customers that the business is opting to use renewable energy resources (see Figure 7.9). Businesses pay a little more for electricity generated from cleaner sources, but they consider it a strategy to help improve the environment, distinguish themselves from competitors, and appeal to customers with an environmental ethic.[16]

Green Power Switch®

FIGURE 7.9 **Window sticker given to businesses using renewable energy resources**

Signage opportunities in the public sector are envied by many in the commercial sector because the public sector has many highly visible ways to communicate with citizens: signage on roadways and at airports, post offices, schools, libraries, parks, community centers, and more. Opportunities such as these to reach large groups of citizens on a frequent and sustained basis at low costs are hard to come by in the private sector.

Although this example, described on Wikipedia, is among the oldest in this book, it is a great example of the power of an effective sign. On Sunday, September 3, 1967 at 5 a.m. in Sweden, traffic switched from the left-hand side of the road to the right. It was called Dagen H (H day), with the H standing for Hogertrafik, the Swedish word for "right-hand traffic." Arguments for the change seemed clear. All of Sweden's immediate neighbors drove on the right, including Norway. Most Swedes drove left-hand drive vehicles, which led to many head-on collisions when passing on two-lane highways, which are common in Sweden because of its low population destiny and traffic levels. Nonetheless, the change was unpopular with citizens. Signage needed to play a strong role in notification that the program was a go, as well as to provide clear prompts and reminders of the change (see Figure 7.10). Evidently, it did. "On the Monday following Dagen H, there were 125 reported traffic accidents, compared with a range of 130 to 198 for previous Mondays." And no fatal traffic accidents were attributed to the switch.[17]

FIGURE 7.10   Sign used to inform and remind drivers in Sweden to switch to driving on the right side of the road

Personal Communication Channels are those involving two or more persons communicating directly face-to-face, person-to-audience, over the telephone, or through email. This channel of personal influence carries great weight, with the word of mouth subchannel being especially powerful. A study by Burson-Marsteller and Roper Starch Worldwide found that one influential person's word of mouth tends to affect the buying attitudes of two other people on average. That circle of influence, however, jumps to eight when online. Thus "word of Web" has joined "word of mouth" as an important buying influence.[18] Marketers also continue to be interested in a relatively new distinction, one they call "buzz marketing." This strategy starts with a satisfied customer and bases itself on the impact this person could have on other potential customers. Providing an unusually positive customer experience causes customers to then act as "buzz marketing agents, literally working for brands free of charge."[19]

Speaking of reaching people, consider this example of personal persuasive communications. As Hurricane Katrina moved up the East Coast from the Gulf of Mexico in September 2005, officials in Virginia decided to try a different pitch to persuade citizens to evacuate. Rescue workers decided to go door to door as they did in New Orleans but planned in addition that if people resisted the plea to leave, the rescue workers would give them Magic Markers and ask them to write their Social Security numbers on their body parts so they could be identified later. "It's cold, but it's effective," one official told news reporters."[20] Some believe this simple strategy could have persuaded hundreds of people to save their own lives in New Orleans.

Popular Media is one of the least utilized yet most powerful channels. It is well understood that movies, television, radio, music, and even comic strips have a great deal of influence on citizens and are indeed instruments of social change, both positive and negative. Many agree, for example, that the casual and sensational attitude of these media toward sex and drug use in the past has made a major contribution to the problems we have in both of these areas today, especially among youth.[21]

Andreasen and Kotler point to a more positive example: "In the first years of the twenty-first century, the NBC program *The West Wing* has done a great deal to educate the public about important public policy issues. Many social observers believe that this program had done more to explain the issues of the day (the nature of terror-ism, the use of sampling in the Census) than has any other public discussion or media coverage. (Observers have also noted that the program has also done a great deal to counteract the widespread notion that federal government leaders were immoral, self-serving egotists—an unanticipated public relations coup.)"[22]

Corralling these ideas as instruments for positive change some-times can be a simple matter of bringing an issue to the attention of the broadcast or movie industry through a letter, email, or personal visit. For many years, for example, no one in a movie or television episode (including police officers) ever put on a seat belt before driv-ing off. When this fact was brought to their attention, many directors incorporated regular seat belt use as a matter of course.[23] You can also explore a strategy of inserting a branded product or service (e.g., Smokey Bear) in a natural way in some form of the media, a tactic known as product placement.

Keys to Success When Selecting Communication Channels

Clearly there are numerous potential options for where and when your messages will appear. To be successful, you will want to choose those that best support your communication objectives and goals, that are within your budget constraints (of course), and that are a good match for your target audience. As you make these choices, you should also be on the lookout for strong yet uncluttered channels and strive for an integrated approach.

Support Communications Objectives and Goals

As you will read in Chapter 13, a formal marketing plan will establish clear communication objectives in terms of what you intend to influ-ence your target audience to know, believe, and/or do. It will also present a quantifiable goal, stating how many or what percentage of your target audience you want to persuade. These directives will then help guide your choice of media channels as well as their timing and frequency. For example, a state wanting citizens to know about new voting regulations requiring official identification at the polls may want 80 percent of adults eighteen and older in the state to know about the new regulation (reach) and to be exposed to messages at least nine times during a six-week campaign (frequency). This ambitious reach and frequency goal would most likely lead planners to use broadcast media and a variety of television and radio stations.

Allocate Funds Based on Budget Realities

Stating perhaps the obvious, the more reach, frequency, and impact you seek, the higher your budget will need to be. Indeed, media strategies and associated budgets are based on desired and agreed-upon campaign goals (e.g., reach 80 percent of potential voters). In reality, plans are influenced most by budgets and available funding sources. Initial estimates of a draft media plan to achieve a goal may indicate that costs for the desired reach and frequency exceed actual and fixed budgets. In this all too familiar scenario, planners will need to prioritize and allocate funding to media types and vehicles judged to be most efficient and effective. In some cases, it may then be necessary and appropriate to revise campaign goals (e.g., reach 60 percent of potential voters) and/or create a phased approach to campaign implementation (e.g., achieve the 80 percent goal in major metropolitan areas only).[24]

Match Media to Target Audience Behaviors and Characteristics

Perhaps the most important consideration when selecting communication channels will be the target market's *profile* (demographics, psychographics, geographics, and behaviors) and *media habits*. The goal is to choose general media types, specific vehicles, and the timing most likely to reach, appeal to, and influence target audiences. *Compatibility* of your messages with the medium will contribute to the ultimate impact you have. For example, a message regarding safe gun storage is more strategically aligned with a parenting magazine than one on gardening, even though both may have readerships with similar demographic profiles.[25]

Look for Uncluttered Channels

As a consumer, you have no doubt experienced the clutter of traditional communication channels, most likely on television and radio, in magazines and newspapers, on the Internet, and in your mailbox. You may be baffled by how any of this works, exclaiming, "I often remember a commercial but can't for the life of me remember the product or sponsor." It is worth your time to brainstorm with your colleagues, communication professionals, and even your customers to discover new, uncluttered venues. A decade or so ago, no one would have believed that we would be walking around flaunting brands on our t-shirts and hats, even our bodies (with temporary tattoos). And how clever someone was to consider inserting promotional messages in fortune cookies! What haven't they thought of yet? What could you think of?

Strive for an Integrated Approach

Integrated marketing communications is an approach intended to help ensure that your messages are consistent, clear, and compelling. It requires you to carefully integrate and coordinate communications across all marketing communication channels (see Figure 7.11). It means that your key messages in your press release announcing a new initiative are the same as those in your direct mail campaign and that your brochure has the same "look and feel" as your Web site. It requires you to consider all brand contact points the customer may encounter because each will deliver a message, whether good, bad, or indifferent.[26]

At the agency level, some organizations appoint a marketing communications director who has overall responsibility for the organization's communications efforts. Outcomes are rewarding with more consistent communications and ultimate impact for the agency.

At the program level, although the scope is narrower, the task is the same: ensuring that each channel carries consistent messages about your offer, delivered in a tone and style that supports your desired brand image.

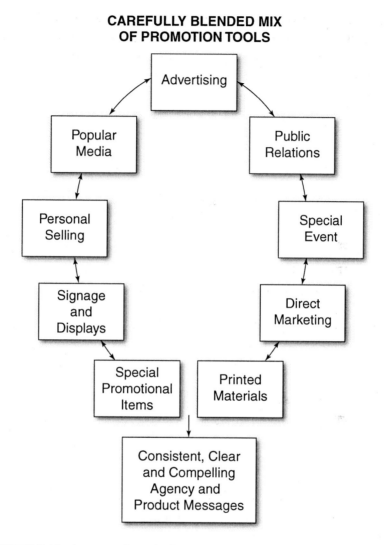

CAREFULLY BLENDED MIX OF PROMOTION TOOLS

Advertising

Popular Media

Public Relations

Personal Selling

Special Event

Signage and Displays

Direct Marketing

Special Promotional Items

Printed Materials

Consistent, Clear and Compelling Agency and Product Messages

FIGURE 7.11 **Integrated marketing communications**

Summary

Promotion, the fourth "P" in the marketing toolbox, is persuasive communication, distinguished by its intent to ensure that target audiences know about your offer, believe they will experience the benefits you promise, and are inspired to act.

Based on decisions that you will have already made in your marketing planning process regarding your offer (product, price, and place), communication strategies will be developed based on the unique profile and characteristics of your target audience and will be designed to support marketing objectives, goals, and a desired brand identity.

Three major components of communications were explored: messages, messengers, and communication channels.

Message development can start with articulating what you want your target audience to know, believe, and do as a result of your communications. Recommendations are to keep it simple, focus on customer benefits, use words that create vivid images, make it easy to remember, and ensure that style and tone fit the brand.

Messengers are those who actually deliver your messages or who you want target audiences to perceive as the one behind your communications. In some cases, your agency itself will be the sole sponsor. Other options on the table include using a spokesperson, including partners in a prominent way, or using a character or mascot as a core element of your campaign. It was recommended that these decisions be guided by three influential factors: perceived expertise, trust, and likeability of the potential messenger.

Communication channels, also referred to as media types, are where promotional messages will appear. Major media types for public sector agencies include advertising, public relations, special events, direct marketing, printed materials, special promotional items, signage and displays, personal selling, and popular media. Within each of these major channels, there are multiple options, which are referred to as media vehicles. Keys to communication success are to select media types and vehicles that will support communications objectives and goals, that are prioritized based on budget realities, and that match your target audience behaviors and characteristics. You were encouraged as well to look for new, uncluttered channels and to strive for an integrated communications strategy.

One final note. Restrain yourself and others from selecting media channels and vehicles before you have solidified your message strategy. Until you know what you need to communicate, you will not know your best media options. And to those people who keep saying, "We need a brochure," tell them about the stamp that effectively spread the word about HIV/AIDS throughout Nepal.

8

IMPROVING CUSTOMER SERVICE AND SATISFACTION

*"Keeping in touch with the customer's needs will become an ongoing fire service challenge. The ability to continually repackage the organization and how we deliver service will directly regulate our survival in a rapidly changing future. Those flexible souls who can continually redefine their jobs ahead of the change curve will grow and prosper. Those who can't, sadly will become **roadkill on the employment highway**—members who staunchly maintain 'they hired me to fight fire (only)' will become 'sail firefighters'—occupational roadkill that is run over and smushed so flat they can be recreationally sailed like a frisbee."*

Alan Brunacini, Fire Chief
City of Phoenix Fire Department

Although the focus of this chapter is on how you can use marketing principles and techniques to improve customer service and satisfaction, we'll begin by acknowledging fair perspectives and challenges that many people working in the public sector have—perhaps ones you share:

- We are the only office that offers building permits. What difference does it make whether or not the citizen had a pleasant experience? When they need to come back, they'll come back.

- As a bus driver, I don't see a reason to greet and smile at riders like they do at the Subway shop. My performance is measured by whether I get to the next stop on time, without accidents or tickets.

- We know what's in it for Burger King to let you "have it your way," and for Nordstrom to accept returns with no questions asked, and for Amazon.com to keep track of the books you've bought so that they can suggest new ones when you log on. We know that what's in it for them is more sales, increased profit, and ways to beat the competition. We don't get funded based on sales. We don't (and can't) make profits. And we don't have competitors.

- My understanding is that customer satisfaction is a function of expectations versus performance. If we meet expectations, a customer is satisfied. Given that most people don't expect much from government, I don't see what all the fuss is about.

After meaningful benefits for improved customer satisfaction have been identified, you move on to read about five major practices that will support your success in realizing them. We begin, however, with another inspirational story.

Opening Story: Phoenix Fire Department— "A Peace Corps with a Tank of Water"[1]

The logo on the side of the Phoenix Fire Department's fire trucks says *who they are*:

"Our Family Helping Your Family" (see Figure 8.1)

Their mission statement, a simple five-word sentence, says *what they do*:

"Prevent Harm. Survive. Be Nice."

Their manuals and training materials say *how they do it*:

"Respond Quickly. Solve Problems. Provide Personal Treatment."

Their Fire Chief, Alan Brunacini, says *why they do it*:

"For the people, pets and pictures."

FIGURE 8.1   Phoenix Fire Department truck with slogan "Our Family Helping Your Family"

Challenges

When Alan Brunacini was four years old, he watched a big fire in a tire store and made his career choice—to become a firefighter. And when he joined the Phoenix Fire Department in 1958, he became a typical firefighter, where the name of the game was to be quick and solve the problem. At that time, firefighters were technicians, and customers were victims. By 1978, he had advanced through the ranks to Fire Chief, which is his role today (2006), 28 years later—a notable accomplishment given that the average tenure of a fire chief in the U.S. is about two and a half years!

He can point to a defining moment around 1990 that shaped the next fifteen years for the Fire Department. It came from reading (really reading) letters from citizens. What he finally noticed in the letters was that they rarely wrote about the systems, equipment, and technical skills, considered heretofore the core products of the department. Instead, they raved or ranted about how they were treated by the troops. They talked about an additional product that was delivered—caring—and a new important piece of equipment—a heart. Customer service became the next logical area of focus for a department committed to ongoing development. It meant to Brunacini that customer needs, perceptions, and feelings were now a primary driver for how the service delivery system would look and behave. "After all, buildings and homes don't vote. People do."[2]

Strategies

Brunacini is now sought out weekly for presentations and conversations and has inspired others around the country with his bold customer service philosophies.

First, he shares that the Fire Department adds value to every encounter, which is demonstrated in the following stories, ones that embody Brunacini's interpretation of the MBO management model to mean Management by Opportunity rather than Management by Objective. (Note that the terms "Mr. Smith" and "Mrs. Smith" are generic phrases for the customer and that these true stories are told in the present tense. This is intentional. They apparently happen every day in Phoenix.)

Phoenix Fire Department: Beyond Service

A major fire occurs at a lumberyard in Phoenix at 1:30 a.m. When it's under control, a Deputy Chief (DC) is assigned to deal directly with the owner. From his cell phone on the scene, he calls Mr. Smith, describes the situation, and establishes a meeting place at the scene.

When Mr. Smith arrives, the DC meets him, gets him through the police line, takes him on a tour, describes the incident action plan, and begins to discuss a recovery plan. After Mr. Smith indicates that the majority of his business is from regular repeat customers over the phone, department communications personnel help develop a plan to do whatever is required to cause the telephones to ring in a temporary office at 8 a.m. The DC sets up a temporary office in a nearby motel, arranges hookup for cellular phones, and coordinates switching over Mr. Smith's business numbers to ring at the motel.

* * *

A self-employed cement contractor is finishing up a nine-yard pour of a driveway when he has a heart attack and collapses. A motorist calls 911, and a team is dispatched to the scene. After standard initial advanced life support treatment is administered, Frank Smith is then transported to a hospital. When the engine company Captain surveys and evaluates the scene, he realizes that a half-finished concrete driveway on a 90-degree day will be costly for the customer. He estimates that cost will be between $2500 and $3000, assuming that most of the work will need to be redone and supplies repurchased. A huddled discussion among the crew indicates that there are two members of an adjacent station who do cement finishing on their days off, so they are asked if they could finish the job. They complete the finishing and edging in 40 minutes. Back at headquarters, the engine Captain calls the hospital and asks them to let Frank's family know that the pickup truck and tools are secured at the station and that they shouldn't worry about the driveway job because "firefighter elves" finished it.

* * *

A collision injury that involves a 67-year-old man (Roscoe Smith) and a 42-pound dog occurs when an inattentive driver in another car runs a stop sign. Upon arrival, medics are assigned to the injured driver, and the Captain introduces himself to the dog, Jake. After rapport is established, the Captain assesses that the dog is okay and then puts him in the cab of the engine. Roscoe, who is still conscious, is most concerned about his dog. The crew assures him that Jake is all right and takes him to the closest trauma center. Meanwhile, Jake is transported to the neighborhood veterinarian, a mile and a half away. After it is determined that he is okay, the Captain then calls the medics at the hospital with the name, location, and phone number of the vet's office, information to be included on Roscoe's medical records so they can reassure him that Jake is okay. On a subsequent trip the next day to the same hospital, they check in on Roscoe to be certain he received the status report that Jake was fine.

Next, this added value strategy relies on attracting and retaining smart and capable fire crews, treating them like you want them to treat customers, and modeling the desired behavior. It includes empowering them to identify and respond to service delivery opportunities right on the spot and to then be positively reinforced. A series of questions assists firefighters in determining what to do. Is it the right thing for the customer? Is it the right thing for our department? Is it legal, ethical, and nice? Is it safe? Is it on your organizational level? Is it something you are willing to be accountable for? Is it consistent with our department's values and policies? And according to the Chief, if the answer is yes to all of these questions, don't ask for permission. Just do it.

Finally, traditional Total Quality Management principles support a customer-oriented system. When a customer makes a complaint, for example, the standard is to quickly contact the person who complained and find out what actually happened. If "we screwed up," develop a new or improved standard to prevent future occurrences and then contact the customer and let them what know what you're going to do to fix this in the future.

Rewards

Chief Brunacini is the first to admit it's been a challenging fifteen years. He has had to overcome a 110-year history of a military management style. He has had to deal with skeptics and critics concerned with added costs and increasing expectations. He responds with the following:

#1. Look at our business outcomes:
- We've never lost a bond levy and are rarely denied resource requests.

- We have one of the highest staff satisfaction levels, safety records, and retention rates in the country.
- We have about 3,000 applicants each year for about fifty openings.

Next question?

#2. If we can increase perceived value with minimal additional costs (sometimes just using the inherent required excess capacity), we can make a dent in the perception that government spends too much money and does too little.

#3. Mr. Smith has paid taxes for 60 years. He deserves to have his dog dropped off at the vet until he can come home from the hospital.

Customer Service in the Public Sector

Customer service and satisfaction efforts, as described for the Phoenix Fire Department, may strike you as "a bit of a stretch." Many public sector managers are probably skeptical about whether your agency could (or should) duplicate their approach and outcomes. Others may even question the fundamental premise that citizen or customer satisfaction matters. They might ask, "What impact does increased customer satisfaction have on funding, revenues, efficiency of operations, performance, and resource allocation for my agency or department?" Without a strong correlation, it's tough to make this a priority.

Some of you have even more basic challenges, asserting, "Show me the problem," and arguing that the quality of customer service is not (much) better in the private sector than it is in the public sector. At a National Customer Service Conference for the Environmental Protection Agency, for example, Ann Laurent, Associate Editor of *Government Executive Magazine*, proclaimed, "The quality of customer service is the same in the private sector as it is in the public sector. Some organizations are good; some are bad. For every Nordstrom, there's a Sears. The difference is that the public sector is more closely scrutinized and reported on more widely."[3]

Benefits of Improved Customer Satisfaction

For purposes of our discussion, you should assume that most governmental agencies have room for improvement in the area of customer service and that it is the allocation of resources to achieve progress that needs to be justified. The following discussions intend to do just that.

Improving Service and Satisfaction Can Increase Revenues

Customer satisfaction levels are most likely to have an effect on the revenues of agencies where citizens have choices for where to go for products, programs, and services (e.g., community centers who rent out facilities for meetings and workshops competing with hotels and conference centers). It is also most likely to impact organizations where "more is better," where frequency of use increases revenues (e.g., basic products and services at a post office, as well as ancillary ones including guaranteed overnight delivery competing with UPS and FedEx).

Consider *public transportation*, for example, which is impacted by both variables. A community transit system has tough competition: the convenience and "love affair" most of us apparently have with our cars. Whether a citizen will give up his or her car and use public transportation will be highly correlated with his or her satisfaction with schedules, routes, numbers of transfers needed, timeliness, courtesy of the driver, cleanliness of the bus (and its riders), location of stops, whether there are shelters for waiting, and even whether there are benches to sit on while waiting. Perceptions and experiences of these aspects of the offer will impact first-time as well as repeat business, both impacting the agency's annual revenues.

Improving Service and Satisfaction Can Support Future Funding Needs

In April 21, 2005, a headline in the *Seattle Times* warned "10 Seattle Schools Targeted for Closure. Sweeping changes aimed at trimming deficit." Reading on, the article explains that the district is faced with a growing budget gap and years of declining enrollment, in part due to birthrate declines but also due to families choosing private schools or moving to the suburbs. Because school districts are funded based on enrollment, the declining enrollment meant the district needed to drastically reduce its budget and was considering school closures and consolidations to reduce operating costs.

For agencies such as *school districts* that rely on government subsidies, and where these subsidies are based on citizen participation levels, customer satisfaction will have an impact. Levels of satisfaction with schools, for example, will be based on everything from classroom size, to how far a child is bussed (or not), to special offerings such as advanced science classes, to how administrators and their staff respond to parent and student concerns. When expectations are not met, parents consider other choices they have to fulfill their unmet needs, including private schools or moving to the suburbs or a different school district.

As another example, the U.S. *Farmers' Market Nutrition Program* is a program with a purpose to increase the use of fresh, unprepared, and locally grown fruits and vegetables among clients of the Women, Infants and Children program and at the same time expand their use and awareness of farmers' markets. It is funded by federal as well as local matching funds. Eligible recipients are issued coupons that can be redeemed only for unprepared fruits, vegetables, and herbs at farmers' markets. Whether or not the family goes to the farmers' market and actually uses their coupons, however, will be impacted by a number of variables including perceived convenience of transportation and parking, choices of produce, and how they are treated when they offer farmers their coupons instead of cash. Because redemption levels are reported and will be considered when allocating funds in the future, state program managers are motivated to measure levels of client satisfaction with the program and explore ways to increase redemption rates.

Improving Service and Satisfaction Can Enhance Operational Efficiencies

Can a case be made that happier customers lead to increased operational efficiencies? We think so, and it involves a systems approach.

Customers appreciate the benefits of increased operational efficiencies, often resulting in outcomes such as shorter lines, minimal wait time, and hassle-free experiences. Your agency can benefit from these conditions as well, having to expend fewer resources delivering service. The key to success is to design, monitor, and adjust processes and procedures based on customer needs, preferences, and behaviors. It counts on customers being more compliant during future exchanges. It requires an ongoing (never-ending) commitment to feedback and adjustments.

Consider the nature of *airport security lines* and what agencies and their employees around the world have done to speed up the process. Each adjustment and enhancement that has been made seems rooted in a unique understanding of the customer's barriers and motivations. Providing a plastic bag for pocket change and keys at the beginning of the line motivates passengers to empty their pockets earlier. Lines are cued and curved more like banks and Disney World, recognizing the time savings if passengers can be directed to the next available checkpoint. Signage with universal icons for prohibited carry-on items and videos, rather than brochures and fact sheets in a hundred languages, demonstrate the need to remove laptops before reaching the conveyor belt. The security agent provides a final convincing reminder to remove our shoes and a motivating message that it might help us avoid a potential, more thorough search. We are even given trays to enable us to quickly unload and retrieve our personal items. Then the system works better, and we as passengers experience a shorter wait. Knowing that the compliance behaviors work, most of us are even more prepared the next time we come. Our satisfaction then reinforces our behaviors and continues to increase the agency's operational efficiency.

Similar concepts can be and are applied to *community health clinics* seeking greater efficiencies, with universal desires for patients to keep appointments, to arrive on time with any important records or information, and to then follow recommended treatment plans. Understanding that "we are only human," a reminder call or card increases patients' chances of keeping appointments and bringing important items. When patients are seen at their appointed arrival time, it is likely to increase the chances that they'll arrive on time for their next appointment, dissipating the perception that they'll just have to sit and wait when they arrive anyway. To increase compliance with treatment plans, standards have been created and implemented by some for follow-up treatment calls and even visits, providing increased motivation and reinforcement.

Both examples demonstrate that customers are more likely to require fewer resources when their barriers to desired behaviors are removed and when they experience benefits for "behaving" correctly that they value (e.g., shorter lines and improved health).

Improving Service and Satisfaction Can Improve Performance Measures

Many, if not most, governmental agencies develop and publish performance measures or indicators to assist in determining priorities for the future as well as to judge progress toward strategic goals and objectives over a period of time. The point is to determine whether and how improved customer satisfaction can have a positive impact on performance measures.

The *U.S. Census Bureau's* recognition of the need for customer satisfaction in order to reach performance goals helps to demonstrate the point.

In the Bureau's 2004–2008 Strategic Plan, one goal is most relevant for our discussion: "*Strategic Goal 1*: Meet the needs of policymakers, businesses and nonprofit organizations, and the public for current measures of the U.S. population, economy and governments."[4] This goal is supported by several objectives, with one being most applicable to customer satisfaction: "*Objective 1.3*: Ease the reporting burden on respondents." The agency recognizes that success of data collection depends on the cooperation and participation of those who provide the data—individuals, families, businesses, and governments—and that minimizing the reporting burden on respondents will increase their cooperation and subsequently decrease operational costs (e.g., for troubleshooting) and increase performance (e.g., meeting targeted response rates).

Several strategies and means to support this objective are specified in the plan based on understanding (once more) the barriers and benefits for participation among customers:

- Facilitate and simplify reporting by expanding electronic reporting capabilities and options, such as responding to recurring surveys through electronic means.
- Use respondent-centered approaches to data collection to facilitate participation and to ease response.
- Align data collection procedures with the record-keeping practices of households and businesses to encourage participation.
- Take full advantage of federal, state, and private sector information to eliminate redundant data requests.

Performance is measured, in part, by return rates. For Census 2000, the final mail return rate was 78.4 percent, an increase of three percentage points over the final return rate in 1990 of 75.0 percent.[5]

Practices to Support Customer Satisfaction

Now that a case has been made for potential benefits from improved customer service, consider the following five major practices utilized in the commercial sector to accomplish this goal—ones most relevant to public sector agencies.

#1: Support Employees to Deliver Great Service

Any discussion about improving customer satisfaction must begin with an acknowledgment of the key role that employees play, especially those on the front line serving the customer. Consider these highly leveraged customer contact points: a policeman ticketing a driver, a librarian at a help desk, a child protective services case manager making a house call, an IRS staff member answering a hotline for questions, a teacher disciplining a student, an employment security counselor helping a teen with a job application, a director conducting a tour at a national museum, and an agent searching a passenger at an airport security checkpoint. Each represents opportunities for creating satisfied customers, building loyalty, and engendering positive word of mouth—or not. Understanding the "make or break" nature of these moments, successful marketing companies have reversed the traditional organization chart, placing the customers at the top and front-line people, those who meet and serve customers, next. Middle managers are positioned to reflect the critical support they provide to frontline people so they can serve customers well. And at the base is top management, charged especially with hiring and supporting great managers. Kotler and Keller illustrate this reverse pyramid in Figure 8.2.

Given the importance of positive employee attitudes, service companies direct their attention and resources to attracting the best employees they can find, developing sound (but simple) training programs, and providing support and recognition for great performance. For Nordstrom, long considered a popular case for studying customer service principles, these are more than ideals. They are a reality.

Robert Spector has conducted extensive research on Nordstrom and clearly maps the company's philosophies and practices in a book he coauthored with Patrick McCarthy, *The Nordstrom Way to Customer Service Excellence*: "What makes Nordstrom unique is its culture of motivated, empowered employees, each with an entrepreneurial spirit. Nordstrom encourages, preaches, demands, and expects individual initiative from these people who are on the frontlines; people who have the freedom to generate their own ideas (rather than wait for an edict from above) and to promote fashion trends that are characteristic of that store and region of the country. The best Nordstrom sales associates will do virtually everything they can to make sure a shopper leaves the store a satisfied customer."[6] Several of their recommendations seem most relevant for public sector agencies and are reminiscent of the opening story about the Phoenix Fire Department:

- **Hire the Smile. Train the Skill**—Spector and McCarthy assert that the qualities that Nordstrom looks for in its employees couldn't be more basic. It wants its salespeople to be *nice,* and they quote Bruce Nordstrom to underscore the point: "We can hire nice people and teach them to sell, but we can't hire salespeople and teach them to be nice."[7]

- **Lead by Example**—An illustrative story is shared in the book about an employee who was inspired by an unforgettable demonstration of the Nordstrom way. She observed Bruce

(a) Traditional Organization Chart

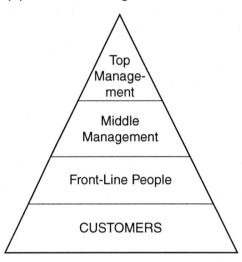

(b) Modern Customer-Oriented Organization Chart

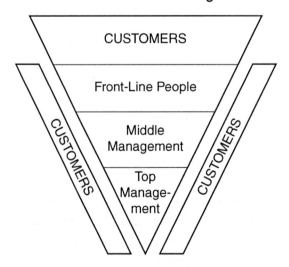

FIGURE 8.2   The Reverse Pyramid Organizational Chart [8]

Nordstrom walking through her department one day and spotting a can of pop on the counter. He evidently just picked it up, put it in a wastebasket, and then continued on his way. What impressed the employee was that he never asked who put it there or why no one removed it. He took care of it himself, the essence of the Nordstrom way.

- **Empower Employees to Act Like Entrepreneurs to Satisfy the Customer**—Though some consider the term "empowerment" a cliché, "at Nordstrom, it's a vital reality."[9] When others understandably ask whether practices such as empowering employees to accept returns unconditionally can be abused or get out of hand, Spector asserts that the response is honest and simple. "Sure it does, but central to the Nordstrom philosophy is a desire not to punish the many for the dishonesty of a few."[10] This philosophy holds true for employees as well as customers.

- **Celebrate Heroic Acts**—Recognizing and showcasing outstanding acts of customer service is a cultural norm at Nordstrom. When fellow employees witness great acts, they write up a story and share it with their manager. This activity as well as the subsequent recognition does more than make the recipient feel good (and appreciative to a colleague). It sends a clear message throughout the company that the way to advance in the company is to give great customer service.

#2: Ensure That Infrastructures and Systems Help, Not Hinder, Service Delivery

Many believe in well functioning systems as the key to customer service, asserting that when things go wrong, it is just as likely or even more likely that there's a system problem rather than a human one. Whether or not systems are more important than a service-oriented culture, we know they're as critical to customer satisfaction as a well-intentioned employee's ability to serve their customer. The role of the marketer (or the marketing mindset) is to sense levels of customer satisfaction and to help pinpoint contact points and procedures that should be explored for potential improvement.

Singapore's Changi Airport receives customer satisfaction awards and accolades on a regular basis, having been recognized for numerous years as the Best Airport in the World by *Condé Nast*

Traveler Magazine, by readers of the *Daily Telegraph* and the *Sunday Telegraph*, a U.K. newspaper, and the "Top Overseas Airport" in the *Wanderlust* Travel Awards among others.[11] Perhaps these outcomes are rooted in a vision of being the world's best airport and global air hub and, more importantly, a focus on providing speedy and hassle-free clearance, what many customers want most. It is reported that passengers take less than three minutes to clear immigration, claim their baggage, and go through customs procedures. Departing passengers are said to find a similar convenience, expedited by a systems approach. A recent example (2004) of a technological improvement to their systems was the installation of a new software tool designed to simplify check-in, especially during peak travel periods.[12]

One of Britain's fastest-growing crimes is *identity fraud*, not only costing the U.K. an estimated £1.3 billion a year but also costing victims up to 300 hours of their time to put their records and their lives back together.[13] New systems to provide more security (and thereby increased customer satisfaction) were announced in March of 2005, with the introduction of biometric "ePassports," which will provide stronger identity authentication through inclusion of a chip containing a scanned image of the holder's unique facial features. In addition, all first-time adult passport applicants will undergo a face-to-face interview. The plan also calls for the introduction of a "lost, stolen, and recovered" passport database, which will link information on lost and stolen passports with law enforcement and border posts throughout the world. It is perceived that this strengthened U.K. system will contribute to international security and law enforcement, as well as help ensure that U.K. citizens can travel easily around the world.[14]

For this last example of infrastructure changes to improve customer satisfaction, consider the *emergency phone number* used in the U.S., "911". Imagine the frustration and distraction for staff when the number is used for such calls as reporting lost pets, stolen bicycles, pot holes, burned out street lights, abandoned vehicles, or to find out if someone is in jail. And imagine as well the frustration for citizens who have a problem and don't know who else or what number to call. Several cities across the nation are now offering an alternative for residents who have non-emergency but important calls a "311" service. The intent is to improve responsiveness to citizens when they need information and to support callers by steering them in the right direction, making city government more efficient and effective and more like "one-stop shopping" for its citizens.

#3: *Consider or Enhance Customer Relationship Management Systems*

After managers in the public sector overcome the barriers of terminology, many find Customer Relationship Management (CRM) systems to be quite applicable to improving customer satisfaction. CRM systems include special software and sometimes hardware that enables the organization to access and monitor real-time as well as historical detailed individual customer information. The architecture of a CRM system includes operational as well analytical components and involves collaboration in order to capture customer data through the variety of customer contact points.

In Queensland, Australia, for example, the *Department of Child Safety* believes their new integrated client-management system will help them more effectively track and manage cases as youths move through the courts and state-sponsored care programs. In the past, the department relied on faxes to exchange information with law-enforcement agencies and courts around the country, and that information was then manually entered into computers. This new system enables agencies to exchange client data electronically, with beneficial outcomes including more time for workers to spend with clients, which may mean that kids are reintegrated into home environments more quickly.[15]

U.S. government spending on CRM systems was predicted by INPUT, a Virginia-based firm providing government market information, to increase from $230 million in 2001 to more than $520 million in 2006, an annual growth rate of nearly 18%. This growth has been driven largely by the 1998 Government Paperwork Elimination Act, which requires agencies to provide electronic options for paper-based processes, including transactions with customers such as bill payment. Understandably, this spending is expected to be highest among civilian agencies that have large customer service transactions with extensive customer data, such as the Internal Revenue Service and the Social Security Administration.[16]

#4: *Discover the Benefits of Total Quality Management*

Total Quality Management (TQM) was developed in the mid 1940s by Dr. W. Edward Deming, who was known for his use of statistics to achieve quality at a reduced cost. Several concepts are core to the theory, including one most applicable to our discussion regarding customer service ... *quality is defined by the customer and achieved through continuous improvement*. Although Japanese manufacturing companies were among the first to adopt Dr. Deming's theories, he caught the attention of many American companies in the 1970s and 1980s and a few public sector agencies as well, as described by a former Mayor of Madison, Wisconsin, Joseph Sensenbrenner, in a *Harvard Business Review* article in March-April 1991, titled "Quality Comes to City Hall."

> While Mayor of Madison, Wisconsin, from 1983 to 1989, Sensenbrenner attended a presentation by Deming, who was 82 at the time. An early analogy presented by Deming struck home. It was his revolutionary (at the time) perspective that the potentially fatal flaw causing market share loss for U.S. companies was our system of "make-and-inspect," which if applied to making toast would be expressed as: "You burn. I'll scrape."[17] The critical issue to which he was referring was that instead of correcting defects "downstream," we needed to get our "upstream" processes under control. And to do this, an organization must practice proven quality improvement techniques- techniques that begin with pleasing customers.
>
> An inspired Sensenbrenner began experimenting. His first stop was the city garage, and his first daunting goal was to decrease vehicle repair turnaround time. He took it a "Deming" step at a time. He first gathered data from individual mechanics and from the repair process itself. He found that many delays resulted from the garage not having the right parts in stock. The parts manager said the problem with stocking parts was that the city purchased many different makes and models of equipment virtually every year, estimating that the current fleet included 440 different types, makes, models, and years of equipment. He also learned that this situation was due to a city policy to buy whatever vehicle had the lowest sticker price on the day of purchase. The parts purchaser agreed with the mechanic that fewer parts

to stock would make the job easier but proclaimed that central purchasing wouldn't allow it. Central purchasing pointed the finger at the comptroller, and the comptroller then pointed to the city attorney. At this apparent "end of the road," the city attorney replied that this was "of course" possible and that all that was needed was (more) detailed written specifications in advance. In fact he assumed they were doing that all along.

Sensenbrenner reported, "The result of these changes was a reduction in the average vehicle turnaround time from nine days to three and a savings of $7.15 in downtime and repair for every $1 invested in preventive maintenance—an annual net savings to the city of Madison of about $700,000."[18]

This first exercise confirmed for Sensenbrenner that the source of the slow turnaround was indeed upstream, caused by a relationship of the city to its suppliers, not downstream, where the worker couldn't find a missing part. It also confirmed that the Deming quality strategy was not simply a matter of adopting a new set of slogans or a new accounting system. It required teamwork, breaking down barriers between departments, and involving employees in choosing the most cost-effective tools and materials for their jobs. And he found that employees were delighted that someone was listening to them instead of merely taking them to task.

#5: *Monitor and Track Customer Expectations and Satisfaction Levels*

One of the most important roles that marketing can play in improving customer satisfaction is to provide customer input and feedback. Marketers who stay close to the customer can provide insight on customer expectations, preferences, and needs to those who are designing programs and systems, measure and report on satisfaction (or dissatisfaction) with performance, and then make recommendations on areas for focus and on strategies for improvement.

One of the primary tools that public sector organizations have adopted for measuring and tracking customer satisfaction is the periodic survey. Using the results of these surveys, managers gain perspectives on how citizens view and experience their services.

The Institute for Citizen-Centred Service in Canada stresses, however, that although these measurement and assessments are very valuable, they are most effective when the results can be compared and evaluated against something, a process known as benchmarking. They suggest several benchmarks including expectations, goals, past performance, an industry standard, or the performance of peers.[19]

One example of a benchmark initiative is the American Customer Satisfaction Index (ACSI), which tracks trends in customer satisfaction and provides insights for companies, industry trade associations, and government agencies. It is produced by the University of Michigan in partnership with the American Society for Quality and CFI Group, an international consulting firm. ForeSee Results sponsors the e-commerce, e-business, and e-government measurements. Having been selected in 1999 by the federal government to be a standard metric for measuring citizen satisfaction, over 60 federal government agencies have used the ACSI to measure citizen satisfaction of more than 100 services and programs.[20]

Another measure that satisfaction (performance) scores might be compared with is perceived need or levels of concern with community or social issues. In his book *How to Make Local Governance Work,* Ned Roberto, a professor of international marketing at the Asian Institute of Management, provides a powerful model for determining citizen priority concerns and needs. He takes it beyond the traditional step of identifying and ranking citizen concerns and problems related to current and potential governmental services. He sees the process as a two-dimensional one—as he professes, "it is not necessarily true that just because a problem is seen as the most serious, it will also be the highest priority problem to the citizens."[21]

To illuminate this perspective, he describes a survey conducted for the City of Cagayan de Oro in the Philippines. The first set of questions asked citizens to rate a list of concerns and needs on a four-point scale in terms of how serious a problem they believed each was for the city. Then an additional series of questions asked respondents to rate perceptions of whether or not the citizen believed the government was doing anything about the problem. Results appear in Table 8.1.

TABLE 8.1   Cagayan de Oro Citizens Priority Problems for City Services (Base-200 = Voter Respondents)

Issues	This Is a Very Serious Problem in the City (1)	City Is Definitely Not Doing Anything About This (2)	Priority Index (3) $(3) = \dfrac{(1) \times (2)}{100}$
Anti-crime services	49%	30%	14.7
Vice control services	46%	18%	8.3
Low-cost housing	43%	29%	12.5
Garbage collection services	35%	53%	18.6
Flood control services	32%	48%	15.4
Potable water supply	30%	31%	9.3
Hospital facilities/services	29%	15%	4.3
Fire protection services	26%	11%	2.9

Source: *How to Make Local Governance Work,* Dr. Ned Roberto, Asian Institute of Management (2002), p. 48.

As findings suggest, the problems rated as most serious (anti-crime services, vice control services, and low-cost housing) did not end up being the highest-priority problems for future focus, based on index scores in Column 3 of Table 8.1. On the other hand, another problem, garbage collection, scored the highest priority because city residents saw garbage collection as very serious (35% rated it as a very serious problem) and more than half (53%) believed that the government was not doing anything about it.

Summary

Through improved customer service and satisfaction, your agency may experience multiple rewards including increased revenues, more support for future funding requests, enhanced operational efficiencies, and improved performance measures. Five major practices to assist in this process include supporting employees to deliver great service, ensuring that infrastructures and systems help (not hinder) service delivery, developing Customer Relationship Management systems (CRM), and employing Total Quality Management (TQM) principles.

Early in this chapter you were hit with a few challenges often heard when promoting a focus in the public sector on improving customer satisfaction. The following summary is intended to give you "ammunition" to address them, should they come up in the future:

> To the person managing the "only" building permit agency in town, we suggest that applying the TQM principles presented, which are grounded in customer feedback and preferences, may make it more likely that your customers will complete your permit forms properly and accurately—the first time—saving you hassle and time and increasing your performance measures. There may come a day, some hope, when your office might be paid based on the number of permits processed, so the more that are processed, the more (or less) money your agency would receive. You might want to get ready.

> To the bus driver who questioned the value of treating passengers like customers, we hope you were inspired by what happens daily at Nordstrom, and it's not all that unlikely that a "delighted" passenger might send a letter to your agency commending you and that, as a result, you might be featured in the next employee newsletter or even given an opportunity at your annual review to switch to that route and schedule you've always wanted.

> To those who don't see the benefit of letting customers "have it their way," we remind you of the schools that may be closed due to declining enrollments.

> To those who don't see the relevance of Nordstrom's practice of empowering employees to accept returns with no questions asked, we hope you'll reread the stories of the Phoenix, Arizona firefighters who do "just do it" because they know that houses and buildings don't vote on levies and referendums. People do.

> To those who can't imagine how Amazon.com keeps track of customer data and history the way they do, check out a CRM system or software.

> To those who don't believe public agencies have competition, ask the directors of your city's library or the local transit system what keeps them awake at night. For the librarian, it might be Google's databases, and for the transit director, Toyota's Prius.

And to those who don't see why "all the fuss" about meeting expectations when expectations for government services are so low, we hope you now consider the positive side of this equation. This should mean that it probably won't take much to exceed expectations, and by doing so, you create opportunities for your agency to build loyal customers, enjoy positive word-of-mouth, maintain funding, increase revenues, and enjoy the status of a highly regarded government agency.

9

INFLUENCING POSITIVE PUBLIC BEHAVIORS: SOCIAL MARKETING

"In the 1970s, we held the world record for heart disease. The idea then was that a good life was a sedentary life. Everybody was smoking and eating a lot of fat. Finnish men used to say vegetables were for rabbits, not real men, so people simply did not eat vegetables. The staples were butter on bread, full-fat milk and fatty meat ... The biggest innovation was massive community-based intervention. We tried to change entire communities. We would go in, measure everyone's cholesterol, then go back two months later. We didn't tell people how to cut cholesterol; they knew that. It wasn't education they needed; it was motivation. They needed to do it for themselves."[1]

Pekka Puska
Director of the National Institute of Public Health
Helsinki, Finland
The Guardian, Saturday, January 15, 2005

This chapter explores a distinct marketing discipline, one that has been called Social Marketing since the early '70s. This term is used today to specifically refer to efforts focused on influencing behaviors that will improve health, prevent injuries, protect the environment, and contribute to communities. As a fairly new discipline, challenges and questions abound for those of you charged with developing and implementing these programs:

- Social marketing theory encourages us to target people who are the most open to change. As a program administrator, I don't get it. It's people like the obese client I saw here at the community clinic yesterday who refuses to exercise who need the most attention.

- What do I say to citizens who say we have no business telling them they should wear a seat belt or use a condom? They ask, "What's next? Are you soon going to start telling me I can't smoke in my own home?"

- We don't have the kind of funding we need to combat tobacco companies, the liquor industry, or the weed-and-feed commercials. We're not like Pepsi competing with Coke. We're more like David up against Goliath!

- Some of these campaigns like Click It or Ticket that people call social marketing just seem to be laws. Did the social marketer have something to do with passing the law? What? How? When?

Opening Story: From "Fat to Fit" in Finland

In January of 2005, an article by Ian Sample with the following headline and copy appeared in *The Guardian*: "Fat to Fit: How Finland Did It. Thirty years ago, Finland was one of the world's unhealthiest nations ... Now it's one of the fittest countries on earth."[2] Highlights of this country's secrets appear in the following summary of the article, in which the government demonstrates a fundamental understanding of the depth of social marketing tools available and the breadth of their potential application.

Challenges

Holding the world's record for heart disease evidently "shocked" the government into an aggressive effort to dramatically improve the health of the country's citizens.

Cultural challenges in the early '70s were pervasive, however— historic policies dictated that farmers be paid for meat and dairy on the basis of the product's fat content; more than half of middle-aged men smoked and pubs were so popular that it seemed these men did little other than drink; and kids who were the most overweight were dropping out of sports, and those challenged to take on physical activity quickly fired back with their lack of time, the frigid temperatures, and packs of snow they faced several months in the year.

But Finland has a reputation as an innovator and didn't let that reputation down.

Strategies

Sweeping nationwide changes were made in legislation. Tobacco advertising was banned. Farmers were provided incentives based on the amount of protein in their product rather than fat content and were encouraged to grow fruit that would naturally thrive in the climate. Policies were changed in many places, requiring citizens instead of machinery to take responsibility for clearing snow and ice from the pavement in front of their homes.

Money was shifted away from Helsinki to local authorities, making them responsible for promoting physical activity. Activities appealing to local populations were given priority, producing outcomes that led to cleaner swimming pools, more ballparks, more cycling, more Nordic walking, and well-maintained snow parks. Activities that were free or substantially subsidized were emphasized to ensure no one was excluded.

A few unusual personal interventions were tried as well. In towns where the pubs were full of middle-aged men, for example, teams would go in, speak with patrons, and engage them in conversations about what they might be interested in doing for exercise. In one region, nearly 2,000 men were either lent bikes, tempted into a swimming pool, had a shot at ball games or coaxed into cross-country skiing.[3]

There was a marked and deliberate cultural shift in emphasis from competitive and elite sports to health-enhancing physical activity. To encourage youth who had dropped out of sports, for example, schemes sought to dampen their competitive nature, with practices promoted for scores to go uncounted, "victories uncelebrated and winning teams unpromoted."[4]

People were encouraged to incorporate exercise into their daily routines. Campaigns encouraged commuters to walk and cycle more to work. Importantly, messages were backed by changes in infrastructures, adding new walking and cycle paths, as well as money to keep them lit at night and well maintained.

Advocacy in the private sector helped overcome barriers to exercise, including one effort where the government encouraged companies to come up with non-slip shoes, addressing special concerns from seniors about falling on brisk walks. In many cities, in fact, elderly citizens could receive free sets of spikes to clamp on their shoes.

Advocacy with healthcare providers was not overlooked, with government officials encouraging physicians to prescribe levels and types of physical activity to patients, hoping it would be as common as prescriptions of medication. They called the initiative the Movement Prescription Project, counting on the finding that 80 percent of Finns consider health care professionals a reliable source of information regarding physical activity and health.[5]

Partnerships between public sector agencies were formed. In one Finnish town, local officials were concerned about the elderly who were staying indoors, especially during winter when it was dark and the pavements were slippery. To make it easier to exercise, authorities persuaded the transit agencies to have buses stop at senior centers and retirement homes and take them to local swimming pools, most for aqua-aerobics activities. And the swimming pools paid for the bus fare!

Rewards

Did it work?

Authorities reported that the number of men dying from cardiovascular heart disease has dropped by at least 65 percent and deaths from lung cancer by a similar margin. Physical activity has increased, and Finnish men can now expect to live seven years longer and women six years longer than before interventions were employed.

It appears that "Finland now finds itself in the spotlight from health officials across the world who are desperate to find out what it was the Finns got so right."[6]

Social Marketing in the Public Sector

Social Marketing is the use of marketing principles and techniques to influence a target audience to voluntarily accept, reject, modify, or abandon a *behavior* for the benefit of individuals, groups, or society as a whole.[7] Its intent is to improve the quality of life.

Behaviors are always the focus. It is this focus and commitment that distinguishes social marketing from education. The educator can typically "go home" when the target audience can demonstrate they have learned a new skill or retained new information. The social marketer, on the other hand, can't quit until the person actually performs the behavior—most often, on a regular basis. It is this commitment to behavior change (for good) that also distinguishes it from social advertising. Advertising may be one of the communication strategies used to deliver messages, but it is rare that this tactic alone will move people from awareness to interest to action. You'll need other tools in the toolbox as well, those with the familiar ring of the 4Ps.

In the area of *health*, social marketing efforts have been used to reduce tobacco use, increase physical activity, improve nutrition, lower the risk of stroke, prevent heart attacks, curb the spread of HIV/AIDS, help control diabetes, prevent communicable diseases, reduce use of contaminated drug syringes, prevent birth defects, reduce skin cancer, improve oral health, detect breast and colon cancers early, prevent teen pregnancies, and impact other similar health issues supported through changes in individual behaviors.

It is used for *injury prevention*, often targeting issues such as drinking and driving, responsible cell phone usage, drowning, domestic violence, sexual assault, fire prevention, emergency preparedness, safe gun storage, bike helmets, pedestrian safety, seatbelt usage, suicide prevention, workplace injuries, hearing loss, and proper use of car seats and booster seats.

It is critical for influencing citizens to *protect the environment,* with typical focuses on individual behaviors that will improve and preserve our water supply, water quality, wildlife habitats, air quality, and nonrenewable resources.

It is a discipline that can be used to *enhance the community* by persuading citizens to volunteer, be a mentor, stay in school, read to children, give blood, adopt a pet from the humane society, be a foster parent, vote, join a neighborhood watch program, or sign up to be an organ donor.

Who Conducts Social Marketing Efforts?

Most social marketing efforts are sponsored by *public sector agencies*, national ones such as the Centers for Disease Control and Prevention (CDC), Departments of Health, Departments of Social and Human Services, the Environmental Protection Agency, the National Highway Traffic Safety Administration, Departments of Wildlife and Fisheries, and local jurisdictions including public utilities, fire departments, schools, parks, and community health clinics. *Nonprofit organizations and foundations* also get involved, most often promoting behaviors that support their agency's mission, as does the American Cancer Society when they urge people over fifty to get a colonoscopy and Nature Conservancy when they promote actions that protect wildlife habitats. And finally, you'll see *corporations* engaged, as auto insurance companies urge drivers to abstain from cell phone use while driving and home and garden supply stores sponsor workshops on water conservation.

Why Is It So Hard?

For a variety of reasons, this is one of the toughest of all marketing assignments. After all, you will probably be asking people to

- Give up a pleasure (Take shorter showers.)
- Be uncomfortable (Wear a seatbelt.)
- Give up looking good (Let your lawn go brown in the summer.)
- Go out of your way (Take the bus to work.)
- Resist peer pressure (Don't start smoking.)
- Be embarrassed (Have a colonoscopy.)

- Spend more time (Come to a health clinic to get clean needles.)
- Spend more money (Get a home emergency kit.)
- Hear bad news (Get an HIV/AIDS test.)
- Establish new habits (Walk to the grocery store.)
- Give up old habits (Don't top off the gas tank.)
- Change a comfortable lifestyle (Turn down the thermostat.)
- Risk rejection (Take the car keys from a friend you think is drunk.)
- Learn a new skill (Compost food waste.)
- Remember something (Take your bags to the grocery store and reuse them.)

The real problem and big difference is that you don't always have something to give, show, or promise your customer in return—especially in the near term. Try to show someone a future sustainable water supply or healthier fish as a result of their actions (sacrifices).

The remainder of this chapter shares twelve principles that social marketers have found make this tough assignment a little easier and you more successful.

Principle #1: Take Advantage of Prior and Existing Successful Campaigns

Yes, the private sector may have big budgets, but you have something they don't. You can learn from and borrow campaigns that others in the public sector have spent time and money to develop. The marketing director for Pepsi can't ask a counterpart at Coke how their new TV spot is working for them, and if successful, ask to use it. You can.

Begin a social marketing campaign planning process with a search for similar efforts in public sector agencies around the country, even the world. It is one of the best investments of a planner's time. Benefits can be substantial, including learning from others' successes and failures, having access to research conducted in preparation for the campaign, finding innovative and cost-effective strategies, and discovering ideas for creative executions and materials you might want to adapt for your campaign.

Those working in public health have a great tool to find the winners. They have access to results from CDC's Behavior Risk Factor Surveillance System, a nationwide survey that measures and tracks more than twenty health risk behaviors among adults in the U.S. (e.g., tobacco use). A state getting ready to develop a tobacco cessation campaign, for example, can find the states with the lowest tobacco use and contact them to explore what strategies they used to achieve success. They can then test others' materials with target audiences in their own state and make revisions that reflect any unique geographic differences.[8]

Consider the two posters in Figure 9.1, developed to improve water quality. The one on the left was developed by the Puget Sound Action Team in Washington State in 2003. The Southeast Michigan Council of Governments and the Southeast Michigan Partners for Clean Water used this creative concept to develop their own version, the one on the right, in 2004.

FIGURE 9.1   Michigan borrowed a creative concept from Washington State's campaign poster on the left to influence behaviors to keep pollutants out of lakes and streams

Principle #2: Start with Target Markets Most Ready for Action

In a nutshell, the social marketer's job is to influence some number of people to do some desired behavior, which may include abstaining from an undesirable one. It would follow, then, that efforts and resources should be directed toward those people most likely to buy (the low-hanging fruit) rather than those least likely (hardest to reach and move).

A model used frequently by social marketers to describe those most ready for action is the Stages of Change model, originally developed by Prochaska and DiClemente in the early 1980s and tested and refined by many over the past two decades.[9] The original five-stage model has been collapsed by Alan Andreasen into the following four:[10]

- **Precontemplation**—Where people have no intention of changing their behavior and typically deny there is even a problem.

- **Contemplation**—Where people are beginning to think about a change, as something may have woken them up to the fact that they have a problem or a need to change.

- **Preparation/Action**—Where people have decided to do something and are beginning to put things in place in order to act. Some have actually started doing the behavior for the first time, or first several times. But it's not a habit.

- **Maintenance**—Where people are performing the desired behavior on a regular basis although sometimes struggle with "relapses" and will benefit from reminders and recognition.

Although the social marketer has a role to play with each segment, you will almost always get the biggest bang for your buck (number of people adopting the desired behavior) if you target those in the *Contemplation* and *Preparation/Action* stages. Contemplators do not need to be convinced they should pick up after their pet. They just need help (e.g., a pet waste bag in the park). Those in the *Preparation/Action* stage have most likely overcome barriers to change. They just need reminders, reinforcement that they will realize promised benefits, and encouragement to reach desired change levels.

Now it may makes sense to you when physical activity programs target people who are exercising once or twice a week, encouraging them to increase to five, and why nutrition counselors in community health clinics might spend more time with obese clients who have been recently diagnosed with diabetes.

Principle #3: Promote Single, Simple, Doable Behaviors—One at a Time

In this world of information and advertising clutter, you often have only a few moments to speak with your audience before they hang up, leave the room, turn the page, click the mouse, or switch channels. A simple, clear, action-oriented message is the most likely to support your target market. Remember, if you are targeting those ready to change (Principle #2), you won't have to spend as much time, money, and space convincing them they should do something. They're just waiting for clear instructions.

Even if you have twenty-five behaviors you want them to do, it is best to present them one at a time.

Although a wide array of public activities contributes to greenhouse gas emissions, for example, one solution stands out as single, simple, and doable. The *Turn It Off* project in Canada was funded by Environment Canada's Climate Change Action Plan Fund and was developed in conjunction with McKenzie-Mohr Associates and the Departments of Natural Resources and Environment. The desired behavior, to turn off your engine if you will be idling for more than 10 seconds, was directed initially to drivers dropping off and picking up their children from schools and commuters at "Kiss and Ride" lots. "Turn It Off" signs were mounted on concrete bases and placed in highly visible locations at each site. Drivers were asked to make commitments to "turn it off," and those pledging were given window stickers that said "For Our Air: I Turn My Engine Off When Parked." The combination of signs and commitment reduced idling by 32 percent and idling duration by an impressive 73 percent, compared to control sites (see Figure 9.2).[11]

FIGURE 9.2   A single message promoted in Canada to help reduce greenhouse gas emissions

Principle #4: Identify and Remove Barriers to Behavior Change

A list of concerns and real reasons why your target audience members perceive they can't or don't want to do your desired behavior should be considered a gift. Because when you have this, you are more likely to know what to say, what to do, and what to give them that will make it more likely that they will move from contemplation to preparation and from action to maintenance.

Those target audience members in contemplation, by definition, are considering this behavior, but something is typically in the way. It may be a perceived lack of skill (keeping a worm bin alive for composting), a concern with self-efficacy (ability to quit smoking), or a real inconvenience (taking the motor oil to a transfer station). For those already in action, the reason they might not be doing something on a regular basis could be that they simply forget (to floss each night), or it might be something more significant, like they think the desired level of the behavior is "over the top" (eating five to nine fruits and vegetables a day) or even "ridiculous" (following the vet's recommendation to brush your cat's teeth *every* day).

Identifying these barriers can actually be as simple as asking your target audience (in groups or individually): What are some of the reasons you haven't done this in the past? What do you prefer to do instead? What might get in the way of doing this in the future?

A counselor in a community clinic working to influence clients to have family meals together as a way to ensure better nutrition and stronger families might get an earful: We have different schedules. We don't like to eat the same things. I don't really know how to cook. It's more expensive. We wouldn't know what to talk about. I work all day, come home, and then find I don't have anything in the cupboard, so we just go get fast food.

On the other hand, a city utility wanting citizens to take a five-minute shower might only hear one big reason, one they could respond to pretty quickly (see Figure 9.3).

FIGURE 9.3 **This hourglass fixture can be attached in the shower as a response to citizens wanting to help conserve water but not knowing when the desired five-minute shower is up.**

Principle #5: Bring Real Benefits into the Present

Benefits are something your target audience wants or needs that the behavior you are promoting can provide. Though simple in theory, the practice is not easy. Two strategies will assist you.

The first is to understand the *real benefits* that are being sought. Bill Smith at the Academy for Educational Development in Washington, DC asserts that these benefits may not always be so obvious and that defining them is one of the greatest challenges of consumer research. For example, "The whole world uses health as a benefit. [And yet] health, as we think of it in public health, isn't as important to consumers—even high end consumers—as they claim that it is. What people care about is looking good (tight abdominals and buns). Health is often a synonym for sexy, young, and hot. That's why gym advertising increases before bathing suit time. There is not more disease when the weather heats up, just more personal exposure."[12]

Your next assist is to focus on near-term benefits, those that will be realized as soon after the behavior as possible. Michael Rothschild at the University of Wisconsin asserts that this is because rewards are "worth less in the future" and at the same time "costs are less onerous in the future."[13] He speaks of "the tyranny of small decisions," where "people tend to choose what is best for them in the short-run, and ignore the long-run implications."[14] To succeed, he advises that marketers should *bring future value closer to the present.*

This principle was exemplified in a project in Wisconsin sponsored by the Wisconsin Department of Transportation/Bureau of Transportation Safety and the National Highway Traffic Safety Administration, for which Rothschild was the principal investigator. The program's objective was to reduce drunk driving among 21- to 34-year-old single men living in rural areas who were driving home after a night of drinking in bars and taverns. The key insight came when they told program planners that if the planners wanted to give them a ride home, they would also need to give them a ride to the bar. The service, branded "Road Crew," provides rides from homes to bars and back home again and is loaded with immediate benefits—looking *cool* being picked up by a limo and having *fun* riding with others between bars. At the same time, many costs were eliminated, reducing the negative image associated with leaving your car at the bar overnight or the worry many felt when driving home intoxicated.

The campaign's slogan "Road Crew, Beats Driving" and advertising highlighted these immediate no hassle, fun, and cool benefits (see Figure 9.4).

Early results indicated the program was persuasive, with almost 20,000 rides given to potential drunk drivers between July 1, 2002 and June 30, 2003. These rides were estimated to have prevented 15 alcohol-related crashes on area roads, a 17 percent reduction. Further calculations indicated the program also provided a good return on investment, with costs to avoid a crash estimated at $15,300 compared with the average cost of an alcohol-related crash in Wisconsin of approximately $56,000.[15] Since mid-2003, the programs have continued as self-sufficient operations, not using any

FIGURE 9.4 **Near-term benefits of letting the Road Crew do the driving were highlighted in this successful effort to reduce drinking and driving in rural Wisconsin.**

government funds. (For more information and a short video, go to www.roadcrewonline.org.)

Principle #6: Highlight Costs of Competing Behaviors

Now you switch to the other side of the exchange equation where you focus on identifying the competition for your behavior and the costs your target market may (or may not yet) associate with them.

The competition in social marketing is the behavior your target audience prefers, might be tempted to do, or is currently doing—instead of the one you would like them to do. And the competition can be tough. For physical activity, it may be working through a lunch hour; for flossing teeth, it might be watching television; for putting a child in a car seat, it may be holding them in your lap; for using natural fertilizers, it may be a greener, weed-free lawn; for giving blood, it may be going straight home from work to spend time with your family.

After the competition is identified, the next question to explore is what costs your target market associates with "buying" the competing behavior rather than yours. These may be direct costs associated with the behavior (e.g., cancer from smoking), or they might be the loss of benefits they would otherwise enjoy if they performed your behavior (e.g., weight loss from physical activity).

This sixth principle urges you to explore and then highlight important costs the target audience believes they will have to pay if they favor the competition. Consider, for example, the costs listed in Figure 9.5 that Snohomish Health District in Washington State highlighted when parents smoke around their children in their homes or cars.

These specific costs were chosen when parents indicated they knew it might be harmful but were "shocked" at the actual statistics that had been verified by medical associations. A follow-up survey with 500 households six months into the campaign found that among those who saw the campaign, 21 percent who had allowed smoking in their car changed their rules and 17 percent who used to allow smoking in their home changed their habits.[16]

Please Decide to Smoke Outside

More than 6,000 children die each year in the United States from exposure to secondhand tobacco smoke. Exposure to tobacco smoke is reported to raise a child's risk of:

- Ear infections by 19%
- Tubes in the ears by 38%
- Asthma by 43%
- Bronchitis by 46%
- Tonsillectomies by 60%–100%
- SIDS by 200%

FIGURE 9.5   Key messages used in Snohomish County, Washington to encourage parents to smoke outside instead of in the home or in their cars

Principle #7: Promote a Tangible Object or Service to Help Target Audiences Perform the Behavior

Although tangible objects and services may be considered an optional component of a social marketing effort, they are sometimes exactly what is needed to help the target audience perform the behavior, provide encouragement, remove barriers, or sustain behavior. They provide opportunities to brand and make the campaign more concrete, creating more attention, appeal, and memorability. Examples are varied, with some offered directly by a public agency and others only promoted by the agency as a part of a campaign:

- Helpline for domestic abuse
- Laminated instruction card for breast self exam for placement on shower nozzle, even providing a water-soluble pen to note when completed
- Colored chopping blocks to increase safe food handling: yellow for poultry, red for meat, and green for vegetables
- University escort at night if you don't have someone to walk with back to the dorm after class
- Disposable cigarette butt pouches

- Stylish walking sticks (rather than a cane) to help prevent senior falls
- A magnifying glass attached to pesticide containers to help read the instruction and warning labels

The City of Johannesburg (Joburg) in South Africa featured a news article covering the services of a local company on their official Web site, a company they evidently believe will help reduce injuries and deaths from drinking and driving—at no cost to taxpayers. "You are a driver, you like drinking and you usually drink and end up driving under the influence. You know one day—rather—one night—you will be nabbed? Relax. Now you can guzzle like a fish, jump into your car and get home safely without the police bothering to plunge the dreaded breathalyzer into your mouth. That's because you're not in the driver's seat, but sitting next to a chauffeur from *Toot-n-Scoot*, a rare Johannesburg company that dispatches drivers on scooters to take people home once they are sizzled." The novelty of the concept is that the driver arrives at the client's car on a scooter, which is then collapsed and put in the "boot of your car." After dropping you off at your house, the driver removes the scooter and heads off to the next call. This *Toot-n-Scoot* service was first offered in 2003, and charges for the service range from R50–R150 (R=Rand), depending on the distance (about $10–$30 U.S.).[17]

Principle #8: Consider Nonmonetary Incentives in the Form of Recognition and Appreciation

The principle here is to consider what you can give to your target audience in recognition and appreciation for their behavior change—acknowledging the extra time they spent (e.g., sorting office paper), the habits they broke (e.g., topping off a gas tank), the pleasures they gave up (e.g., taking a shorter shower), the discomfort they experienced (e.g., wearing a life vest), the risks they took (e.g., suggesting that a neighbor use only natural fertilizers), the extra money they spent (e.g., buying an emergency kit), or the embarrassment they felt in the process (e.g., asking for an HIV/AIDS test).

In this case, we are referring to "gifts" that your agency or one of your partners gives, often unexpected and having some psychological value to your customer:

- A *yard plaque* saying "Backyard Wildlife Sanctuary" mailed to a homeowner for pledging to follow natural yard care practices
- A *lapel pin* for employees who use alternative transportation to commute to work
- A *certificate* presented to attendees completing a CPR class offered at the fire station
- A *thank you* call to a parent from a school principal expressing appreciation for volunteer work
- A *bracelet* for the designated driver, also signaling that they get a free non-alcoholic drink at restaurants and bars working in partnership with governmental agencies
- An *award* presented at a city council meeting to a local business for its increased recycling efforts
- A *"high five"* given by lifeguards at a public beach to kids wearing a life vest
- A *window sticker* for businesses who adopt environmentally friendly practices
- A *letter* from a director of a community health clinic congratulating a client for being smoke-free for thirty days
- An *article* in a business journal recognizing corporations who have supported a local beach cleanup effort

This tactic has several advantages. It is typically less expensive than offering monetary incentives such as discounted or free products and services (e.g., coupons for a child's life vest). It can be quite effective in influencing the target audience to sustain the desired behavior into the future because it has the potential to function well as a prompt or reminder (e.g., the Backyard Wildlife Sanctuary sign reminding the homeowner that he or she committed to keeping the bird bath clean). And perhaps most powerfully, it can make the desired behavior more visible and appealing to others, even creating the perception of a social norm for the behavior (e.g., the lapel pin indicating that the employee is doing his or her part for air quality and traffic congestion).

Principle #9: Have a Little Fun with Messages

Using humor to influence public behaviors can be tricky, especially for the government. There are times when it isn't appropriate for the target audience (e.g., victims of domestic violence). There are agencies with a brand personality where humor doesn't quite fit (e.g., the military in a time of war). There are some messages that are so complex they could be lost or overridden by a humorous approach (e.g., how to baby-proof your home). And there are certain behaviors that are more likely to be inspired by some other emotion (e.g., when getting people to evacuate before an impending hurricane).

You are encouraged, however, to look for opportunities where it might be appropriate for the audience, where it wouldn't be inconsistent with your brand, and where it may be just the right emotion to garner the attention, appeal, and memorability you want in your campaign.

Pet waste is a subject that most people would probably like to avoid. But many communities have a little fun with it, as they do in Austin, Texas. The city's Watershed Protection Department makes Mutt Mitts available in *Scoop the Poop* boxes in city parks (see Figure 9.6). They believe citizens are responding to their plea. Based on the number of mitts distributed in one year alone, they estimate that they removed 135,000 pounds of waste and its related bacteria from watersheds.[18]

FIGURE 9.6 **Having a little fun in Texas with messages to pet owners**
(http://www.ci.austin.tx.us/watershed/downloads/scoopsign.pdf)

Principle #10: Use Media Channels at the Point of Decision Making

Many social marketers have found that an ideal moment to speak to your target audience is when they are about to choose between alternative, often competing behaviors.[19] They are at a fork in the road, with your desired behavior in one direction and their current behavior, or potential undesirable behavior, in the other. The social marketer wants a last chance to influence this choice, and being at the point of decision making with your messages can be powerful (see Figure 9.7).

Consider the impact of the placement of these "just-in-time" messages:

- The use of the ♥ symbol on menus signifying a smart choice for those interested in options that are low in fat, cholesterol, and/or calories
- The idea of encouraging a parent who smokes and wants to quit to put their child's photo inside the wrapper of their cigarette pack
- A stencil on a storm drain reminding citizens that what they are about to put down the drain (e.g., motor oil) will go directly to lakes, rivers, and streams

FIGURE 9.7 A just-in-time message at a boat ramp on a lake to increase the chances that someone will decide to bring a lifejacket along

Principle #11: Get Commitments and Pledges

A commitment or pledge to perform a behavior has been shown to significantly increase the likelihood that your target market will actually follow through.

Behavior psychologist Doug McKenzie-Mohr considers commitments and pledges one of the major tools you can use to influence behavior change, one that can produce dramatic results. He emphasizes the importance, though, of starting with small initial requests because research has proven that those who agree to a small step are more likely to agree to a subsequent larger one. For example, a sampling of registered voters were approached one day prior to a U.S. presidential election and were asked, "Do you expect you will vote or not?" All agreed that they would vote. Relative to voters who were not asked this simple question, their likelihood of voting increased by 41 percent.[20]

He offers several tips to leverage the effectiveness of this tool: emphasize *written over verbal commitments* (e.g., signing a pledge to use alternate transportation once a week), ask for *public commitments* (e.g., having names advertised in a newspaper), seek *commitments in groups* (e.g., signing as a member of a church congregation), *use existing points of contact* to obtain commitments (e.g., when people purchase paint, ask them to sign a commitment that they will dispose of any leftover paint properly), *don't use coercion* and instead seek commitments when people appear already interested in an activity (e.g., those attending a natural yard care workshop), and *use the most durable forms and formats to display commitments* (e.g., a sticker on recycling containers rather than a listing of names in a newsletter).[21]

In Portland, Oregon, this commitment tool and small steps principle was used successfully to reduce the usage of hazardous household products among families with preschool-age children. Metro's Household Hazardous Waste program partnered with three childcare facilities to pilot and evaluate a program targeting parents. The project included seven weeks of onsite educational displays and materials as well as three commitment actions for facility staff and adult family members: a pre-project survey measuring participants' current knowledge and use of hazardous household products, a pledge to use an alternative household cleaner (see Figure 9.8), and a post-project survey to evaluate use of hazardous household cleaners after participating in the project. Results reflected in Table 9.1 were encouraging, indicating that the commitment strategy changed the behaviors of about half of study participants.

Greener Cleaner Pledge
Pledge to give up one nasty, gnarly household cleaner!

Get a 16 oz greener cleaner made just for you!

How does this pledge work? If you can pledge to stop using one of your household cleaners for a few months, we will make one for you to have and use.

YOUR PLEDGE (choose one!)

☐ Change out a **tub and tile** cleaner for a
   general purpose greener cleaner!

☐ Change out **a glass cleaner** for a greener
   cleaner glass cleaner!

☐ Change out a **general household cleaner**
   for a general purpose greener cleaner!

Or...

☐ I don't use conventional store bought cleaners but would
   like to try a ☐ general purpose greener cleaner or
☐ greener cleaner glass cleaner.

Name _____

Signature_____

**Can we call you and ask you about how well the greener
cleaner worked?** ☐ YES ☐ NO

Phone number (optional): _____

Thank you!

FIGURE 9.8   Pledge form used in Portland, Oregon with parents of children in a childcare facility

TABLE 9.1 Survey results among participants in a pilot project in Oregon using commitments to reduce use of hazardous household cleaning products

Use fewer hazardous cleaning products now	More selective in use of cleaning products	No change, because already had prior awareness and use of non-toxic alternatives	Use about the same number and kind of products as before toxic alternatives	Can't say whether the project had any effect on use of hazardous products
39%	18%	14%	21%	8%

Principle #12: Use Prompts for Sustainability

A prompt in a social marketing environment serves an important purpose—a reminder. McKenzie-Mohr and Smith in their book *Fostering Sustainable Behavior* caution that this tactic is not likely to change attitudes or increase motivation; rather, it will simply remind your target audience to engage in a behavior they have already decided they want to do. In these cases, the primary barrier is "the most human of traits—forgetting."[22]

Prompts are typically visual or auditory in nature, can be used for a variety of behaviors, and can take one of many forms: a *label* on a public bathroom towel dispenser suggesting to "Take only what you need," a *sign* at a gas station reminding a customer to check their tire pressure, *Post-it Notes* left by cleaning staff at a university reminding faculty to turn off their computer monitors when leaving at night, a *grocery store clerk* asking a customer in the checkout lane if they brought their own bag, a *refrigerator magnet* reminding homeowners what week they should put out their food waste containers, *tent cards* on tables at restaurants explaining that you won't automatically be served water, *messages* on fast-food bags reminding patrons to dispose of litter properly, *posters* in bar restroom stalls graphically depicting someone bending over "the porcelain god" serving as a reminder to drink moderately, a *sticker* for a calendar indicating it's time to check the smoke alarm batteries, an *email* alert from a utility signaling the homeowner it's time to turn the compost bin, and *a letter* from the state health department encouraging a parent of a toddler to check whether their immunizations are up to date.

To be effective, McKenzie-Mohr and Smith suggest that the messages should be self-explanatory (e.g., turn off the light) and located as close in time and space as possible to the targeted behavior (e.g., placing the prompt to turn off the light directly on a light switch).

You might also want to try creative tactics to engage and interact with citizens, as they certainly did in the Netherlands at a theme park where tales of Danish Hans Christian Andersen are featured. One sculpture of a whimsical character is connected with an infrared sensor so that every time a person passes by, it is activated and says, "Got litter?" Kids are especially fond of feeding this guy, and the nice effect is that kids often actively search the area for stuff to feed it. After all, every time the kids throw in something, he says "Thank you!" Another similar approach is used in Washington State with a litter receptacle fondly referred to as the Garbage Goat (see Figure 9.9).

FIGURE 9.9   This vacuum powered Garbage Goat at Riverfront Park in Spokane, Washington, "eats" anything that comes close to his mouth. (Photo courtesy of Gary Nance, Spokane, WA)

Applications Upstream

Up to this point in the chapter, discussions have focused on influencing individual behaviors. In a metaphoric sense, the strategic focus for addressing social issues has been *downstream*—on individuals who have a problem (e.g., high blood pressure), who are contributing to the problem (e.g., taking computers to the dump), or who are not part of the solution (e.g., giving blood). Many believe we have been placing too much of the burden for solving these social issues on individual behavior change and missing opportunities to alter infrastructures and other environmental factors, even legal actions, that make change easier and more likely—opportunities that are *upstream*.

Alan Andreasen in his book *Social Marketing in the 21ˢᵗ Century* describes this expanded role for social marketing well: "Social marketing is about making the world a better place for everyone—not just for investors or foundation executives. And, as I argue throughout this book, the same basic principles that can induce a 12-year-old in Bangkok or Leningrad to get a Big Mac and a caregiver in Indonesia to start using oral rehydration solutions for diarrhea can also be used to influence politicians, media figures, community activists, law officers and judges, foundation officials, and other individuals whose actions are needed to bring about widespread, long-lasting positive social change."[23]

Consider the issue of the spread of HIV/AIDS. Downstream, you focus on decreasing risky behaviors (e.g., unprotected sex) and increasing timely testing (e.g., during pregnancy). Now, in your mind's eye, move upstream and notice groups and organizations and corporations and community leaders and policy makers that could make this change a little easier or a little more likely, ones that you then choose as your target market for a social marketing effort. You could encourage pharmaceutical companies to make testing for HIV/AIDS quicker and more accessible. You could work with physicians to create protocols to ask patients whether they have had unprotected sex and if so encourage them to get an HIV/AIDS test. You could advocate with offices of public instruction to include curriculums on HIV/AIDS in middle schools. You could support needle exchange programs. You could provide the media with trends and personal stories. You might look for a corporate partner that would be interested in setting up testing at their retail location. You could organize meetings with community leaders such as ministers and directors of nonprofit organizations, even provide grants for them to allocate staff resources to community interventions. If you could, you would visit hair salons and barbershops, engaging owners and staff in spreading the word with their clients. You might testify before a senate committee to advocate for increased funding for research, condom availability, or free testing facilities.

The process you follow and principles that guide you will be the same ones you used for influencing individuals. You have "simply" changed your target market.

Summary

Social marketing principles and techniques are most appropriate when the purpose of your marketing efforts is to influence behaviors intended to improve health, prevent injuries, protect the environment, or contribute to communities. Behaviors are always the focus. Some describe this discipline as the toughest of all marketing assignments because you will be asking target audiences to do something for which you are not always able to give them or show them something in return, especially in the near term.

Twelve principles will help make this task easier and you more successful:

#1: Take Advantage of Prior and Existing Successful Campaigns

#2: Target Markets Most Ready for Action

#3: Promote Single, Simple, Doable Behaviors—One at a Time

#4: Identify and Remove Barriers to Behavior Change

#5: Bring Real Benefits into the Present

#6: Highlight Costs of Competing Behaviors

#7: Promote a Tangible Object or Service to Help Target Audiences Perform the Behavior

#8: Consider Nonmonetary Incentives in the Form of Recognition or Appreciation

#9: Have a Little Fun with Messages

#10: Use Media Channels at the Point of Decision Making

#11: Get Commitments and Pledges

#12: Use Prompts for Sustainability

Although most social marketing campaigns to date have focused primarily on influencing individual behaviors, experts are now urging you to move your target market lens upstream, zooming in on organizations, groups, corporations, policy makers, law makers, and others who have an impact on infrastructures and who can make it a little easier, cheaper, convenient, and even fun and popular for individuals to "behave."

10

FORMING STRATEGIC
PARTNERSHIPS

"Social change is too important to be left to chance. Today in Jordan, a network of public and private agencies are working together to address water-related issues on a scale not previously considered possible—at a fraction of the cost. In January 2005, the Mansoura city park opened—the last of six in Jordan featuring a natural environment in the Middle East. One NGO donated land. Another designed the landscaping. A third designed the Interpretation Center. The private sector provided partial funding. An architect and engineer employed by the city will provide maintenance. The Ministry of Agriculture supplied plants. The Ministry of Water and Irrigation provided oversight, and USAID provided the funding. The whole program was coordinated and managed by the Academy for Educationa l Development, working at scale from the very beginning and employing the logic that if you increase the number of diverse players responding simultaneously to a specific problem and then increase the collaboration among those players, what you get is increased impact on the economy, environment and people's lives."

Gregory R. Niblett, Senior Vice President and Director
The AED Social Change Group
Academy for Educational Development

215

This chapter is all about mutually beneficial relationships, ones that bring critical resources to your efforts and in return provide valuable benefits for your partners. If you are like most public sector managers, you know that partnerships are helpful. What you don't know as well is how to find the right partners and realize their full potential.

The reality is you need each other. You need resources that only the private sector has, and they have needs only you can fulfill. You need resources that only nonprofit organizations have in abundance, and they can't get their job done well without you. And you also need other public agencies supporting your efforts, and they are bound to call on you for the same.

A marketing mindset is key to finding and winning the best partners to make this happen. Seeing and approaching potential partners as customers will make it more likely that you will focus your efforts on the most attractive prospects and increase the chances they will say yes.

This opening story demonstrates these principles well.

Opening Story: Improving Jordan's Water Problems—For the People, By the People, Through Partnerships

Challenges

One of the most water-poor nations on earth, in 1999, the Hashemite Kingdom of Jordan was in the midst of its worst drought in more than a century. Population growth from high birth rates coupled with unprecedented refugee immigration had placed intolerable pressures on water resources. Demand for water in the Middle East had reduced the Jordan River to a narrow, polluted stream. Millions of liters of water were being lost through antiquated infrastructure, leaking toilets, outdated plumbing systems, and inappropriate fixtures, in some cases accounting for one third of total water bills. Government had also limited household access to water to just one day per week.

Believing they were already making as many sacrifices as they could to conserve water, Jordanians felt there was little more they could do. Just six percent of the population believed that their personal actions could help alleviate water shortages. Many felt that Jordan's neighboring countries were to blame, not understanding that water shortages were a chronic problem throughout the entire Middle East. Knowledge about water-saving plumbing devices was negligible, as was knowledge about other techniques for conserving water at home.

Despite active efforts from the government's Public Relations Office to educate the public, more needed doing. Most experts recognized that government efforts and communications alone could not hope to address Jordan's water-use challenges. Yet, environmental NGOs suffered from a lack of donor support, and only one NGO specializing in water issues existed in Jordan Thus, community-based leadership in dealing with Jordan's water crisis was virtually nonexistent.

Strategies

In the year 2000, the Jordanian Ministry of Water and Irrigation (MWI) and the Academy for Educational Development (AED) launched an initiative with big intentions: to reduce water consumption in Jordan by the largest consumers; to change knowledge, attitudes, and practices regarding water efficiency in the larger population; to improve advocacy and efforts to deliver water demand education and programs; and above all, to build a deep, nationwide foundation for wholesale change. The initiative, conceived of and funded by USAID, was called Water Efficiency and Public Information for Action (WEPIA).

Initial WEPIA research identified the primary drivers of Jordan's poor water-efficiency environment—and underscored the need for a comprehensive response on multiple fronts. But funding allocations limited the WEPIA staff to nine members. How could so few people address a problem that clearly required the involvement of so many? From the outset, WEPIA worked to build a coalition of organizations and individuals to create change.

Program staff developed partnerships with other organizations, which in turn spearheaded key initiatives. After only a few months, WEPIA staff had built relationships with hundreds of stakeholders and decision makers throughout Jordan. In June 2000, they met in Amman for WEPIA's strategic planning summit. Together they crafted new solutions to Jordan's endemic water problems. Participants included engineers, behavioral scientists, government officials, media experts, university professors, donor agency and NGO representatives, public and private schools, women's programs, lawyers, activists, and large consumers and suppliers from the private sector. Thus the nine-member WEPIA staff grew to a virtual ninety strong, forming a dynamic, interdisciplinary force, ready to act. The ninety participants returned to their own offices with a plan they had helped develop and their own roles clearly delineated.

The new approach represented a significant departure from past approaches. It would reduce demand, not focus on supply. It would rely on collaborative action rather than discrete initiatives, inspire actions including retrofitting of buildings and homes, disseminate water-saving devices, amend policies and laws, incorporate water-efficiency lessons into every school grade, stimulate media promotion, and even integrate messages into sermons at mosques.

In one such project, 112 poor women, most of whom had never worked outside of their homes, purchased water-saving devices at cost, sold the devices to friends and neighbors, and kept the profits. Another program, a joint effort with Jordan's Ministry of Planning, offered community grants to help increase water efficiency to over 98 community-based organizations, farmers' cooperatives, women's groups, and other groups primarily among the rural poor. An award-winning media campaign created by Prisma, a Jordanian advertising agency, focused on how water efficiency could bring economic gains for the average Jordanian. WEPIA's new messenger, Abu Tawfir, represented this possibility to all Jordanians through cartoons accompanied by water-saving tips on television, radio, and billboards and in newspapers and magazines. His name, an ingenious choice meaning "papa miser," represented in animated form a typical Jordanian family. He was part comic, part real, and all Jordanian (see Figure 10.1).

Rewards

This collaborative approach had multiple effects. It energized and strengthened Jordan's weak nonprofit sector. It applied social marketing concepts to change individual behaviors, and it helped create the standards and infrastructure needed to make water efficiency a reality. The results have been astounding. By 2004,

FIGURE 10.1 Abu Tawfir is the messenger for Jordan's water-saving message appearing on billboards at 75 locations around the country

- Ninety percent of citizens were fully aware of the extent and cause of Jordan's water shortage and knew three strategies for improving water efficiency.

- The number of people believing they could do something about Jordan's water crisis grew tenfold.

- The percentage of those who knew about aerators climbed from 9 percent to 73.8 percent.

- Sales of aerators—at one time practically nonexistent—skyrocketed. During one stage of the campaign, one company sold 1,750 aerators in a single day.

- School curricula were rewritten to focus on interactive lessons in water demand management.

- Jordan graduated its first 15 female licensed plumbers under a revamped vocational training system.

- Each community grant yielded an average water savings of 45 percent. Average increase in income, per grant, for each family was 27 percent.

Most importantly, it saved water:

- Retrofitting reduced water use of Jordan's largest users by 18 percent.

- Modernization of national plumbing codes saved 1.4 million liters of water each year.
- Estimated outdoor use of water dropped from 20 million liters per year to 11 million.
- Annual water deficits are projected to decrease by 50 million liters per year.

By the time the WEPIA program ended in 2005, Jordan had emerged as a leader in water efficiency for the entire Middle East region. Ultimately, it would vastly improve water-efficiency capabilities and competencies across Jordanian society. And it would give Middle Eastern countries an innovative model for creating sustainable, measurable results of their own.[1]

Benefits of Strategic Partnerships

Partnership trends between public sector agencies and private as well as nonprofit organizations are not easy to measure with certainty. It appears, however, that directional signals indicate the numbers must be going up.

Charitable giving in the United States, for example, is at an all-time high. According to the Giving USA Foundation, estimated charitable giving from corporations, foundations, individuals, and bequests reached $248.52 billion for 2004, a new record for the United States.[2]

Corporations are getting more strategic, however, about giving, choosing partners and initiatives that reflect an increased desire for "doing well *and* doing good." You'll find more corporations picking a few strategic areas of focus that fit with their corporate values and that support business goals. A study conducted by Cone Inc. in 2000, for example, found that 69 percent of companies planned to increase future commitments to social issues.[3] Perhaps this is an indication that corporations have their fingers on the pulse of their customers, as another Cone study reported that 84 percent of Americans said they would be likely to switch brands to one associated with a good cause if price and quality are similar.[4]

Benefits for All

As summarized in Table 10.1, all partners can gain as they give, an essential condition if these exchanges are to take place and be sustained over time. Examples for each are described in remaining sections of this chapter.

TABLE 10.1 What Partners Give to and Get from Partnerships with Public Agencies

Partners	Give to the Partnership	Get from the Partnership
Private Sector	• Cash • In-kind services • Products • Access to distribution channels • Access to customers • Increased visibility for communications • Advocacy • Volunteers	• Technical expertise • Increased brand preference • Increased sales • Community goodwill • Social impact • Increased employee attraction, retention, and satisfaction
Nonprofit Sector	• Technical expertise • Talent • Local networks • Volunteers • Credibility • Access to distribution channels • Advocacy	• Increased resources • Increased visibility • Technical expertise • National networks and contacts of the public agency • Support for agency mission and goals
Other Public Agencies	• Clout • Access to target markets • Technical expertise • Access to distribution channels	• Support for agency mission and goals • Increased resources • Increased visibility • Technical expertise

Partnerships with the Private Sector

In our book *Corporate Social Responsibility: Doing the Most Good for Your Company and Your Cause* (New York: Wiley, 2005), six distinct corporate social initiatives are identified, ones that corporations undertake to contribute to a social issue, most commonly in the area of health, basic needs, injury prevention, community development, and the environment. They include Cause Promotions, Cause-Related Marketing, Corporate Social Marketing, Corporate Philanthropy, Community Volunteering, and Socially Responsible Business practices.

Corporations have a variety of resources to contribute to public agencies, regardless of the type of initiative:

- **Cash** (e.g., Washington Mutual providing grants for teacher education)
- **Expertise** (e.g., Dell employees working at a regional electronics recycling event)
- **Access to distribution channels** (e.g., 7-Eleven displaying litter prevention messages in stores)
- **In-kind services** (e.g., a home and garden store printing a utility brochure on water conservation)
- **Merchandise** (e.g., a bike helmet manufacturer contributing bike helmets to a community clinic serving low-income families)

Partnerships with public sector agencies range from those representing long-term relationships (e.g., American Express and the Statue of Liberty) to ones that are more short-term (e.g., McDonald's printing childhood immunization schedules on tray liners). In the following sections, the nature of each social initiative is described more fully, with examples of public/private partnerships for each. The point is for you to be aware of the many options that corporations have for giving and the potential benefits they are seeking in the relationship.

Corporate Cause-Promotion Partnerships

A cause promotion is one specifically intended to increase *awareness and concern* regarding a social issue (e.g., Levi Strauss & Co.

distributing leaflets about AIDS). It may also focus on persuading people to do something to help: *find out more* about an issue (e.g., Ben & Jerry's promoting their Web site to teach about factors that contribute to global warming), *donate their time* (e.g., *PARADE* magazine encouraging citizens to conduct bake sales to raise money for food banks), *donate money* (e.g., British Airways collecting change on flights from Europe to benefit UNICEF), *donate nonmonetary resources* (e.g., LensCrafters collecting eyeglasses for those in need), or *participate in an event* (e.g., Subway promoting the American Heart Association's annual walk). Persuasive communications are the major focus for this initiative. Corporations sometimes implement these campaigns on their own (e.g., The Body Shop promoting bans on animal testing), but more often they are conducted in partnership with nonprofit organizations and/or public sector agencies, as illustrated in the following example.

Universities and Johnson & Johnson

In 2002, the National Research Center for College and University Admissions surveyed over a million college-bound students and found that nursing ranked only ninth among all professions. This was of special concern due to the nation's critical shortage of nurses, considered by many to be one of the biggest problems facing the health care industry. By 2003, nursing had moved to fourth place, and a Vanderbilt University study specifically cited the Johnson & Johnson Campaign for Nursing as a key factor in raising awareness about this shortage and in promoting positive feelings about careers in nursing.[5] In 2002, Johnson & Johnson launched a multiyear, nationwide effort to enhance the image of the nursing profession and worked in partnership with colleges and universities to recruit new nurses (see Figure 10.2). Scholarships were an important component of this effort, and as of May 2005, the company had raised $7 million for fellowships, scholarships, and grants and provided links to a variety of resources for additional scholarships on their Web site, discovernursing.com.[6]

FIGURE 10.2   Johnson & Johnson's campaign materials for enhancing the image of the nursing profession

Corporate Cause-Related Marketing Partnerships

In cause-related marketing campaigns, a corporation commits to making a contribution or donating a percentage of revenues to a specific cause based on product sales. This link to product sales or transactions most distinguishes this initiative, which contains a mutually beneficial understanding and goal that the program will raise funds for the cause and has the potential to increase sales for the corporation. Partnerships with public sector agencies most often involve contributions to a foundation that supports a public agency or institution, as was the case in the following example.

A National Monument and American Express

The *Statue of Liberty*, a national monument managed by the U.S. National Park Service, can trace its support from *American Express* back to 1885 when the company raised money through a call to employees to help fund the Statue's pedestal.[7] Then, in the early 1980s, they launched the first and best-known national cause-related marketing campaign to fund the restoration work on the Statue in preparation for its centennial celebration in 1986. Instead of just writing a check to help with the cause, American Express tried a new approach, and the marketing world was watching. They pledged that every time cardholders used their cards, the company would make a contribution to a fund to restore the Statue of Liberty, as well as an additional contribution for every new card application. The campaign generated $1.7 million in funds for the "the lady," a 27 percent increase in card usage, and a 10 percent jump in new card member applications.[8]

Then in 2003, they rolled out yet another fundraising initiative, pledging a minimum of $3 million to make critical safety improvements so that the monument could again be accessible to the public.[9] The Statue had been closed since September 11, 2001. The company pledged one cent for every purchase made on an American Express Card, up to $2,500,000 from December 1, 2003 through January 31, 2004. A ceremony in August of 2004 celebrated the improvements, the reopening, and the contribution American Express made to help make this happen.

Corporate Social Marketing Partnerships

In corporate social marketing, a corporation supports the development and/or implementation of a behavior change campaign, most often to improve public health, safety, the environment, or community well-being. Behavior change is always the focus and intended outcome. Most commonly, social marketing campaigns are developed and implemented by professionals working in federal, state, and local public sector agencies. Support from private sector companies is often critical to increasing the reach and frequency of campaign messages, as it was in the following example.

Health Canada and Pampers

In 2000, Health Canada announced a new corporate partnership to help reduce the incidence of Sudden Infant Death Syndrome (SIDS), the leading cause of death in Canada for infants between four weeks and one year of age. Procter & Gamble's Pampers brand included a new message in English, French, and Spanish on their two smallest diapers. The message read, "Back to Sleep," the sleeping position that evidence has shown helps reduce the risk of SIDS. In addition, Pampers supported the creation of a promotional door hanger distributed through hospitals in Canada and Wal-Mart stores. Pampers also promoted SIDS awareness and the "Back to Sleep" message in their own television and print advertising campaigns (see Figure 10.3).

Pre- and post-campaign measures made it clear the partnership had bolstered the agency's impact over prior efforts. Survey results showed that awareness that the proper position to place a baby during sleep is on his or her back increased from 44 percent in 1999 to 66 percent in 2001. The number of professionals who advised putting the child to sleep on his or her back increased from 21 percent to 67 percent, and most importantly, the number of caregivers and parents that placed their babies on their back went from 41 percent to 69 percent.[10]

FIGURE 10.3   Promotional materials supported by Procter & Gamble (Source: Health Canada. Reproduced with the permission of the Minister of Public Works and Government Services, Canada, 2006)

Corporate Volunteering Partnerships

Distinguishing corporate community volunteering as an initiative is not difficult, as it alone involves employees of a corporation personally volunteering at local organizations (e.g., at recycling centers) and for local cause efforts (e.g., removing ivy in public parks). Volunteer efforts may include employees volunteering their expertise, talents, ideas, and/or physical labor. Corporate support for employee volunteering ranges from programs that simply encourage their employees to give back to their communities to those representing a significant financial investment and display of recognition and reward. Types of volunteer partnership opportunities with the public sector are numerous, including those where volunteers from corporations can serve on citizen advisory committees (e.g., giving input to a five-year strategic plan for a school district), help staff community events (e.g., organizing a pancake breakfast at a city's summer celebration), host activities at corporate facilities (e.g., natural gardening workshops at nurseries), and staff phones for a special hotline (e.g., pediatricians from a medical group answering calls regarding benefits of childhood immunizations).

As you will read in the following example, tying volunteer work to the company's core business and products is always popular—for the company, the volunteers, and the recipients.

Public Schools and Washington Mutual

Washington Mutual—or WaMu, as it is known—is a national financial institution with a more than a 115-year legacy of contributing to communities where it does business. In 2003 alone, employees volunteered 44,000 times for a total of 184,000 hours of community service. Many employees volunteer for schools, organizing projects ranging from helping teachers in the classroom and sprucing up school grounds to conducting school supply drives. Employees worked on the projects either solo or in teams. One financial education activity is the WaMoula for L.I.F.E.™ (Lessons in Financial Education) program, consisting of free, one-hour courses introducing young students to the concept of money and teenagers to the concept of credit management.

As an example, in Pasadena, California, WaMu volunteers arrived at Eugene Field Elementary wearing CAN! shirts, visors, and handmade medallions shaped like giant coins and made their presentation on financial literacy fun through rap songs (see Figure 10.4).[11]

FIGURE 10.4   Washington Mutual employees volunteering in the classroom. (Photo courtesy of Washington Mutual © 2005, Washington Mutual, Inc. All rights reserved.)

Corporate Philanthropy

Corporate philanthropy is perhaps the most traditional of all corporate social initiatives, representing a direct contribution by a corporation to a cause, most often in the form of cash grants, donations, and/or in-kind services. Most agree that the character of corporate philanthropy has matured over the decades, primarily in response to internal and external pressures to balance concerns for shareholder wealth with expectations to demonstrate responsibility for communities that have contributed to the corporation's livelihood. As a result, contributions that support business objectives, such as the following one that showcases the company's products, are becoming the norm.

A National Park and General Electric Foundation

In May 2002, the GE Foundation, the philanthropic organization of the General Electric Company, announced a new program in cooperation with the National Park Service and the Yellowstone Park Foundation to restore the night sky over Yellowstone in Bozeman, Montana. The program, timed to celebrate the 100th anniversary of the Old Faithful Inn, targeted the "sky glow" in the Old Faithful village. Based on an audit conducted with the National Park Service, GE agreed to donate 50 anti-glare fixtures, and the Foundation made a 2002 grant of nearly $100,000 to support the overall effort to bring back the dark skies over Yellowstone. Over a three- to five-year period, support was expected to amount to $200,000, including GE Foundation grants and in-kind donations. According to a GE spokesperson, "the media and headline writers liked the irony that a light bulb manufacturer would take the initiative to lower light levels."[12]

Socially Responsible Business Practices

A key distinction for socially responsible business practice initiatives is a focus on activities that are discretionary, not those that are mandated by laws or regulatory agencies. They are also not ones that are simply expected, as with meeting moral or ethical standards. Corporations adopt and conduct these business practices and investments as a means to support social causes that improve community well-being and protect the environment. They can take many forms and often include partnerships and alliances with public sector agencies and programs, as illustrated in the following example.

Environmental Protection Agency and Motorola

Motorola's environmental vision statement calls for the company to fully support sustainable use of the earth's resources. Responsible business practices are concentrated in three major areas: protecting the land, protecting the air, and conserving water.[13]

Programs designed to protect the land include a program called Waste-Wise, a voluntary U.S. EPA program where organizations eliminate costly municipal solid waste, benefiting their bottom line and the environment (see Figure 10.5). Since joining the WasteWise Program in 1994, Motorola's U.S. manufacturing sites are reported to have recycled almost 125,000 tons of waste. Motorola has also developed packaging reuse systems, such as the Compack™ system, eliminating over 140 tons of packaging waste each year with an estimated savings of approximately $4.3 million annually.[14] To contribute to protecting the air, in 1992 Motorola was the second electronics firm in the world to eliminate the use of chlorofluorocarbons (CFCs) from manufacturing processes.[15]

FIGURE 10.5   Motorola participates on a voluntary basis in the U.S. Environmental Protection Agency's waste reduction program.

Partnerships with the Nonprofit Sector

Public sector partnerships with nonprofit organizations are even more typical and sometimes more mutually beneficial. This may be because they are often less controversial than those between private sector companies and public agencies (e.g., a fast food restaurant sponsoring an agency's nutrition education program). It may be because they more often represent common organizational missions (e.g., food banks and local health and human service agencies). It may also be that public sector managers are more familiar with nonprofit partners and are more comfortable with approaching them.

In this next section, you will read about public/nonprofit partnerships that are helping a state reduce costs associated with their foster care system, convincing women to breastfeed exclusively for six months, increasing revenues on college campuses, and extending the reach of the U.S. Department of Homeland Security. There is a marketing angle for each one.

Improving Programs and Services

Nonprofit organizations are great resources for technical expertise, expertise that can assist governmental agencies in improving programs and services and as a result increase participation and citizen satisfaction and even decrease costs, as illustrated in the following example.

Department of Family Services and Casey Family Programs

Even though in 2003 the state of Wyoming already exceeded national standards in moving children from foster care to adoption in less than two years and preventing children from re-entering the foster care system, they wanted to do better. They needed to. At that time they were placing youth in foster care at a rate six times higher than the national average, and it was costing the state $32 million each year. In December of 2003, Governor Dave Freudenthal announced they would be forming what they considered to be an unprecedented partnership in the social services arena. They would be working with a national nonprofit foundation, Casey Family Programs, to improve services for abused and neglected children in the foster care system and for children at risk of abuse or neglect. Wyoming's Department of Family Services (DFS) Director explained the intent and hope for the partnership: "Casey has developed many of the best practices for helping children and families succeed, and we hope Casey can help DFS, communities and providers expand this capacity in Wyoming." Casey Family Programs is the largest national foundation whose sole mission is to provide and improve—and ultimately prevent the need for—foster care and will draw on its 40 years of experience and expert research and analysis to improve the state's child welfare practice and policy.[16]

Providing Talent

Nonprofit organizations can also bring tremendous and special talent to the table, and public agencies are fortunate when they are included in partnerships like the one in the following example.

U.S. Department of Health and Human Services and the Ad Council

Although many Americans are aware of the importance of breast-feeding, the United States has one of the lowest breastfeeding rates in the developed world. This is in spite of evidence from recent studies showing that babies who are breastfed are less likely to develop ear infections, respiratory illness, diarrhea, and childhood obesity. And it is behind the partnership between the U.S. Department of Health and Human Services, Office of Women's Health, and the Ad Council's National Breastfeeding Awareness Campaign. The federal government set a goal to increase the number of mothers breastfeeding at six months postpartum to 50 percent by 2010. In 2005, we are only at about 33 percent. Campaign messages are intended to address confusion about the recommended duration and lack of belief that the added benefits are really that significant. All campaign ads drive home the message: "Babies were born to be breastfed" and highlight real, tangible benefits—with a little humor (see Figure 10.6).[17]

The Ad Council is a private, nonprofit organization that marshals volunteer talent from the advertising and communications industries to deliver critical messages to the American public, most often those sponsored by public agencies. For more than 60 years and with the help of some of the most talented advertising professionals in the country, the Ad Council has helped create some of our country's most memorable slogans, such as "Friends Don't Let Friends Drive Drunk" and "A Mind Is a Terrible Thing to Waste."[18]

Sharing Distribution Channels

Nonprofit partners can add value to existing distribution channels and at the same time experience increased support for their own agency's

BREASTFEED FOR 6 MONTHS. YOU MAY HELP REDUCE YOUR CHILD'S RISK FOR CHILDHOOD OBESITY.

Recent studies show babies may be less likely to develop childhood obesity when exclusively breastfed for six months. Call 800-994-WOMAN or visit www.4woman.gov to learn more. Or talk to your healthcare provider. Babies were born to be breastfed.

U.S. Department of Health and Human Services

FIGURE 10.6   Poster for a breastfeeding campaign in partnership with the Ad Council

mission and goals. Being able to sign up to be an organ donor when getting a driver's license adds convenience for the potential donor and increases donors for nonprofit organizations supporting this cause. High school ID cards that have the names and phone numbers of local nonprofit organizational resources on the back add value to the card as well as the teens and the nonprofit agencies listed. Postal carriers across the nation get a chance to help the communities they see firsthand when they participate annually in a one-day food drive, collecting nonperishable food donations left by mailboxes and then delivering them to local community food banks, pantries, and shelters. They can also extend the reach and influence of governmental agency efforts (e.g., community health clinics posting HIV/AIDS awareness posters in churches).

The partnership described in the next example is a classic win-win-win, with university administrators happy with increased sales and bottom-line profits, students finally satisfied with a socially responsible option, and a charity-run gourmet coffee company making inroads into a coveted distribution channel.

Universities and a Coffee Company

Pura Vida Coffee is a gourmet coffee company that is 100 percent charitably owned and 100 percent certified Fair Trade, Organic, and Shade-Grown. The company uses all of its resources to benefit at-risk children and their families in coffee-growing countries, and through its commitment to Fair Trade, it helps ensure that farmers are paid a living wage for their harvest and have access to affordable credit. Some would say, "All the world needed was another coffee company!" But this isn't just another coffee company. It is one that combines the tough-minded focus of a business with the tender-hearted nature of a nonprofit, and as of the summer of 2005, over 70 campuses nationwide (many of which are public institutions) are now serving Pura Vida Coffee, providing both dining hall dispensers as well as standalone espresso kiosks (see Figure 10.7). According to the company's president and co-founder John Sage, there has been an overwhelming positive response, which even makes

FIGURE 10.7   Pura Vida Coffee on college campuses

him hopeful that "the trend toward enlightened consumerism continues to grow and flourish and that the term Caveat Emptor (Buyer Beware) will give way to Prosum Emptor (Buyer Do Good)."[19]

Promoting Causes and Public Behavior Change

Nonprofit partners have a variety of resources that can be tapped to assist governmental agencies in promoting social causes and public behavior change. Volunteers certainly extend the reach, as they did in the following example.

U.S. Department of Homeland Security and the American Red Cross

The U.S. Department of Homeland Security and the American Red Cross seem like natural partners for an effort to increase public awareness about the importance of preparing for emergencies and to encourage individuals to take action. In 2004, Secretary of Homeland Security Tom Ridge's comments at an American Red Cross Annual Convention echoed this premise: "Homeland Security cannot begin and end at the doors of our federal department building in Washington, D.C. Washington can be expected to lead, but we cannot, nor should not, micro-manage the protection of our country. Instead, it must be a priority in every city, every neighborhood, and every home across America ... I've often said that for the homeland to be secure, our hometowns must be secure. So it follows that the Red Cross—dedicated to the protection of our communities for generations—is integral to this goal."[20]

Through this partnership, Homeland Security and the American Red Cross work with local, state, and federal government organizations, as well as the private sector, to highlight the importance of public emergency preparedness and present a variety of opportunities for citizens to learn more about preparing for emergencies, including natural disasters and potential terrorist threats. The Red Cross, with a nationwide network of nearly 900 locally supported chapters, one million volunteers, and 35,000 employees, brings critical resources to the table, as chapters across the country are already engaged in helping people create a family disaster plan so that each person knows what to do, where to go, and how to contact loved ones.[21]

Partnerships between Governmental Agencies

Although this is perhaps the most common and well-understood type of partnership, it is worthy of highlighting the potential marketing benefits. You may recall that these were included in Table 10.1, earlier in this chapter: increased clout, access to target markets, technical expertise, and access to distribution channels. A few examples may help make these seem real.

Washington State's Litter Prevention Campaign

Consider Washington State's litter prevention campaign mentioned in earlier chapters, the one that includes a hotline for citizens to call to report litterers. The campaign is managed by the state's Department of Ecology, but key to its success is the partnership with the Department of Licensing and the State Patrol. As you may recall, citizens who are reported for littering get a letter in the mail that describes the day, the time, the location, and the type of litter that a citizen saw being tossed out of their car or truck. Cooperation with the Department of Licensing is then critical to access the records of the registered owner of the vehicle. The letter then arrives in an envelope with the return address of the Washington State Patrol, printed on their letterhead, and the signature block reads "Washington State Patrol Chief." Imagine if instead the "criminal" got a letter from the Washington State Department of Ecology. Would it be opened as fast or at all?

New Zealand's Drowning Prevention Effort

It is hard to imagine a successful drowning prevention effort (anywhere in the world) that wouldn't include a coalition of governmental agencies. In New Zealand, with one of the highest rates of drowning in the Western world, a strategy to decrease drownings includes participation from a suite of governmental agencies as well as nonprofit organizations and private corporations, each providing unique areas of expertise as well as resources. Governmental agencies alone include representatives from the Maritime Safety Authority, city councils, schools, public health, and internal affairs.[22] This is not surprising, given the need for an understanding of governmental policies and processes, knowledge about drownings incidents and water safety, access to teaching core water safety skills in schools, political influence, and of course, funding.

Difficulties and Risks in Partnerships

These partnership examples may have left you feeling hopeful and inspired. Many of you, however, have experiences or have heard from others that the picture isn't always so rosy. This is true, and this section's brief discussion of the potential pitfalls for your agency may help you see them coming. After these warnings are posted, you will read in the following section about strategies to avoid some of these pitfalls and minimize others.

Regardless of the type of partnerships (public/private, public/non-profit, public/public), there are universal realities that impact your net gains from the effort. First, they take more *time* than going it alone— time for finding a partner, getting to know each other, joint decision-making, and approvals. It may have sounded like it happened overnight, but developing strategies with Pampers to support the Back to Sleep campaign no doubt required additional research, formal agreements, and coordination for Health Canada. Second, as with most relationships, success will include *compromise*. A company providing in-kind printing services, for example, may be willing to do this only if their contribution is acknowledged on the front of the brochure using their logo and brand colors, rather than being briefly mentioned in a closing paragraph. A third major downside is the potential that your corporate or nonprofit partner may subsequently have "fallen from grace" or be the subject of *negative publicity*, even for some minor deviation. No doubt this has the potential to cast a dark shadow over your agency as well, as it would on the Environmental Protection Agency if Motorola violated some major hazardous waste disposal guideline.

There are additional, more unique potential concerns with each of the relationship types. Regarding the *private sector*, citizens seem to be "naturally" cynical towards these gestures of goodwill. It often seems their first reaction is, "Why are they doing this?" Their next one is, "If they really cared about the issue and the cause, why do they make me mail back my box tops or use a coupon to give to the cause?" The reality is that public partnerships with private sector corporations will have to pass the "smell test" with potential consumers and dissipate any thought that the company is just trying to advertise their way out of something (e.g., a partnership between a children's videogame corporation and a health department to reduce childhood obesity). In relationships with *nonprofit organizations*, there are additional potential concerns: the public agency may be flooded with requests from other, similar nonprofit organizations, communications may be harder to control given the national networks of some nonprofits, and agency resources may be more drained because those from the nonprofit may be more scarce. When partnering with *other governmental agencies*, the major downside can be the additional time and effort often required for approval and decision making. Though this was noted for partnerships in general, it may be especially true given the more political, bureaucratic, and complex nature of this sometimes tangled network.

A Marketing Approach to Winning Great Partners and Reducing Risks

The following ten recommendations from *Corporate Social Responsibility* (Kotler and Lee) have been summarized to not only address the aforementioned potential risks of partnerships but to also make it more likely you will find great partners and realize their full potential benefits.[23] To illustrate each, we will use a hypothetical state health department's quest for partners to assist in increasing timely childhood immunization rates. Notice the application throughout of fundamental marketing principles, from determining a clear focus on objectives to approaching and treating potential partners with a customer mindset to developing and implementing targeted and effective campaigns.

> #1 *Start by developing a list of additional resources that your agency needs in order to meet a specific program's goals and objectives, resources such as increased funding, technical expertise, increased visibility, enhanced distribution channels, credible endorsements, and others.*

Assume a state public health department has a goal to increase the percentage of children who are fully immunized on time by the age of six from 72 percent to 80 percent in a two-year time frame, an increase of almost ten percent. Assume as well that rates have hovered around 70 percent for the past five years. A work group composed of state and county health department representatives believes that they have great materials and strategies (e.g., a direct mail campaign that reaches parents of children one month prior to the due date for their next immunization) but that they need additional funding (approximately $200,000) to implement the program statewide. The legislature has indicated they want the health department to explore partnerships with private and nonprofit organizations to help make this happen.

#2 *Identify a short list of organizations that these social issues might have a connection with, something that relates to their business mission, products and services, customer base, employee passions, communities where they do business, and/or corporate giving history.*

The work group first makes a list of organizations they think might have some interest in the issue of childhood immunizations and might be likely to provide financial or in-kind support for the mailing. With a keen eye on the potential partner's mission, customer base, and any prior relationships, initial categories include financial institutions, grocery stores, retail stores, foundations, and other select governmental agencies. Within each category, five to ten organizations are identified, ones the team believes might be a good match. They are especially concerned with eliminating any they think would be controversial or raise the "cynical" brow of a parent (e.g., a drug manufacturer or toy store).

#3 *Approach potential partners to find out more about their priority social issues and potential interest in your program issue.*

The health department then commissions a local research firm to conduct brief telephone surveys with 75 organizations on the potential list, exploring priority social issues that their organization supports as well as interest in childhood immunizations. The decision to hire a research firm to do the interviews was based on scarce staff resources as well as the perception that corporate and foundation managers might be more open with a research firm and not as suspicious that it was a sales call. Based on these findings, let's assume that 20 organizations appear to have at least some interest in the issue and indicated they are willing to discuss sponsorships further with a representative from the health department.

#4 *Listen to their business needs.*

At this point, members of the work group meet face-to-face with decision-makers at eighteen of the organizations and have telephone interviews with the other two who are located out of state. Topics of these subsequent conversations include acknowledgement by the health department that they understand there is some interest in supporting childhood immunizations but that first they are interested in knowing what business goals and objectives their organization is currently focused on, with specific attention to those that are marketing related, ones such as interest in building their brand identity, enhancing community goodwill, or increased visibility with specific target markets.

#5 *Share with them the social issues your organization supports, the initiatives you are considering or engaged in, and your strengths and resources. Find out which, if any, they find most appealing.*

During this same meeting, health department representatives then share program materials and the history and outcomes of the program. They show samples of the specific materials included in the mailings that the state is trying to find sponsors for: posters, charts, refrigerator magnets, and immunization cards. They then ask which, if any, might be of interest for sponsorship and what conditions in a proposal would make it more likely they would be interested, conditions such as funding levels and type of acknowledgement for the organization's contribution.

#6 *Prepare and submit a proposal to those most interested in supporting your effort. Present several optional initiatives for potential support, ones that are the best match for their stated business and marketing needs. Be sure to include in this proposal specifics regarding what you won't be able to offer.*

Assume, then, that five of the twenty organizations expressed interest in having the health department prepare and submit a proposal for their consideration, a proposal that would include specifics on sponsorship levels, recognition for the company, timing, number of parents reached by the materials, and length of the agreement. The health department will also include guidelines covering things they will not be able to do, such as providing organizational endorsement for the company or its products or altering content of materials.

#7 *Participate in developing an implementation plan.*

Of the twenty on the short list, it is realistic to imagine that perhaps only three to five organizations end up accepting their proposal, and even this may be after a few points are negotiated, such as the number of years they can commit to the sponsorship. Health department staff members then work more closely and directly with those in the sponsoring organization who will be involved in the day-to-day tasks related to the partnership and who need to be aware of deadlines for printing and copy approvals.

#8 *Offer to handle as much of the administrative legwork as possible.*

Even though the health department now has formal agreements, key to satisfaction and a long-term partnership (rather than a short-term relationship) will be the actual amount of additional time and resources the project ends up requiring of the sponsor. In this scenario, this might mean that the department would agree to have printed materials picked up from the corporation's print facility or deliver brochures to the grocery store partner interested in displaying the immunization schedules in their stores once a year.

#9 *Assist in measuring and reporting outcomes.*

Fortunately, in this scenario, the health department has a biannual survey they conduct with parents to assess satisfaction with mailings, awareness regarding content of materials, and changes in immunization behaviors. All partners were aware of this ahead of time and then were assured they would have results on parental awareness of their support for the program.

#10 Provide recognition for the corporation's contribution, in ways
preferred by the company.

Two of the three major partners are satisfied with the recognition they will receive from having their logo prominently displayed on the materials and a mention of their contribution in a health department publication. One of the partners, however, does not want their name on the materials because they felt this would bring too many additional requests their way, but they were glad to be mentioned in the publication with the narrower distribution.

Summary

This chapter has been about stretching the limits of partnerships, from good to great and from a possibility to a reality.

You read about mutually beneficial public/private partnerships that helped increase water supplies in Jordan, encouraged more students to choose a career in nursing, provided needed funding for a national monument, persuaded parents and caregivers to reduce the risks of SIDS by putting infants on their backs to sleep, brought professional bankers to high school classrooms to teach financial management to students, and reduced waste headed for landfills. You read about public/nonprofit partnerships that are likely to decrease costs for foster care, increase breastfeeding, increase revenues for universities and colleges, and increase the number of households that have a family disaster plan. You read about public/public partnerships that are helping decrease litter and prevent drownings.

Finally, you read about potential risks and how a marketing approach can help minimize downsides and assist you to find, negotiate, and win with partners.

PART III

MANAGING THE MARKETING PROCESS

11

Gathering Citizen Data, Input, and Feedback

"It has been fascinating to witness how research has given the average citizen a voice in developing South African tobacco control legislation for the 21st century. In 1997, the National Department of Health was concerned about the World Health Organization's warning that millions of women in developing countries were converting to tobacco use in spite of cultural prohibitions. We were tasked with determining how vulnerable black African women were to becoming tobacco users, even though they had the lowest rate of smoking (7%).

Many barriers had to be overcome to reach women in volatile, high crime township areas, and interview them in their home language, Xhosa. Our solution was to train local women to do the field work, providing them with employable skills and jobs. They also contributed to the translations and shared insights about what the findings meant, thus ensuring that African women's concerns were accurately conveyed in their own words."

Amy Seidel Marks, Ph.D.
Graduate School of Business, University of Cape Town

Marketing research as a tool for decision making is not usually questioned as much for its benefits as it is for its costs. You may have witnessed or even participated in tense debates reflected in the following comments aimed at discouraging a marketing research endeavor:

- By the time we get the survey designed and through the approval process, we will have missed the deadline to use the funds allocated for the campaign in the first place!

- The $35,000 you want to spend on research to determine who's littering and where and when and why will have to come out of the media budget. That could mean as many as ten fewer billboards carrying our anti-litter message.

- The last time I was involved in a study like this, the report that came back had two inches of computer tables, twenty five pages of explanation about statistical technique, and a three-page summary of findings. Where's the beef?

As you read this opening story, consider the high opportunity cost that would have been experienced if project managers had let challenges such as these get them down.

Opening Story: Building a Healthy Nation through Research in South Africa

Black women are a strategically important market for tobacco companies in South Africa, comprising over 39 percent of the population and constituting a key market for fast-moving consumer products like cigarettes and snuff. Traditionally, tobacco use has been perceived to be taboo for these women, and those who use it do so secretly or only with trusted others. Fortunately, as a result, black African women have had some of the lowest rates of smoking in South Africa. Unfortunately, tobacco marketers understand this and aim to change these societal norms.

Challenges

This targeting of black African women is particularly disturbing not only because of the diseases and early death tobacco use produces but also because these women have a significant influence on the consumption behavior of their children, family, and community members. This is compounded by the harmful effects on other household members from exposure to secondhand tobacco smoke and the increased incidence of tobacco-related harm for children during their mothers' pregnancies.

The challenge and balancing act program planners faced was to help female smokers and snuff users quit and, with the same precious resources, combat temptations among nonusers to slip into a smoking lifestyle. Interventions needed to be carefully targeted—right on.

The solution employed was a rigorous marketing research effort to understand the target markets—better than the competition did.

Strategies

A research project in 1999 surveyed 1,314 black Xhosa-speaking women ages 15 to 64 living in the Cape Town metropolitan area to study the knowledge, attitudes, practices, and behaviors of this audience regarding tobacco use. This effort, also known as a KAPB study, was designed to interview women who were smokers and/or snuff users and to compare findings with nonusers. A quarter (25 percent) of those interviewed were smokers, 27 percent were snuff users, 2 percent used both cigarettes and snuff, and just under half (46 percent) did not use tobacco.

Findings revealed that tobacco marketing had indeed been successful in reaching black women, with the majority of respondents reporting personal exposure to tobacco marketing. A third of all the women had recently seen cigarette advertisements, with even more (42 percent) of smokers reporting this. Three-quarters had purchased cigarettes as children on behalf of an adult, and the vast majority knew the current price of a single cigarette. All women had a worrying lack of awareness of the health hazards of tobacco use.

Understanding Nonusers at Risk: More than half (58 percent) of women who did not use tobacco were at risk of converting. Five percent were found to be pro-tobacco in orientation and on the verge of smoking. These women had a more urban and less traditional identity, were less sensitive to others' disapproval, were more exposed to cigarette advertising, had female friends who were smokers, and were more hedonistic and less health-oriented than the other women nonusers. Another 53 percent were found to have only a shallow commitment to remaining non-smokers. They were the most economically disadvantaged among the nonusers and in the midst of social transition. They were significantly desensitized to social taboos against black women smoking and were surrounded by smokers in their families and among female acquaintances.

Understanding How to Help Users: Tobacco users were found to be somewhat older and less educated. They were much more likely to be surrounded by other smokers such as husbands or partners and other family members who smoked. Over half the smokers said that they had smoked during pregnancy, and over a third of the snuff users said they took snuff while pregnant. Conservative estimates indicate that, on average, the women who were smokers spent at least 10 percent of their disposable income on their own cigarettes. Over half of their close female friends were smokers, and they had strong rationales for why tobacco use was beneficial—insights key to intervention messages. They believed smoking could help them lose weight. Snuff users thought that snuff had medicinal value, including pain relief.

Rewards

This rigorous research effort led to clear findings and recommendations.

It reinforced current tobacco-control legislation in South Africa, helping to ensure that regulations would be implemented, including banning advertising and smoking in public places as well as increased monitoring of sales to minors.

It led to recommendations that new efforts should be undertaken to develop strategies to counter smokers' beliefs about the benefits of smoking, increase awareness of health risks, and enable tobacco users to identify and understand which of their own health problems are related to their tobacco usage.

It provided insight that efforts need to delink smoking from modernity and a progressive orientation and link being tobacco-free with the things black women value most, whether it is personal dignity, family welfare, upward mobility, or access to personal and social development.[1]

Marketing Research in the Public Sector

Marketing research defined formally is "the systematic design, collection, analysis, and reporting of data relevant to a specific marketing situation facing an organization."[2] Those among you who use citizen data, input, and feedback for marketing decision making and evaluation on a regular basis probably can't even imagine how you could be effective without it. Those among you who have not will be amazed at how much easier this tool makes it for you to make decisions, obtain approvals, and report results.

Data on citizen behaviors and profiles can be critical in the marketing planning process. A utility, for example, will benefit from detailed census data on neighborhoods where it plans to work with single-family household residents to take steps to reduce rainwater runoff from roofs into sewers and drains. A Department of Transportation will count on using data on causes of automobile accidents when deciding among several options for reducing traffic-related injuries and deaths. And the Office of National Drug Control Policy will no doubt need to utilize data regarding current major distribution channels for drugs to develop effective intervention plans.

Citizen input will be especially insightful when developing the strategic marketing mix (4Ps). It can help you to determine the features of products, programs, and services (e.g., when developing a strategic plan for a school district), decide what incentives or disincentives will be most persuasive (e.g., what it will take to curtail tax evasion), choose among options for distribution channels and citizen access (e.g., when considering Sunday hours for liquor stores), and it will be crucial when developing campaign messages, choosing messengers, and selecting media channels. And it can help avoid producing and launching products and programs not likely to be a hit with citizens (e.g., the Susan B. Anthony $1 coin that looked like a quarter and had no special section in cash register drawers).

Feedback from citizens is a core component of program and campaign evaluation and is often used to assist in assessing satisfaction with programs and services, recall of and reaction to campaign messages and ways to do better "the next time" (e.g., Medicare drug bill in the U.S.), or when a campaign is rolled out.

This chapter presents a summary of marketing research terminology, primarily serving as a reference point for a common language, one that will assist you in future discussions with colleagues and contractors. It may also serve as a starting point in decision making regarding the appropriateness of a variety of potential research methodologies.

Research Defined by When It Is Conducted

Marketing research terminology sometimes refers to when research is conducted and used in the planning process. Three such terms are common: formative research, pretesting, and monitoring and evaluation.[3]

Formative Research

As the label implies, formative research refers to *research that is used to help form strategies*, especially understanding a target audience and developing the marketing mix. In March 2005, the U.S. Census Bureau, for example, promoted on their American FactFinder Web site an opportunity for users to participate in an online usability study to gain citizen ideas on how to improve the Web site.[4] This information could then be used to inform a variety of product improvement efforts such as determining what additional data citizens wanted to be able to access on the site, improving navigation, and meeting additional needs for producing custom reports. In social marketing efforts, formative research most often focuses on identifying audience barriers and motivators to behavior change (e.g., reasons why citizens might not want to have their children walk to school one day a week and what might assuage their concerns).

Pretest Research

This research at a subsequent phase in the planning process is conducted to *test draft strategies and tactics prior to production and implementation*. Most commonly, it is used to help choose among a short list of alternative strategies (e.g., which of three slogans for Homeland Security are most likely to resonate with citizens). It can help assure you (or not) that chosen strategies and tactics have no major flaws (e.g., discovering that a recommendation from a health department to exercise one hour a day, seven days a week raised eyebrows as to whether officials were "out of touch with reality"). It is particularly useful in determining whether a certain approach will reach and influence your particular target market (e.g., whether the bookmobile hours and locations being considered will appeal to seniors).

Monitoring and Evaluation

After a program or campaign has been launched, marketing research can be used to gauge performance relative to your goals and objectives. When this research is *conducted while the campaign is still underway*, it is often referred to as monitoring, and it helps you to make course corrections "midstream." After a project is completed, research can be *conducted to provide a final assessment* of the effort and is then referred to as evaluation.[5] (Chapter 12, "Monitoring and Evaluating Performance," provides more detail on monitoring and evaluation techniques.)

Research Defined by Source of Information

Information to inform your campaign is typically found in one of two ways. It may already exist somewhere, having been collected at another time for another purpose, in which case it is referred to as a *secondary research* source. *Primary research*, on the other hand, refers to data gathered for a specific research project for the first time.

Secondary Research

It is wise to start your research investigation by examining some of the rich variety of secondary data that is most likely currently available to determine whether you can glean enough insights and information without conducting more costly primary research. Secondary data certainly can provide a starting point and includes specific sources such as your agency's internal records, databases, prior surveys, and even anecdotal comments (e.g., reports that a customer service department provides on types of calls received). Looking outside the organization, a rigorous search and literature review can be conducted for journal articles and surveys conducted by other organizations with your target audience and/or relative to your specific issue.

Many cities across the U.S., for example, are interested in increasing commercial recycling rates. A program manager at a city utility faced with this challenge might begin this journey by reviewing internal data regarding business customers and their current recycling rates and utilization of city recycling services and how this varies by type of business (i.e., retail vs. manufacturing). Next, a search would be undertaken to identify journal articles and surveys conducted by others that provide insight into barriers that businesses have to recycling and experiences that others have had with strategies such as education, new services, and offering incentives and disincentives.

Primary Research

When the needed data does not exist or is outdated, inaccurate, incomplete, or unreliable, you'll want to consider the potential benefits and costs of conducting a primary research project.[6]

That city manager interested in increased commercial recycling rates has a variety of primary research options to learn more about the customer. He or she could ride along with waste management collectors and observe the actual locations and types of dumpsters being used, conduct in-person interviews with supervisors to explore barriers and solutions, commission anonymous surveys with owners to get candid information, and then follow this up with a focus group to pretest specific strategies. He or she will weigh these options and their potential costs against insights they will provide and the value placed on recyclable materials diverted from landfill.

Research Defined by Technique

Primary data can be collected using a variety of techniques. The following brief descriptions and examples simply introduce the range and nature of tools available and can serve as a reference point for further exploration.

Observational Research—Primary data is gathered by observing target markets in action. This technique can be used to enrich understanding of your audience (e.g., watching what warehouse employees do with leftover cardboard packaging), or it might be used as a means to evaluate campaign efforts (e.g., recording the number of drivers wearing seat belts before and after a campaign in a specific geographic area).

Ethnographic Research—This technique often includes observation as well as face-to-face interviews with study participants. As an anthropological discipline, it is considered a holistic research method, founded in the idea that to truly understand target markets, the researcher will need an extensive immersion in their natural environment. For example, a researcher might spend several days on a farm observing farmers' activities, seeking to understand what it would take to influence them to collect and cover manure piles to protect water quality.

Experimental Research—As one of the most scientifically valid research techniques, the purpose of this approach is to capture cause-and-effect relationships by selecting similar groups of subjects, exposing them to different treatments, controlling extraneous variables, and then checking whether response differences are statistically significant.[7] This approach might assist border patrols, for example, in deciding whether kiosks actually reduced or increased processing and wait time.

Behavioral Data—Data related to actual citizen behaviors is collected and analyzed, as in the case where data on taxpayers is used to understand differences between those submitting their forms and payment online versus by mail, in an effort to increase online utilization.

Focus Group Research—This popular methodology provides useful insights into customers' thoughts, feelings, and even recommendations on potential strategies and ideas for future efforts. Thought of by some as a group interview, a focus group typically involves inviting eight to ten people to gather for a couple hours with a trained moderator who uses a discussion guide that focuses the discussion—hence the name "focus group." Participants are carefully selected based on certain demographic, psychographic, or other considerations and are often paid a small sum for attending. This technique would be useful, for example, for a school district interested in understanding more about how retired citizens would like to be involved in classroom volunteering.

Mail Surveys—This survey technique offers the advantage of collecting large amounts of information at a low cost per respondent and is sometimes the best way to reach people not wanting to participate in personal, less anonymous interviews. Its disadvantages are that response rates are often very low and the researcher has little control over the quality of the mailing list sample (i.e., who fills out the survey at the mailing address). This technique might be appropriate and useful, for example, for providing ideas on what programs residents want most in a new community center.

Telephone Surveys—This technique is one of the best methods for gathering information quickly and has higher response rates than most mail questionnaires. Interviewers can explain difficult questions and even skip ones that don't apply. On the downside, costs per respondent are higher. The Centers for Disease Control and Prevention utilize telephone surveys, for example, to track national trends in health-related behaviors such as levels of physical activity.

Online/Internet Surveys—This technique is the fastest-growing option, providing opportunities to send surveys through email, include a questionnaire on a Web site, introduce questions to a chat room or bulletin board, hold an online focus group, and learn about individuals by following how they *clickstream* through your Web site and move to others.[8] Although it can be inexpensive, faster, and more versatile than some techniques, it can be prone to technological problems, and samples can be small and skewed.

In-person Individual Interviews—This most flexible but expensive method typically involves an arranged interview where the respondent is often contacted for an appointment and sometimes paid a small amount for their time. It offers the advantages of a focus group such as being able to show participants sample ads, but it also removes any concerns for group influence and provides a greater opportunity for in-depth questioning.

Intercept Interviews—Sometimes individual interviews are not prearranged and involve stopping people in places such as shopping malls, street corners, airports, or post office lobbies. Though less expensive, respondents may be more hurried, and extra care needs to be taken so that the sample is not biased in some way (e.g., interviewing people who look more approachable). A state department of business and economic development might make use of this tool at an airport gate, for example, to understand the demographic profile of visitors and explore their purposes for visiting and related behaviors such as shopping and entertainment while visiting.

Mystery Shopping—Often used as a technique to measure customer satisfaction, testers pose as customers or potential customers and report on strong and weak points experienced when interfacing with an agency's personnel, applying for programs and services, or purchasing products.

Finally, you may also hear the terms "qualitative" and "quantitative" mentioned in research discussions. **Qualitative** techniques refer to studies where samples are typically small and are not projectable to the greater population, with a focus on identifying and seeking clarity on issues. You won't be disappointed with this strategy if you and others are clear that it is a powerful technique for understanding issues in more depth and do not expect to use it when you need quantifiable and scientifically representative findings. Focus groups, personal interviews, observation, and ethnographic studies are often qualitative in nature. **Quantitative** tools, on the other hand, are used when you need hard counts, representative samples, and the ability to project results to larger populations with statistical reliability. This is when telephone, mail, and online interviews are more typical.

Steps in the Research Process

Nine steps are traditionally followed in a primary research project. As you will read, you begin with the end in mind.

#1: Determine Purpose—What decisions will this help us make? Why are we doing this?

Primary research should be conducted when it will help you make better decisions than the ones you would make without the research. A community center interested in offering (and filling) exercise classes for seniors, for example, will need to make smart decisions regarding length of class, time of day offered, type of instructor, preferred type of exercises, what to charge for the class, a name for the class, key messages to be used in communications, and ways to get the word out.

#2: Identify Informational Objectives—What specific information do we need to make this decision or answer the questions we have?

This step gets you closer to determining questions you will want to ask your target audience. For the senior exercise class, for example, program managers would benefit from knowing specifics such as what would motivate seniors to attend the class and what might keep them from enrolling. They would also want to test which of several pricing options, times of day for the class, instructor qualifications, and types of exercises are most appealing. They would also want to test several potential names, key messages, and media channels.

#3: Determine Audience—Who do we need the information from to answer the questions?

At this point, the target population that will be sampled is defined. Having articulated responses to steps one and two in this process, the target audience may seem obvious. The community center, for example, will want to conduct research with seniors in their community they have identified as the most likely to enroll in such a class, and they may be described by age, income, gender, ethnicity, physical abilities, benefits sought and/or related behaviors (e.g., already attend some other event at the community center).

#4: Select Research Technique—What is the most efficient and effective way to gather this information?

As presented in prior sections of this chapter, a variety of techniques are available. A specific method should be selected that will best meet the informational objectives at the lowest possible cost. One or more techniques will be chosen, based on whether results need to be statistically reliable and projectable to larger populations. For the community center, a focus group to identify issues and a telephone or mail survey to provide projectable findings would most likely help make decisions regarding the features, pricing, hours, and communications for the class.

#5: Develop Sample Plan—How many respondents should we survey? Where do we get names? How do we select (draw) our sample so that our results are representative of our target market?

A sample is the segment of the population you select for marketing research purposes to represent (at varying levels of reliability) the population you are studying. Clearly, large samples give more reliable results than small ones, although it is not necessary to sample the entire target market or even a large portion to get projectable results. An important decision at this step is how the sample is chosen. In a *probability* sample, each population member has a known chance of being included in the sample, and researchers can calculate confidence limits for sampling error. When this technique costs too much or takes too much time, a *nonprobability* sample is used, even though the sampling error cannot be measured. Five major types of samples are described in Table 11.1, with examples referring back to the community center interested in offering senior exercise classes.[9]

#6: Pretest Draft Instruments—When tested with a small sample of respondents, how well does the instrument work?

A research instrument is now developed (e.g., a draft telephone survey or self-administered questionnaire) and pretested with a small sample of intended respondents. Of special interest are whether questions make sense, responses can be easily recorded, skip patterns are smooth, and the length is as intended. Is the introduction or explanation of the survey successful in engaging potential respondents, or does it instead turn them away or cause them to hang up? Appropriate revisions are then made. For the community center, the questionnaire used for the telephone survey could be tested with a sample of four to six respondents and then revised if needed.

#7: Field the Research—Who will conduct the research, and what is the timing?

You are now ready to collect the data. Options for implementation range from hiring a marketing research firm to doing it yourself. A fielding plan should be developed, outlining milestones such as timing for a targeted number of completed interviews, recruitment timeframes, dates for focus group discussions, and desired completion date.

#8: Analyze Data—How will data be analyzed and by whom to meet the needs of planners and other audiences?

TABLE 11.1   Types of Samples[10]

	Probability Sample
Simple random sample	Every member of the population has an equal chance of selection. (Names are selected from a city's telephone directory, and calls screened for senior citizens.)
Stratified random sample	The population is divided into mutually exclusive groups (such as age groups), and random samples are drawn from each group. (A sample of 60- to 64-year-olds is drawn to compare with 75- to 84-year-olds.)
Cluster (area)	The population is divided into mutually exclusive groups (such as city blocks), and the researcher draws a sample of the groups to interview. (One sample is selected from addresses north of the community center and another from addresses south of the community center.)
	Nonprobability Sample
Convenience sample	The researcher selects the most accessible population members. (Seniors already attending some event at the community center are asked to participate in a focus group.)
Judgment sample	The researcher selects population members who are good prospects for accurate information. (Program planners ask physicians for names of seniors likely to be interested.)
Quota sample	The researcher finds and interviews a prescribed number of people in each of several categories. (Focus groups are recruited to ensure at least three males in each group and a mix of income levels.)

Each methodology (technique) suggests its own type of analysis. Qualitative research (e.g., focus groups) is analyzed more in terms of issues that participants raised, preferences that they expressed, and ideas that they generated. Caution is often needed to refrain from quantifying or projecting these findings, such as concluding that half the participants loved Option A for the class name and only a fourth preferred Option B. A more appropriate analysis in this case is why they preferred the options they did. On the other hand, quantitative analysis of large sample surveys focuses on more statistical techniques and decision models to interpret and represent the findings and often requires professional research assistance.

#9: Write a Report and Present Recommendations—What information should be included in the report, and what format should be used for reporting?

Reports should be designed with the audience in mind. A typical report will begin with a standalone executive summary that leads with a statement of purpose for the research, a brief description of methodology, a summary of findings, and concludes with recommendations relating back to decisions and questions that the research was intended to address. A separate section of the report then presents more detailed findings, tables, and perhaps specific verbatim comments made by respondents. An appendix includes information on the sample and a copy of the survey instruments and any documents shared with respondents.

A Word about Low-Cost Research

Timeframes, price tags, and lack of funding for research projects often stop them in their tracks, especially in the public sector where managers are challenged to show "profitable" rationales for the undertaking. Although clarity of purpose and intended use for the research can assist you in gaining support, consideration should be given to the many inexpensive and quick approaches that, as Andreasen asserts, may not lead to certainty but will at least improve the decision to a degree that justifies the cost.[11] Among those mentioned in his book on *Marketing Research That Won't Break the Bank* are the use of available data and techniques such as systematic observation, streamlined surveys, and small-scale samples.[12]

Additional options to explore include shared-cost surveys, where you can pay to add a few questions to a survey being conducted by a research firm for a variety of organizations, targeting an audience you are interested in. Additionally, professors and students at universities may be willing to volunteer their assistance because they may find your research proposal of interest and of benefit to their current projects and studies.

Summary

Terminology used in research sometimes refers to when the research is conducted in the planning process (*formative, pretest, monitoring,* or *evaluation*), the source of the information (*secondary* versus *primary* research), or the technique used to collect the data (*observation, ethnographic studies, experimental approaches, behavioral data, focus groups, mail surveys, telephone surveys, online/Internet surveys, in-person interviews, intercept interviews,* and *mystery shopping*). It was further explained that *qualitative* research refers to studies where samples are typically small and not representative of larger populations. On the other hand, *quantitative* tools are used when you need hard counts, representative samples, and the ability to project results with statistical reliability. Traditional steps in the planning process were described, beginning with a clear statement as to what decisions the research will support:

#1: Determine Purpose for the Research

#2: Identify Informational Objectives

#3: Determine Audience to be Surveyed

#4: Select Research Technique

#5: Develop Sample Plan

#6: Pretest Draft Instruments

#7: Field the Research

#8: Analyze Data

#9: Write a Report and Present Recommendations

12

MONITORING AND EVALUATING PERFORMANCE

"In tight fiscal times, our numerous outreach and education programs were being criticized for not having any 'proof' that they were working. Management wanted to know if they should keep investing in what they viewed as a public education strategy or whether it was time to shift into a more regulatory mode. The political and operational costs of outreach programs are considered low, but without evidence that these programs were paying off, there was real suspicion whether they were worth it.

*I suspected that the programs were good based on anecdotal information, but we needed to create a robust measurement tool that would hold up to management skepticism. Creating the Environmental Behavior Index allowed the programs to get detailed data on household attitudes and behaviors to improve their work in the field **and** allowed management to have defensible data showing the real impact in the population at large—over time."*

Michael Jacobson, Performance Measure Lead
King County Department of Natural Resources
and Parks, Washington State

Throughout this book, you have read of challenges you face when developing and implementing marketing-related activities in the public sector. However, many pale in comparison to the topic of evaluation, not only because it is one of the least understood but also because it is one of the most requested and hotly debated. You have probably witnessed some of the following states of confusion and dilemmas in your own agency:

- I don't understand how you know whether marketing contributed to what happened compared to other factors. We don't know whether our public meetings with citizens created the reduction in crime in that neighborhood, but that's what the boss wants to know.

- How can we possibly justify thousand of dollars to report on what good our marketing expenditures did? We're already getting heat for how much we spent on the campaign alone.

- To be honest, I'm worried about the results. I've got this sinking feeling that this didn't do any good and that we won't see that we moved the needle one bit. Then what?

By the conclusion of this chapter, you will have insights on how to address these challenges and more importantly a model to share with others next time you face these issues, one that was successfully applied in our opening story.

Opening Story: An Environmental Behavior Index—Helping to Quantify What Happened and Decide What to Do Next

Challenges

King County, Washington and its Department of Natural Resources and Parks are committed to protecting the environment *and* conserving taxpayers' dollars. The questions administrators decided to tackle in the fall of 2004 were, "How do we do both?" and "How do we know how we're doing?"

At that time, the department was allocating resources to several dozen programs designed to influence environmentally friendly yard care, recycling, waste disposal, and purchasing practices among county residents. The goal was to develop a common evaluation tool that would measure current behavior levels for each of the programs being promoted, with an interest in determining which behaviors had the greatest market opportunities for growth (increased participation) and, when overlaid with environmental impact, should be considered for continued or increased resources. The tool was also meant to help the Department track progress over time of the various behaviors to support its performance management system.

Strategies

In the spring of 2005, a telephone survey of 1,001 county residents was conducted to assess current levels of participation in 29 key environmental behaviors being promoted by the Department. For each of these behaviors, respondents were asked a series of questions that resulted in their household being categorized as one of the following:

> **Bright Green**—Do the desired behavior all or most of the time
>
> **Light Green**—Do the desired behavior only some of the time
>
> **Yellow**—Do not do the desired behavior but have thought about it
>
> **Brown**—Do not do the desired behavior and are not considering it
>
> **Grey**—Do not know about the behavior or what their household is doing
>
> **White**—Does not apply (e.g., don't have a yard or lawn)

Programs were then ranked (from 1 to 29) based on the greatest number of *Light Green* and *Yellow* households, those viewed as most likely and most open to change—to conduct the behavior on a regular basis, at the desired level (see Figure 12.1).

Rewards

Results of the survey have helped the Department in several important ways.

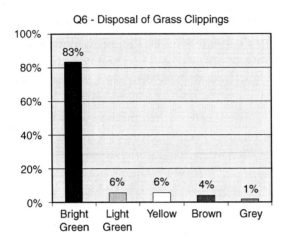

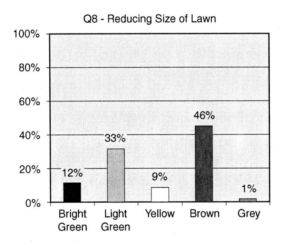

FIGURE 12.1 As indicated by the percentage of those in the light green and yellow categories on this bar chart, only 12 percent of households appear to be "available/open" to increased regular disposal of grass clippings compared with 42 percent for reducing the size of their lawn.

First, as hoped, it helped with prioritizing programs for resource allocation, with findings indicating that for 15 of the 29 behaviors, at least 20 percent of households in the county were either considering doing this behavior (the Yellows) or were doing it some but not all of the time (the Light Greens). Examples of markets of opportunity included increased use of energy-saving light bulbs (with 56 percent light green or yellow), proper washing of cars (33 percent), and giving experience gifts rather than "stuff" to reduce waste (23 percent). The environmental impact of each behavior, funding sources, operational feasibility, and the need for strategies beyond education were also to be considered when changing funding allocations among programs.

Second, it provided valuable data for programs when *developing marketing plans*. Target markets (Light Greens and/or Yellows) for specific behaviors can be described in terms of unique demographic, geographic, and related-behavior variables—data that was collected for respondents and their households. The Light Greens for using only natural or organic fertilizers, for example, were more likely to be college-educated males with children six and under living in the household. This then can assist in the development of more targeted, effective, and efficient marketing strategies, ones most likely to influence intended behavior change.

Rankings also assisted in developing *public communications*. Press releases, brochures, and Web sites reinforced behaviors that appeared to be cultural norms (e.g., 81 percent indicating they used recycling containers at home), focused on those with low awareness (e.g., with 67 percent indicating they hadn't heard of the EnviroStars program recognizing environmentally friendly businesses), and corrected apparent confusions and misunderstandings (e.g., prescription drugs should not be put down the toilet or sink but should be put in the garbage or returned to a pharmacy that accepts used medications). Information from the Environmental Behavior Index is also reported to the public as part of the Department's performance management report.

Finally, this first survey now serves as an outcome-based performance measurement *baseline for monitoring and tracking changes* over time. Knowing these current levels, managers can set goals for numbers of households to increase behaviors, and then outcomes can be measured against these goals on a periodic basis. Levels of change can then be calculated, and costs (in taxpayer dollars) supporting this change can be analyzed relative to outcomes and anticipated environmental benefits.

Measuring Marketing Performance

Measuring marketing performance is one of the most complex, even frustrating, of all marketing tasks. It is often expected and then questioned; it can be applauded and then forgotten.

In an ideal scenario, you can step forward and report on the return on your marketing investment of time, money, and other resources to develop and carry out marketing programs—an uncommon situation indeed.

This chapter is intended to help by outlining components of an evaluation plan, posed in the form of questions you'll want to answer in a sequential way, starting with the toughest one:

- Why are you conducting this measurement and for whom?
- What will you be measuring?
- How will you conduct these measurements?
- When will these measurements be taken?
- How much will it cost?

Your evaluation plan is developed before your final marketing implementation plan as it will need to be covered in your budget and noted in your action items.

One distinction is important up front: the difference between the term "monitoring" and the term "evaluation."

Monitoring generally refers to measurements that are conducted sometime after your new program and/or promotional campaign has been launched but before it is completed. Often you do this to determine whether you need to make mid-course corrections that will ensure that you reach your ultimate marketing goals (e.g., 50 percent of businesses filing their tax returns online). You may want to analyze whether you are reaching your target audience and how they are responding. Of interest may be how management and staff are viewing the effort, whether your competition has reacted, and what to do about it.

An *evaluation* is a measurement and final report on what happened, answering the bottom-line questions: Did you reach your goals? Can you link outcomes with program elements? Were you on time and on budget? How do costs stack up against benefits? Were there any unintended consequences that will need to be considered going forward—maybe even handled now (e.g., increase in cigarette butt littering as a result of restrictions on smoking at entrances to public facilities)? Which program elements worked well to support goals? Which ones didn't pull their weight? Was there anything missing? What will you do different next time, if there is a next time?[1]

Why Are You Conducting This Measurement and for Whom?

First, determine why and for whom you are conducting this measurement. There are several possibilities:

- To fulfill an expectation for reporting on campaign outcomes
- To fulfill funding or grant requirements
- To make changes mid-course or before a campaign rollout
- To do better next time
- To get more or continued funding

As may be apparent, methodologies and reports will vary depending on your answer to this first question. If you are conducting this measurement to fulfill some grant requirement, you will be guided by pre-established specifications. If, on the other hand, your audience is primarily internal and your main purpose is to do better next time, you will want to be diligent in your evaluation of each campaign component and interested in understanding what contributed to your outcomes and what didn't, as was the case in the following example.

In preparation for a campaign to reduce chewing gum litter in the U.K. scheduled for the spring of 2006, a four-week campaign pilot was conducted in 2005 in three local towns. Pilot campaigns used catchy advertisements, which included the message "Thanks for binning your gum when you're done," offered alternative disposal solutions such as gum pouches, and highlighted the threat of fines (see Figure 12.2). These pilot strategies had been based on formative research that identified reasons why some people drop gum (i.e., they didn't know it was a problem) and what might motivate them to change behavior (i.e., the threat of enforcement). Results from one of the pilots indicated that gum litter had been reduced by 80 percent. The Minister for Environmental Quality believed "the pilots last year gave us a good idea of

FIGURE 12.2   Campaign to reduce chewing gum littering in the U.K.[3]

what worked and what didn't." Information and experience gained informed a wider rollout and assisted in the development of a guide for local authorities on "how to tackle this sticky problem."[2]

What Are You Measuring?

What you will measure to achieve your research purpose is likely to fall into one or more of three categories: *outputs*, *outcomes*, and/or *impacts*. As you will read, efforts and rigor required vary significantly by category.

Output Measures

Perhaps the easiest and most straightforward measures are those thought of as marketing outputs, sometimes also referred to as process measures. As the label implies, these measures are ones that reflect levels of marketing activities, as quantifiable as possible. Most fall in the category of promotional efforts because the word "output" focuses on messages sent from your agency to the marketplace.

Common output measures, usually available in records and databases, include:

- **Number of materials distributed** (e.g., number of brochures on identity theft handed out at a city's police department and community centers)
- **Reach and frequency of advertising** (e.g., number of citizens estimated to have been exposed to state-sponsored radio spots and busboards regarding identify theft and the number of times they would have been exposed to them)
- **Number of impressions from other communication channels** (e.g., number of customers at a grocery store who would be exposed to messages on grocery bags regarding identify theft)
- **Mentions and airtime in the news media** and anticipated numbers of people reached by them (e.g., number of minutes of news coverage on a local television station and numbers of people typically viewing that program)

- **Numbers of special events** held and anticipated numbers of people reached at these events (e.g., number of presentations made by police officers at local community groups such as Rotary Clubs and numbers of people attending)
- **Resources expended** noting time and money (e.g., amount of money spent to develop and implement identify theft campaign elements and amount of time staff spent managing the campaign)
- **Other marketing-related activities** with some exposure among target audiences (e.g., number of links you were able to establish on related Web sites such as those of local police departments)

Notice that output measures say nothing about customer or citizen response to your efforts. They only reflect your "flurry of activities"—what campaign elements you put out there, what it cost you, and the estimated number of citizens (ideally, target audience members) exposed to them.

Outcome Measures

What most of you and those you work with also want to know is how citizens responded (outcomes) to what you did (outputs). Were your messages and materials even noticed? Was anyone listening to your ad on the radio or your speaker at special events? Were you able to create partnerships or generate contributions to support funding? Did these activities change levels of knowledge, attitudes, beliefs, or levels of citizen satisfaction? Did they inspire people to find out more? Most importantly, did they influence citizen action, reflected in increased purchases, participation, compliance, or behavior change? In each case, your focus is on answering the challenge "So what happened?"

If you are following a systematic marketing planning process, you'll find this identification of outcome measures easier because likely factors to be measured are rooted in your goal and objective statements.

Consider Maine's *Think Blue* campaign to protect water quality. Formative research conducted before a 2004 campaign revealed that the majority of Mainers had no idea what a watershed is, where storm water goes, or what is polluting the water in neighborhoods. Campaign outputs included radio and television ads, a Web site, a print piece, hosting or supporting local events, and forming partnerships.

But their definition of success was to be determined by outcomes based on results from surveys conducted with target audiences. Results were encouraging:

- **Campaign awareness**—Two months after the end of the campaign, of those surveyed, 14.4 percent of Maine adults remembered the ads and the message; 8.7 percent said the ads were about storm water runoff.

- **Changes in knowledge, attitudes, or beliefs**—Awareness that soil erosion is a source of water pollution increased from near zero to 6 percent; concern with water quality increased by 8 percent.

- **Changes in behavior or behavior intent**—26 percent of the adult Maine population said they had taken or were likely to take one or more of the recommended actions to reduce storm water pollution.

- **Creating partners or campaign contributions**—Multiple agencies and organizations in the state contributed funding to the media campaign and to support special events—leveraging the Department's money, staff time, and resources.

- **Increases in customer satisfaction**—Although this outcome was not measured for this campaign, an example would be if they included a question in their survey regarding citizen satisfaction with what the state was now doing to protect water quality.

As with the King County Environmental Behavior Index mentioned earlier in this chapter, these outcomes can now assist program managers when setting goals and objectives for future campaign outcomes.

Impact Measures

You will probably get a thankful nod from administrators when you provide a recap of your marketing program activities and expenditures (outputs). When you then go on to describe and quantify citizen response to your efforts (outcomes), you will most likely capture and hold their attention. If and when you are able to take it to the next level and report on the actual impact these citizen actions had on social, economic, and/or environmental conditions, however, they will applaud your efforts—as they should.

Notice in the following list of potential impacts from your marketing efforts the more rigorous questions that you will need to answer:

- **Cost savings**—How much money does the E-ZPass program save each year in operational costs?

- **Increases in net revenues**—Has the increase in admission revenues at the Louvre paid back the costs for improvement yet? When might it?

- **Funding and levies approved**—Do we know whether the community presentations the police department gave actually contributed to the levy passing?

- **Lives saved**—We understand there has been an increase in life vest usage. But has there been a decrease in drownings or near drownings as a result?

- **Diseases prevented**—How many cases of HIV/AIDS were prevented as a result of the increases in testing we achieved with our target audience?

- **Water quality improved**—Are the salmon healthier because the use of chemical lawn fertilizers has decreased in homes on the waterfront?

- **Water supply increased**—How much more water do we have in the reservoir as a result of the number of low-flow toilets we subsidized?

- **Air quality improved**—Are there fewer asthma attacks in the county as a result of the decrease in woodburning fires?

- **Landfill reduced**—How many acres of land did we preserve as a result of our 25 percent increase in recycling?

- **Wildlife and habitats protected**—Are there more baby crabs in the waters of Maine as a result of citizen actions to reduce storm water pollution?

- **Animal cruelty reduced**—Are pets living longer and with fewer injuries and diseases as a result of the increased fines in Turin, Italy?

- **Crimes prevented**—How many fewer assaults do we have in the park since we started blasting classical music over the loudspeakers?

How Will You Measure?

You have three major informational resources to assist you in your efforts to measure outputs, outcomes, and/or impact: internal records and databases, citizen surveys, and scientific/technical surveys.

Internal records and databases are perhaps the most relevant and reliable way to measure and report on outputs such as the number of brochures distributed on how to reduce your electric bill or the number of visitors to the post office who might have seen the notice regarding the availability of passport applications. In some cases, you can also use records and databases to track outcomes, as you would if you wanted to know the number of citizens and businesses filing tax returns online before and after your campaign this past year. With some planning and preparation, you could also use this resource to determine impact, as you would when analyzing any decreases in HIV/AIDS infections and correlating these with increases in testing.

Citizen surveys may be the best and sometimes the only way for you to determine outcomes from your marketing efforts. Your target audience will need to tell you whether they are more informed (e.g., on where to go for more information on property tax increases), whether they are motivated (e.g., are now considering use your port for cargo ships), whether they have changed a belief or attitude (e.g., that the schools need to be remodeled), or whether they indeed changed a behavior (e.g., drove one fewer time a week). As noted in Chapter 11, "Gathering Citizen Data, Inputs and Feedback," a variety of techniques may be appropriate including surveys conducted by phone, mail, online, or face-to-face. Some may be accomplished most effectively through observation surveys (e.g., watching for increases in pedestrian use of crosswalks).

Scientific or technical surveys may be the only sure method to assess the ultimate impact of your efforts. If you are really charged with reporting back on the difference your efforts made in improving air quality, water quality and supply, the health of fish and wildlife, and/or the value of diverted materials from the landfill, you will need help designing and implementing reliable scientific surveys that not only indicate changes but can also link these changes to your marketing efforts. You will also need this approach when making the case that decreases in diseases (e.g., obesity) can be linked to increases in desired public behaviors (e.g., physical activity).

It should be noted that you will most likely need to provide data from any, if not all, of these sources to those developing financial models (the ultimate measurement tool) for your agency, assisting you and others in a final economic assessment of past and potential future activities.

When Will You Measure?

With a clear sense of why, what, and how you will be measuring your performance, your next decision is when. Options reflect this timing.

Pre and post surveys, as the name implies, are conducted at some point prior to your campaign and then again at some point after it is completed—or at least a phase of it. A state launching a new slogan for attracting tourism, for example, may conduct a pre and post survey to determine any intended changes in attitude towards the state and intent to visit, linked with exposure and proven recall of the campaign. When resources or other factors make both measurements unlikely, a *post survey* alone might be conducted, which is still useful but more challenging in its ability to link outcomes with outputs.

Longitudinal surveys track and measure changes over a period of time, most often studying changes in a specific population group. The U.S. Department of Labor, for example, conducts a set of longitudinal surveys designed to gather information at multiple points in time on labor market activities, assisting those analyzing unemployment statistics and employment-related activities by geographic areas, age groups, and gender.[4]

Periodic surveys may be used for monitoring as well as evaluation of efforts. One evaluation measure of a state's litter campaign, for example, may be a scientific litter survey conducted every two years that measures changes in the amount and content of litter on targeted state highways and county roads and then overlays data on location of campaign activities such as road signs.

How Much Will It Cost?

Finally, you identify costs that will be associated with developing and conducting your monitoring and/or evaluation activities to be included in your final marketing budget.

When significant, these will include staff time to manage the process and, if relevant, will certainly include staff time to field the survey (e.g., time to conduct observational surveys on household recycling practices) or conduct the analysis (e.g., time needed to develop financial models).

It is not uncommon that you will end up contracting with an outside research or consulting firm to conduct these measurements. The need for quantifiable results will increase the numbers and therefore the time required to survey citizens, and the need to ensure a lack of bias may lead to a third-party choice.

Summary

Questions to answer when you are developing a plan to monitor and evaluate the performance of your marketing efforts are straightforward. Why, what, how, and when will you be measuring, and how much will it cost? It is the answers that are tough, especially when deciding the "what," as you will no doubt be torn between the desire to report on the return on your agency's investment and the need to just get it done; the desire to be accurate and the need to stay within budget; and the desire to learn from your mistakes as you go forward and the need to "look good" today.

Measuring your outputs (marketing activities) is more tedious than complex, usually "just" requiring you to develop a records and database system that will document the nature, quantity, frequency, and exposure of your efforts in the marketplace—most often those promotional in nature.

Measuring the outcomes of these activities in terms of citizen response is a little less certain and more resource intensive, as you strive to measure and then report on responses to your marketing program elements. For these measures, you will typically need to survey citizens to determine changes in intended knowledge, attitudes, and behaviors and use methodologies that can correlate your activities with theirs.

And then there's the "best of show," awarded because you measured and reported on the impact your efforts had on your agency's scorecard—indicators of accountability, including those that are social, economic, and/or environmental in nature. You know the harsh realities of this endeavor. It will take more time, more money, and more stamina, as even the most well-intentioned methodologies will be subject to peer and management scrutiny. Regardless, you are encouraged to make progress in this arena, settling at times for narrowing the focus of your measurement on only a few of your efforts, a pilot, a single geographic area, or a single target audience. Remember, a small step is still a beginning.

13

DEVELOPING A COMPELLING MARKETING PLAN

"My name is Joseph Perello. You can call me Joe. Since my appointment last April by Mayor Bloomberg as New York City's Chief Marketing Officer, I also tell people they can call me 'the luckiest guy in the world.' ... In 1949 E.B. White wrote in 'Here is New York' that there are actually three different New Yorks (Natives, Commuters and Settlers). I would like to propose there is a fourth New York—the idea of New York. This fourth New York is what the millions of people who don't live here experience when they hear the words, 'New York City.' It is what makes people feel connected to the City, even if they have only visited for a few days or have never been here at all. The idea of New York is, in many ways, our greatest asset."[1]

Joseph Perello
Chief Marketing Officer, New York City
Address to The Economist's 2nd Annual Marketing Roundtable
March 25, 2004

This final chapter provides a framework that organizes most of the major topics that have been addressed throughout this book (Segmentation, Target Marketing, Positioning, the 4Ps, and Evaluation), ones representing key components of a marketing plan and ones relying on a variety of timely research efforts. It presents a traditional outline for a marketing plan and provides descriptions of major components. It is intended to be a practical template for you to use when developing marketing plans—whether five or fifty pages in length.

It is also hoped that it will make clear the benefits of taking the time to develop a formal plan, benefits that might address common challenges you are most likely to face:

- The last time I brought up the idea of developing a marketing plan, everyone said we didn't have time. We just need to get the brochure out!

- We don't have a marketing department, so who's going to write the plan? I'm a program manager and have no marketing background.

- It doesn't seem to me this marketing stuff is measurable, and we are under real pressures to show impacts on the triple bottom line: social, economic, and environmental indicators.

In the opening story, imagine how hard it would be for this department manager to succeed without a solid marketing plan.

Opening Story: New York City Marketing Starts Spreading the News

Challenges

In April 2003, Mayor Bloomberg announced the appointment of Joseph Perello as Chief Marketing Officer to head a department—NYC Marketing—with the specific mandate of developing and executing plans to maximize the full marketing potential of the City's resources. It is believed to be the first city in the world to develop an actual marketing office and Chief Marketing Officer position.

Perello and his department were given three primary marketing objectives:

1. Generate alternative means of revenue for New York City.
2. Support City agencies and important City initiatives.
3. Promote New York City around the world to grow jobs and tourism.

At first glance, this might look like an easy assignment, with research ranking New York City thirteenth out of 2,400 different brands and acclaiming positive attributes like "unique, fun, energetic, intelligent, independent, dynamic, glamorous, authentic, charming, socially responsible, kind and innovating."[2] The problem is the same research indicated other, less positive attributes: "tough, rugged, arrogant and unapproachable," ones that could make this journey a little bumpier.[3]

The department faced internal challenges and public sensitivities as well. "When people first heard about the idea of marketing New York City," Perello noted, "their first thought was that we would be renaming the Brooklyn Bridge after a bank or plastering a company's propaganda all over the City. That is not going to happen. The Mayor and New Yorkers would never stand for it."[4]

Strategies

First, the department became the *guardian of the image* of New York City, relying on proven business models that other like organizations with strong emotional properties leverage, ones such as Disney and the Olympics. It meant there would need to be rigorous and coordinated efforts to build, expand, and protect the City's image and use it effectively to drive tourism to and economic development of New York.

The department became the *City's exclusive internal marketing agency* for corporate sponsorships, marketing, licensing, media, advertising, media management, and brand management. They offered their services to more than 50 other city agencies and departments, maximizing promotional opportunities that each possesses, increasing efficiency in government, and providing additional revenue for essential services. They consolidated efforts to make use of citywide assets, ones such as their 5,800 bus shelters, 250,000 light pole banners, 12,000 phone booths, 300 newsstands, 12,000 taxis, 1,600 public parks, and 5,000 buildings, not to mention the 35 million visitors, 8 million residents, and 3.5 million workers in the City.

They embarked on an ambitious effort to *develop world-class partnerships,* interested in selecting only eight to ten world-class companies that would capture the essence of the City and help tell the story of New York around the world. It is anticipated that through these public/private initiatives with like-minded corporate citizens, the department would be able to deliver revenue to the City without raising taxes and that city services would be improved, which would improve the lives of New Yorkers.

Rewards

Several notable accomplishments were reported in the department's first couple years:

- A collaboration was formed with **The History Channel**, valued by the City at $19.5 million.
- A multi-year deal with **Snapple** was to guarantee the City $106 million in cash and $60 million in marketing and promotional value, where Snapple, among other agreements, would be the exclusive provider through vending machines of bottled spring water and 100 percent fruit juices in the City's 1,200 schools.
- **Virgin Airlines** was successfully enticed by promotional opportunities and tax incentives to locate its new U.S. headquarters in downtown New York City.
- In 2005, the **Country Music Awards** were lured to the City for the first time.
- A **Made in NY Incentive Program** provides marketing incentives to supplement the City and state tax incentives for feature films and televisions shows to be filmed primarily in New York City.

These partnerships and agreements appear to be delivering on the original premise that this new department and model could generate net revenue and visibility for the City by taking advantage of previously unrealized resources and promotional opportunities. Perello warns, however, that this type of innovation "requires being unreasonable. And expecting unreasonable things to happen."[5]

Marketing Planning in the Public Sector

Developing a marketing plan requires a systematic process, one that begins with analyzing the current situation and environment, moves on to establishing marketing objectives and goals, identifying target audiences, determining a desired positioning, and designing a strategic marketing mix (4Ps), and then wraps up with developing evaluation, budget, and implementation plans (see next page).

Sometimes the plan is created for a specific program, product, place, or service within an agency (e.g., increasing the number of visitors to a national park), a specific geographic market (e.g., major cities in the Southeast), or a specific segment of the population (e.g., youth). Sometimes, though less frequently, plans are created for an entire agency or entity (e.g., U.S. Department of the Interior). Plans are most often developed for a one- to three-year period, with annual updates.

Those who have taken the time to develop a formal plan realize numerous benefits. Most importantly, they are more likely to meet their agency's performance goals (e.g., increase postal revenues). The planning document itself can also address any important internal objections regarding "marketing." Readers of the plan will see evidence that recommended activities are based on strategic thinking. They will understand why specific target audiences have been selected—and represent efficient and effective use of resources. They will see what anticipated costs are intended to produce in specific, quantifiable terms that can be translated to an associated return on investment. They will certainly learn that marketing is more than advertising. They will be delighted (even surprised) to see that you have a system, method, timing, and budget to evaluate your efforts. And they can't help but notice that you have recognized and engaged others within the agency in assisting with the plan's implementation.

Who develops the marketing plan? Ideally, a lead person with a team that includes a program manager, a representative from your communications or public information office, potentially someone from the finance area of your agency, and when relevant, members of external partner organizations and someone from the "field" or operations who can provide valuable input regarding the customer's perspective, the feasibility of potential strategies, and the important buy-in you'll need for implementation.

Marketing in the Public Sector
Marketing Plan Outline

1.0 Executive Summary
Brief summary highlighting major marketing objectives and goals the plan is intended to achieve; target audiences and desired positioning; marketing mix strategies (4Ps); evaluation, budget, and implementation plans.

2.0 Situation Analysis
    2.1 Background information and plan purpose
    2.2 SWOT: Strengths, Weaknesses, Opportunities, Threats
    2.3 Competition: Direct and Indirect
    2.4 Past or similar efforts: activities, results, and lessons learned

3.0 Marketing Objectives and Goals
    3.1 Objectives (e.g., increases in utilization of services, participation levels, product sales, behavior change, compliance levels, market share, customer satisfaction, customer loyalty)
    3.2 Goals: Intended results that are quantifiable, measurable, and specific

4.0 Target Audience
    4.1 Profile: demographics, geographics, behaviors, psychographics, size, readiness to buy
    4.2 Perceived barriers and benefits related to marketing objectives

5.0 Positioning
How you want the program or agency to be seen by target audiences

6.0 Marketing Mix: Strategies to Influence Target Audiences
    6.1 Product
        Physical goods, services, events, people, places, agency, ideas
        Components: Core, Actual, and Augmented
    6.2 Price
        Monetary costs (fees)
        Monetary and nonmonetary incentives and disincentives
    6.3 Place
        How, when, and where programs, products, and services can be accessed
    6.4 Promotion
        Key messages, messengers, and communication channels

7.0 Evaluation Plan
    7.1 Purpose and audience for evaluation
    7.2 What will be measured: output, outcome, and impact measures
    7.3 How they will be measured
    7.4 When they will be measured

8.0 Budget
    8.1 Costs for implementing marketing plan
    8.2 Any anticipated incremental revenues or cost savings

9.0 Implementation Plan
Who will do what, when

Situation Analysis

In this section of your plan, you present relevant background information, an analysis of organizational and market forces you will consider when determining marketing strategies, and a review of performance and lessons learned from past, similar efforts.

Background Information and Plan Purpose

Begin this section with a summary of factors that led to development of the plan. Why are you doing this? It might have been precipitated by a decline in utilization of services (tourists), a public health crisis (obesity), an increase in risk behaviors (use of methamphetamines), a desire to revitalize a brand (community transit), the need to respond to a new competitive offering (from FedEx), or an opportunity to offer a new program or service that meets some public need (the ability to get a temporary visa online). By including a clear statement of purpose and focus for the plan at this point, you will have a reference and rallying point for subsequent planning decisions (e.g., a purpose to increase literacy and a focus on early learning).

Strengths, Weaknesses, Opportunities, Threats (SWOT) Analysis

Relative to the purpose and focus of the plan, you'll then want to conduct a quick audit of forces in the internal and external environment that are anticipated to have some impact on or relevance for subsequent planning decisions.

Make a list of major *organizational* strengths to maximize and weaknesses you need to minimize, including factors such as available resources, management support for the project, current alliances and partners, delivery system capabilities, agency reputation, and issue priority.

Then make a similar list of *external forces* in the marketplace that represent either opportunities you can take advantage of or threats you need to prepare for. These major trends and events are typically outside your influence as a marketer but must be taken into account, with major categories including cultural, technological, demographic, economic, political, and legal forces.

Competitive Analysis

Now scan the strengths and weaknesses of the competition, considering both direct as well as indirect players. Direct competitors are those whose offerings are similar to yours (e.g., bookstores for libraries). Indirect competitors are those that fulfill the target audience's need—but in a different way (e.g., television for libraries).

Review of Past, Similar Efforts

Finally, take a brief moment to reflect on past, similar efforts, reviewing outcomes and noting lessons learned, either by your organization or a similar one.

Marketing Objectives and Goals

With your eye on the purpose for your plan and a keen awareness of the marketing environment, you are now ready to declare more specific intentions—your marketing objectives and goals.

Marketing objectives are more detailed than your statement of purpose and should be expressed in terms of a desired behavior or action, change in brand image, or increased knowledge that you want to achieve. Examples are varied:

- Increase purchases of packaging products offered at post offices
- Increase volunteers for after-school tutoring programs
- Increase utilization of online vehicle license renewals
- Decrease number of fans driving home drunk after sports events
- Decrease car thefts in high-crime neighborhoods
- Create awareness of new Medicare prescription options
- Improve perception of law enforcement officers

Marketing goals are quantifiable and measurable expressions of your marketing objectives. They answer the question, "How many car thefts do you want this plan to prevent, or what percentage of vehicle owners do you want to renew their license online as a result of this effort?" They should be realistic and include a time frame (e.g., by the year 2010), addressing the question "by when." Recognize that what you determine here will guide your subsequent decisions regarding target audiences and marketing mix strategies. This decision will also have significant implications for budgets and will provide clear direction for evaluation measures later in the planning process.

Target Audience

As you recall from earlier chapters, you will select target audiences by first segmenting the market, evaluating segments, and then choosing one or more as the focal point for positioning and marketing mix strategies. A rich description of that target audience should be provided in this section of your marketing plan.

Ideally, you will describe your target audience in such a way that "you'd know them if they walked into the room." This means you provide a *demographic profile* using variables such as age, gender, family size, income, occupation, education, religion, race, and nationality. It is also just as meaningful, in some cases even more so, to provide other team members and campaign planners with information on this segment's *values, lifestyle,* and *personality* characteristics. Information regarding *related behaviors or purchases* will be inspiring, as will any insights you have on when and where your target audience might be *most open* to your messages or likely to notice them (e.g., messages regarding invasive plants might be of most interest to attendees at an annual flower and garden show).

Also describe the potential *benefits* that your target audience perceives they will receive, or wants most to receive, as a result of taking the actions your marketing plan will attempt to influence. Those working on your campaign materials will benefit immensely from knowing "what's in it for them." Importantly, benefits vary by target audience segment and should therefore be researched. One commuter segment targeted by a transit agency may care most about cost savings, while another is motivated by doing their part to protect the environment, and yet another is looking for a chance to read more books. What is your target audience looking for that you should highlight? Some planners even further segment the market based on "benefits sought," recognizing implications for different positioning and marketing mix strategies.

Every great "salesperson" is also eager to know what *barriers* or concerns the target audience has that might keep them from acting. Knowing that this will assist in developing a compelling positioning for your offer as well as the right marketing mix. A public utility wanting households to put kitchen oils and grease in containers to be recycled will need to address confusion over what types of containers are safe and appropriate to use, objections to having to take it to a special recycling center, and a challenge as to why it even matters.

Positioning

After identifying, describing, and understanding the target segment, this part of the marketing plan briefly describes the desired positioning for the program, service, agency, or other product offering at the focal point of the plan. This is an essential step prior to developing your marketing strategy because a successful strategy is always built on STP—Segmentation, Targeting, and Positioning.[6]

This desired positioning can be described using a few sentences, even bullet points, that clarify how you want your offer to be viewed by your target audience. It should include a *value proposition*, the cogent reason why the target market should "buy" your offering.[7] The aim is to determine and articulate a distinct position, one that highlights benefits and diminishes barriers unique for your target audience and one that places you in a favorable light relative to the competition. It should define appropriate *points-of-difference* as well as *points-of-parity* relative to direct as well as indirect competitors.[8] As you may recall from Chapter 6, "Creating and Maintaining a Desired Brand Identity," the EPA wanted consumers to see ENERGY STAR® products as a way to save money and help protect the environment at the same time, CDC wanted tweens to see exercise as cool and fun, and officials in Texas wanted their litter prevention effort to be seen as bold and as a reflection of great state pride.

Marketing Mix

Now open your marketing toolbox, one containing four familiar tools by now: Product, Price, Place, and Promotion (4Ps). It is the blend of these elements that constitutes your marketing mix strategy, one you will design with an intention to produce the response you want from your target market. Because separate chapters have been dedicated to each of these elements, the following comments focus on information you would include regarding each in a formal marketing plan.

Product

Describe core, actual, and augmented product levels. The *core product* consists of benefits the target audience will receive as a result of acting and are ones that you will highlight. The *actual product* includes aspects of features, name, quality, style, design, and packaging associated with the product. The *augmented product* refers to any additional features, objects, and/or services that you will include that will add perceived value to the transaction.

Price

Mention any *monetary costs* (fees) charged for products, programs, and services and, if offered, note *monetary incentives* to stimulate action. Also stress any *monetary disincentives* such as fines, *nonmonetary incentives* such as recognition, and *nonmonetary disincentives* such as negative public visibility.

Place

Place decisions relate to ones where you have chosen to deliver your offer and the means that citizens have to access it. You will delineate what distribution channels will be utilized, choosing among options including physical locations, phone, fax, mail, mobile units, drive-thrus, Internet, videos, home delivery/house calls, places where potential customers shop, dine, and hang out, kiosks, and vending machines. You will also include decisions on when these channels are "open for business," the amount of wait time, and any aspects of locational ambiance (e.g., cleanliness of a lobby).

Promotion

In this section, you will describe your persuasive communication strategies, covering decisions related to key *messages* (what you want to communicate), *messengers* (any spokespersons, sponsors, partners, or actors you use to deliver messages), and *communication channels* (where promotional messages will appear).

It is important to present the marketing mix in the sequence just noted, beginning with a description of the product and ending with a promotional strategy. After all, the promotional tool is the one you count on to ensure that target audiences know about your product, its price, and how to access it, decisions that you will make prior to communication planning.

Evaluation Plan

In this important part of your plan, especially for administrators, you outline what measures will be used to evaluate the success of your effort and how and when these measures will be taken.

It begins with explaining the purpose and audience for the evaluation because this information has guided your choices. These were driven, at least in part, by your marketing goals, established earlier in the planning process. It may include one or more of the following measures mentioned in Chapter 12, "Monitoring and Evaluating Performance":

- *Output measures* will identify what marketing activities and resources you will be reporting back on (e.g., numbers of brochures handed out).

- *Outcome measures* will focus on citizen response, noting what actions you will be measuring, reflected in levels of behaviors (e.g., numbers of attendees at a senior exercise class) or changes in knowledge, beliefs, or attitudes.

- *Impact measures* take it to the next level, answering those tough questions like "What good did all this do?" Your intended measures might be reflected in targeted revenue increases for the agency as a result of selling road services to local cities, improved traffic congestion, reductions in teen pregnancy, improvements in school readiness, improved water quality, decreases in traffic injuries, reduction in crime, or increased support and approval for a governmental project.

Expenses for evaluation will be noted in the budget section of your plan, and action items, including when measures will be taken, are reflected in your implementation plan.

Budget

Costs associated with developing and implementing the marketing plan are delineated in this section. Although preliminary budgets may have been revised based on realities of funding sources, only a final budget is then presented—one reflecting confirmed product, price, place, and promotional-related costs. You will include incremental costs for product development, any pricing incentives, and added costs related to distribution channels as well as development and dissemination of communications.

This is where you note any anticipated incremental revenues or cost savings, ones that can then be paired with marketing costs to produce an anticipated return on investment. Analysis can then be conducted on the marketing cost "per transaction," "per behavior change," or "per new customer." Over time, a database with these historic indices can be created that will provide a rational, relative means to determine efficient and effective use of marketing-related expenditures.

Implementation Plan

You will wrap up your plan with a document that specifies *who* will do *what, when,* and for *how much*. It transforms marketing strategies into actions. Some even consider this section "the real marketing plan" since it provides a clear picture of marketing activities, responsibilities, timeframes, and budgets. It can serve as a standalone piece that can be shared with important internal groups, especially those who will be impacted by campaign activities as well as target market response (e.g., phone centers).

Tasks will include any developmental activities such as production of materials as well as important launch dates for communication elements. It provides the map that charts your course, enabling timely feedback when you have wavered or need to take corrective actions. It certainly incorporates planned evaluation activities, ensuring they get implemented.

Formats for plans vary from simple schedules incorporated in the executive summary of the marketing plan to complex ones using special software programs. The ideal plan identifies major activities that would be undertaken over a period of one to three years.

Summary

The process of developing a marketing plan may be as important as the plan itself.

By design, it encourages strategic thinking, beginning with establishing a purpose and focus for the plan and a description of "Where we are." This then leads to identifying "Where we want to go," expressed in terms of marketing goals and objectives. Strategies are selected for "How will we get there," including choosing target markets, a desired positioning, and a special mix of the 4Ps, a blend especially designed to capture your target market. Don't wrap up until you have your evaluation and implementation plans in place, outlining "How we will know we've arrived" and "How we will keep on track."

Sharing the plan with others adds even more value, serving as a testament that your actions are based on strategy, that your budgets are aligned with goals, and that you have structures in place that will ensure accountability.

Though presented here as a sequential process, in reality you have most likely experienced or will experience that it is spiral in nature. Don't be surprised or discouraged if you get all the way to an evaluation plan and find you need to redefine your goals or that you add up the costs of your ideas during the budgeting process and find you need to rethink some of your wild promotional ideas. Remember this is a dynamic management tool, not a dust-gathering document.

REFERENCES

Chapter 1

1   Osborne, David and Gaebler, Ted. *Reinventing Government: How the Entrepreneurial Spirit Is Transforming the Public Sector.* Addison-Wesley, 1992, pp. 20-21, 45-48.

2   Ibid., p. xxi.

3   Ibid., p. x-xi.

Chapter 2

1   The United States Postal Service: An American History 1775-2002, Introductory Letter. Publication 100, September 2003, United States Postal Service, Washington D.C.

2   *The United States Postal Service: An American History 1775-2002.* Publication 100, September 2003, United States Postal Service, Washington D.C. p. 25.

3   2004-2008 USPS Five-Year Strategic Plan (September 2003) (accessed at USPS.com), www.usps.com.

4   Philip Kotler and Kevin L. Keller, *Marketing Management*, 12th ed. (Upper Saddle River, NJ: Prentice Hall, 2005), pp. 15–23.

5   Peter F. Drucker, *Management: Tasks, Responsibilities, Practices* (New York: Harper & Row, 1973), pp. 64–65.

6   Alan Andreasen and Philip Kotler, *Strategic Marketing for Nonprofit Organizations*, 4th ed. (Upper Saddle River, NJ: Prentice Hall, 1991), p. 125.

7   Ibid.

8   Philip Kotler and Gary Armstrong, *Principles of Marketing*, 9th ed. (Upper Saddle River, NJ: Prentice Hall, 2001), pp. 193–197.

9   Ibid.

10   Everett M. Rogers, *Diffusion of Innovations*, 5th ed. (New York: Free Press, 2003).

11   Philip Kotler and Gary Armstrong, *Principles of Marketing*, 9th ed. (Upper Saddle River, NJ: Prentice Hall, 2001), pp. 245–261.

12   Ibid., pp. 259–262.

13   Ibid., pp. 266–267.

14   John Zagula and Richard Tong, *The Marketing Playbook: Five Battle-Tested Plays for Capturing and Keeping the Lead in Any Market* (New York: The Penguin Group, 2004).

15   Kotler and Keller, *Marketing Management*, p. 372.

16   Kotler and Armstrong, *Principles of Marketing*, p. 371.

17   Philip Kotler, Ned Roberto, and Nancy Lee, *Social Marketing: Improving the Quality of Life* (Thousand Oaks, CA: Sage, 2002), p. 264.

18   Kotler and Keller, *Marketing Management*, p. 20.

19   Robert Lauterborn, "New Marketing Litany: 4P's Passe; C-Words Take Over," *Advertising Age*, October 1, 1990, p. 26.

20   Andreasen and Kotler, *Strategic Marketing*, p. 617.

21   Andreasen and Kotler, *Strategic Marketing*, p. 618.

22   American Marketing Association, 2004.

Chapter 3

1   Philip Kotler and Gary Armstrong, *Principles of Marketing*, 9th ed. (Upper Saddle River, NJ: Prentice Hall, 2001), pp. 72–73.

2   Philip Kotler and Kevin L. Keller, *Marketing Management*, 12th ed. (Upper Saddle River, NJ: Prentice Hall, 2005), p. 699.

3   International Obesity Task Force, "Childhood Obesity," May 4, 2005, http://www.iotf.org/childhood/.

4   United Press International: Food: "TV chef transforms U.K. school meals," March 22, 2005, http://www.upi.com/view.cfm?StoryID=20050322-101930-7242r (accessed May 2, 2005).

5   Sydney Morning Herald, "Jamie gives school meals the wooden spoon," March 24, 2005, www.smh.com.au.

6   Ibid.

7   International Herald Tribune, "Chef whips U.K. school cafeterias into shape," April 25, 2005, Sarah Lyall, *The New York Times*, http://iht.com/bin/print_ipub.php?file=/articles/2005/04/24/news/cook.php.

8   Ibid.

9   Ibid.

10   Ibid.

11   United Press International: Food: "TV chef transforms U.K. school meals," March 22, 2005, http://www.upi.com/view.cfm?StoryID=20050322-101930-7242r.

12   Future School News, http://www.futureschool.ca/news/industrynews.cfm?ArticleID=633 (accessed May 2, 2005).

13   Sydney Morning Herald, "Jamie gives school meals the wooden spoon," March 24, 2005, www.smh.com.au.

14   United Press International: Food: "TV chef transforms U.K. school meals," March 22, 2005, http://www.upi.com/view.cfm?StoryID=20050322-101930-7242r.

15   International Herald Tribune, "Chef whips U.K. school cafeterias into shape," April 25, 2005, Sarah Lyall, *The New York Times,* http://iht.com/bin/print_ipub.php?file=/articles/2005/04/24/news/cook.php.

16   Sydney Morning Herald, "Jamie gives school meals the wooden spoon," March 24, 2005, www.smh.com.au.

17   International Herald Tribune, "Chef whips U.K. school cafeterias into shape," April 25, 2005, Sarah Lyall, *The New York Times*, http://iht.com/bin/print_ipub.php?file=/articles/2005/04/24/news/cook.php.

18   Kotler and Armstrong, *Principles of Marketing*, p. 300.

19   Silicon Valley Power, City of Santa Clara, California, publication, 2002.

20   http://www.siliconvalleypower.com (accessed May 9, 2005).

21   David Osborne and Ted Gaebler, *Reinventing Government: How the Entrepreneurial Spirit Is Transforming the Public Sector* (Plume, 1993), pp. 193–194.

22   Kotler and Armstrong, *Principles of Marketing*, p. 294.

23   http://www.ezpass.com (accessed May 9, 2005).

24   Kotler and Armstrong, *Principles of Marketing*, pp. 338–353.

25   Ibid., p. 340.

26   Osborne and Gaebler, *Reinventing Government*, pp. 219.

27   http://www.lyricsfreak.com/k/kenny-rogers/77886.html (accessed May 12, 2005).

28   http://www.2good2toss.com.

29   http://www.ojp.usdoj.gov/pressreleases/OJJDP05008.htm.

30   http://www.amberalert.gov/ (accessed May 12, 2005).

31   Kotler and Keller, *Marketing Management*, pp. 322–324.

32   Adapted from Kotler and Keller, *Marketing Management*, pp. 322–331.

33   Ibid.

34   James Nevels, "Reading, Writing, ROI," *Forbes*, March 14, 2005, p. 38.

35   The Communication Initiative—Experiences—Nepalese Health Fairs—Nepal http://www.comminit.com/experiences/pds12004/experiences-457.html (accessed May 19, 2005).

36   Louvre Museum Official Website, http://www.louvre.fr/anglais/palais/museum.htm (accessed May 19, 2005). Other references for this section include Le Musee du Louvre—The Louvre

Museum, http://www.discoverfrance.net/France/Paris/Museums-Paris/Louvre.shtml, and Gedi Online—Louvre, http://www.gedi.cn/en/paris/louvre.html (accessed May 23, 2005).

37   Ibid.

Chapter 4

1   National Highway Traffic Safety Administration, "The Economic Impact of Motor Vehicle Crashes," 2000, Technical Report Documentation. Report date, May 2002.

2   National Highway Traffic Safety Administration, "Programs for Hispanics," http://www.buckleuptexas.com/clickit/ (accessed May 26, 2005).

3   Ibid.

4   U.S. Department of Transportation—NHTSA, "The Facts to Buckle Up America," http://www.nhtsa.dot.gov/people/injury/airbags/buasbteens03/.

5   U.S. Department of Transportation—NHTSA, "Click it or Ticket 2005 Mobilization—Fact Sheet: Safety Belt Use," http://www.buckleupamerica.org/nmay05/fact_sheet.php (accessed May 26, 2005).

6   http://www.nhtsa.dot.gov/people/injury/airbags/clickit_ticke03/ciot-report04/CIOT%20May%202003/pages/Intro.htm (accessed May 26, 2005).

7   U.S. Department of Transportation—NHTSA, "Click it or Ticket 2005 Mobilization—Fact Sheet: Safety Belt Use," http://www.buckleupamerica.org/nmay05/fact_sheet.php (accessed May 26, 2005).

8   http://www.tdot.state.tn.us/ClickItorTicket/.

9   "Not bucklin up? Click it or Ticket program returns," Detroit Free Press, http://www.freep.com/news/metro/belt16e_20050516.htm (accessed May 26, 2005).

10   Ibid.

11   U.S. Department of Transportation—NHTSA, "Click it or Ticket 2005 Mobilization—Fact Sheet: Safety Belt Use,"

http://www.buckleupamerica.org/nmay05/fact_sheet.php (accessed May 26, 2005).

12   NHTSA, Economic Impact of Crashes 2002.

13   U.S. Department of Transportation—NHTSA, "Click It or Ticket 2005 Mobilization—Press Release," http://www. buckleupamerica.org/nmay05/fact_sheet.php (accessed May 26, 2005).

14   "Not bucklin up? Click it or Ticket program returns," Detroit Free Press, http://www.freep.com/news/metro/belt16e_20050516.htm (accessed May 26, 2005).

15   Philip Kotler and Kevin L. Keller, *Marketing Management*, 12th ed. (Upper Saddle River, NJ: Prentice Hall, 2005), pp. 437–450.

16   Philip Kotler and Gary Armstrong, *Principles of Marketing*, 9th ed. (Upper Saddle River, NJ: Prentice Hall, 2001), p. 403.

17   Rama Lakshmi, "A Meal and a Chance to Learn." Special to *The Washington Post*, April 28, 2005.

18   Ibid.

19   Don Edwards Post, "Ten-Hut! The Army's Bungling Recruitment," Washingtonpost.com, Sunday, June 12, 2005.

20   Ann Scott Tyson, "Army Aims to Catch Up on Recruits in Summer," Washingtonpost.com, Saturday, June 11, 2005.

21   *The Week*, May 6, 2005, p. 8.

22   John Ritter, "Towns offer free land to newcomers." *USA Today*, February 9, 2005, p. 1.

23   http://kansasfreeland.com (accessed June 27, 2005).

24   Arthur Stamoulis, "Tax on Plastic Bags Works," The Woodchuck Cafe, http://www.greenworks.tv/woodchuckcafe/archives/feature_plasticbagtax.asp (accessed June 28, 2005).

25   "Irish bag tax hailed success," BBC News, Tuesday, August 20, 2002, http://news.bbc.co.uk/1/hi/world/europe/2205419.stm (accessed June 28, 2005).

26   "Owners told to walk dogs or pay up," *The Courier Mail*, Queensland Newspapers, April 24, 2005, http://www. thecouriermail.news.com.au/printpage/0,5942,15070795,00.html.

27   Peter Edidin, "Birds and bees in Singapore," *International Herald Tribune*, Tuesday, February 10, 2004, p. 2.

28   "Measure of Sustainability Eco-Labeling," http://www.canadianarchitect.com/asf/perspectives_sustainibility/measures_of_sustainablity/measures_of_sustainablity_ecolabeling.htm.

29   http://www.blauer-engel.de/englisch/navigation/body_blauer_engel.htm.

30   King County Animal Services, http://www.metrokc.gov/lars/animal/services/plindex.htm.

31   *The Filthy 15*, http://www.ci.tacoma.wa.us/tacomanews/Filthy15/5647_S_Birmingham.asp (accessed March 7, 2006).

Chapter 5

1   Population Services International (PSI)/Nepal. Author interview, September 2005.

2   Metro Transit—Park and Ride Minneapolis/St. Paul Metro Area, http://www.metrotransit.org/serviceInfo/parkRide.asp (accessed August 24, 2005).

3   Wisconsin Tobacco Quit Line: Fax to Quit Program, http://www.ctri.wisc.edu/HC.Providers/healthcare_QL-Fax2Quit.htm (accessed August 24, 2005).

4   U.S. Census Press Releases, "U.S. Voter Turnout Up in 2004, Census Bureau Reports," http://www.census.gov/Press-Release/www/releases/archives/voting/004986.html (accessed August 24, 2005).

5   "Vote by Mail," Fairvote.org, http://www.fairvote.org/turnout/mail.htm (accessed August 24, 2005).

6   MidCentral District Health Board, New Zealand, http://www.midcentral.co.nz/pub/Releases/Dental-Mobiles.pdf (accessed August 24, 2005).

7   *The Citizen, The Newsletter of Citizens for Maryland Libraries*, Number 3, Summer 2000 (From an article by Jennifer McMenamin in the March 17, 2000 edition of the *Baltimore Sun*).

8   Triangle Transit Authority, http://www.ridetta.org/Home/News_ Events/8-05TTAOnlinePassSales.htm (accessed August 22, 2005).

9   "Jail Adopts Video Visitation," http://governmentvideo.com/ articles/publich/printer_74.shtml (accessed August 26, 2005).

10   Jessica Kowal, "Rapid HIV tests offered where those at risk gather: Seattle health officials get aggressive in AIDS battle by heading to gay clubs, taking a drop of blood and providing answers in 20 minutes," *Chicago Tribune,* January 2, 2004, http://www.aegis.com/news/ct/2004/CT040101.html (accessed May 25, 2005).

11   24/7 Live Help—Utah.gov, http://www.utah.gov/contact.html (accessed August 22, 2005).

12   Washington State Liquor Control Board, "Sunday Sales Begin Sept. 4 in 20 State Stores," August 19, 2005, http://www. liq.wa.gov/releases/pr050819.asp (accessed September 4, 2005).

13   The Government of the Hong Kong Special Administrative Region—Immigration Department, http://www.immd.gov.hk/ ehtml/pledge_p7.htm (accessed September 4, 2005).

Chapter 6

1   Al Ries and Jack Trout, *Positioning: The Battle for Your Mind* (New York: Warner Books, 1986), p. 2.

2   "Branditis" is a term used by Paul Hoskins, director of brand consulting firm Precedent, http://society.guardian.co.uk/think tank/story/0,14097,1229027,00.html.

3   Philip Kotler and Gary Armstrong, *Principles of Marketing,* 9th ed. (Upper Saddle River, NJ: Prentice Hall, 2001), p. 301.

4   Philip Kotler and Kevin L. Keller, *Marketing Management,* 12th ed. (Upper Saddle River, NJ: Prentice Hall, 2005), p. 278.

5   Kotler and Armstrong, *Principles of Marketing,* p. 302.

6   Kotler and Keller, *Marketing Management,* p. 281.

7   Ibid., p. 301.

8   Ibid., p. 284.

9   Ibid., p. 280.

10   Ibid., p. 390.

11   "Smokey Bear Guidelines," February 2004, http://www.smokeybear.com/resources.asp (accessed September 21, 2005).

12   http://www.ams.usda.gov/nop/Consumers/brochure.html.

13   CDC, "Preventing Chronic Disease," http://www.cdc.gov/pcd/issues/2004/jul/04_0054.htm.

14   Kotler and Keller, *Marketing Management*, p. 282.

15   "Don't Mess with Texas" Web site, http://www.dontmesswithtexas.org/ (accessed September 25, 2005). "Don't Mess with Texas" is a registered trademark of the Texas Department of Transportation.

16   Ibid.

17   "Smokey Bear Guidelines," February 2004, http://www.smokeybear.com/resources.asp (accessed September 21, 2005).

18   Hong Kong International Airport Web site, http://www.hongkongairport.com/eng/index.jsp (accessed September 28, 2005).

19   Leon Stafford, "Brand Atlanta to Launch New Advertising Campaign," August 21, 2005, *Atlanta Journal-Constitution*. Quote regarding spending referred to a "Bain Study."

20   Ibid.

21   The official Web site of the Athens 2004 Olympic Games, "How Greece is perceived by the citizens of five major countries," October 19, 2004, http://www.athens2004.com/en/LatestNews/newslist?item=52abbd996b5bffOOVgnVCM4000002b13. (accessed September 28, 2005).

22   National Crime Prevention Council, *Guidelines for McGruff and Related Marks*, "A Capsule History of McGruff and the National Citizens' Crime Prevention Campaign," pp. 22–24.

23   National Crime Prevention Council Web site, http://www.ncpc.org/ncpc/ncpc/?pg=10742 (accessed September 28, 2005).

24   Kotler and Keller, *Marketing Management*, pp. 294–295.

25   "The New D.A.R.E. Program," http://www.dare.com/home/newdareprogram.asp (accessed September 30, 2005).

26   Charlie Parsons, President and Chief Executive Director of D.A.R.E., "The New D.A.R.E. Program," http://www.dare.com/home/newdareprogram.asp (accessed September 30, 2005).

27   "The New D.A.R.E. Program," http://www.dare.com/home/newdareprogram.asp (accessed September 30, 2005).

28   Ries and Trout, *Positioning: The Battle for Your Mind*, pp. 143–147.

Chapter 7

1   Author interview with Social Marketing Leader and Director, Organ Donation Breakthrough Collaborative, via email, November 2005.

2   PSI Profile, Social Marketing and Communications for Health, December 2004, The Ultimate Stamps of Approval: "Postal Campaigns Deliver AIDS Information Beyond Mass Media," www.psi.org.

3   John L. Henshaw, "Safety and Health add value to your Business, Workplace and Life," April 21, 2004, 8th Biennial Governor's Pacific-Rim Safety and Health Conference, http://www.osha.gov/pls/oshaweb/owadisp.show_document?p_table=SPEECHES&p_id=755.

4   Ready.gov—From the U.S. Department of Homeland Security, http://www.ready.gov/index.html (accessed October 5, 2005).

5   Al Ries and Jack Trout, *Positioning: The Battle for Your Mind* (New York: Warner Books, 1986) pp. 11–13.

6   "Law, Regulation & Economy," *Marketing News*, February 15, 2006, p. 4.

7   Herbert C. Kelman and Carl I. Hovland, "Reinstatement of the Communication in Delayed Measurement of Opinion Change," *Journal of Abnormal and Social Psychology* 48 (1953): pp. 327–335.

8   Philip Kotler and Kevin L. Keller, *Marketing Management*, 12th ed. (Upper Saddle River, NJ: Prentice Hall, 2005), p. 546.

9   Chisaki Watanabe, "Japanese shedding ties to ease warming," Associated Press, *The Seattle Times*, Business Section, June 2, 2005.

10 Randy Dotinga, "Military channel reports for duty," *Christian Science Monitor*, http://www.csmonitor.com/2005/0425/p11s01-usmi.htm (accessed October 27, 2005).

11 Kotler and Keller, *Marketing Management*, p. 536.

12 Peace Corps Web site, Media section, http://www.peacecorps.gov/index.cfm?shell=resources.media.psa (accessed October, 31, 2005).

13 See Neil Neroutsos, "Snohomish PUD Tackles Enron: Northwest Utility Uncovers Evidence Showing Widespread Corruption," *Northwest Public Power Association Bulletin*, July 2004, pp. 25–27. Also see utility's Web site at www.snopud.com.

14 "Best Practices in Community Policing" with Wesley Skogan, Professor of Political Science at the Institute for Policy Research at Northwestern University, PBS, August 17, 2004.

15 Hanley and Wood, *Public Works*, June 2005, 136(7), www.pwmag.com, pp. 28–31.

16 Tennessee Valley Authority, "Put Green Power to Work," http://www.tva.gov/greenpowerswitch/green_comm.htm.

17 "Dagen H," Wikipedia, the free encyclopedia, http://en.wikipedia.org/wiki/Dagen_H (accessed October 3, 2005).

18 Kotler and Keller, *Marketing Management*, p. 548.

19 OnPoint Marketing and Promotions, "Buzz Marketing," http://www.onpoint-marketing.com/buzz-marketing.htm (accessed November 1, 2005).

20 John Tierney, "Magic Marker Strategy," September 6, 2005, nytimes.com/travel

21 Alan Andreasen and Philip Kotler, *Strategic Marketing for Nonprofit Organizations*, 6th ed. (Upper Saddle River, NJ: Prentice Hall, 2002), p. 490.

22 Ibid.

23 Ibid.

24 Philip Kotler, Ned Roberto, and Nancy Lee, *Social Marketing: Improving the Quality of Life* (Thousand Oaks, CA: Sage, 2002), p. 307.

25 Ibid.

26   Philip Kotler and Gary Armstrong, *Principles of Marketing*, 9th ed. (Upper Saddle River, NJ: Prentice Hall, 2001), pp. 515–518.

Chapter 8

1   Alan Brunacini, Fire Chief, City of Phoenix, Fire Department, "Essentials of Fire Department Customer Service," 1996, Copyright by Alan Brunacini. Excerpts from this book and an interview with the chief on April 10 and 11, 2005.

2   Ibid.

3   Ann Laurent, Associate Editor, *Government Executive Magazine*, "The Big Picture on Customer Feedback," EPA Customer Service Conference, November 30–December 1, 1999, http://www.epa.gov/customerservice/conferences/proceedings/proceedingsfeedback.htm.

4   U.S. Census Bureau, Strategic Plan 2004–2008, http://www.census.gov/main/www/aboutus.html (accessed April 21, 2005).

5   U.S. Census Bureau, Census 2000 Mail Return Rates, January 30, 2003, Final Report. p. v.

6   Robert Spector and Patrick McCarthy, *The Nordstrom Way to Customer Service Excellence* (Hoboken, NJ: John Wiley & Sons, 2005), p. xiii.

7   Ibid., p. 91.

8   Philip Kotler and Kevin L. Keller, *Marketing Management*, 12th ed. (Upper Saddle River, NJ: Prentice Hall, 2005), p. 140.

9   Spector and McCarthy, *The Nordstrom Way to Customer Service Excellence*, p. 115.

10   Ibid., p. 122.

11   Singapore Changi Airport, http://www.singaporemirror.com.sg/ab_infr_airport.htm (accessed March 3, 2005).

12   Unisys, "Singapore's Changi International Airport Services (CIAS) 'Checking In' with New Unisys Solution to Expedite Passenger Processing," http://www.unisys.com.hk (accessed April 21, 2005).

13 United Kingdom Passport Service, "UK Passport Service: Improving Passport Security and Tackling ID Fraud," Press Release March 24, 2005, http://www.ukpa.gov.uk/textonly/eng lish/t_press_240305.asp (accessed April 25, 2005).

14 Ibid.

15 Tony Kontzer, "Government Agencies Look to CRM Software," *InformationWeek*, December 6, 2004, http://www.infor mationweek.com/showArticle.jhtml?articleID=54800256 (accessed April 7, 2005).

16 "Feds pump up the CRM," MM, March/April 2002, p. 5.

17 Joseph Sensenbrenner, "Quality Comes to City Hall," *Harvard Business Review*, March-April 1991, p. 68.

18 Ibid.

19 Institute for Citizen-Centred Service, "Benchmarking: Benefits and Lessons Learned," http://www.iccs-isac.org/eng/bench-ben.htm (accessed April 25, 2005).

20 The American Customer Satisfaction Index, http://www.theacsi.org/overview.htm (accessed April 27, 2005).

21 Ned Roberto, *How to Make Local Governance Work* (Asian Institute of Management, 2002).

Chapter 9

1 Ian Sample, "Fat to fit: how Finland did it," *The Guardian*, Saturday, January 15, 2005, http://www.guardian.co.uk/befit/story/0,15652,1385645,00.html.

2 Ibid.

3 Ibid.

4 Ibid.

5 Ilkka Vuori, Becky Lankenau, and Michael Pratt, "Physical Activity Policy and Program Development: The Experience in Finland," *Public Health Reports*, May-June 2005, Volume 119, pp. 331–345.

6 Ian Sample, "Fat to fit: how Finland did it," *The Guardian*, Saturday, January 15, 2005, http://www.guardian.co.uk/befit/story/0,15652,1385645,00.html.

7   Philip Kotler, Ned Roberto, and Nancy Lee, *Social Marketing: Improving the Quality of Life* (Thousand Oaks, CA: Sage, 2002), p. 5.

8   Behavior Risk Factor Surveillance System, http://www.cdc.gov/brfss/.

9   J. Prochaska and C. DiClemente, "Stages and Processes of Self-Change of Smoking: Toward an Integrative Model of Change," *Journal of Consulting and Clinical Psychology*, 51, 1983, pp. 390–395.

10   Alan Andreasen, *Marketing Social Change: Changing Behavior to Promote Health, Social Development, and the Environment* (San Francisco: Jossey-Bass, 1995), p. 148.

11   http://oee.nrcan.gc.ca/transportation/idling/material/campaign-resources.cfm?attr=28#stickers, http://toolsofchange.com/English/CaseStudies/default.asp?ID=181.

12   B. Smith, "Beyond 'Health' as a Benefit," *Social Marketing Quarterly*, 9(4), Winter 2003, pp. 22–28.

13   Michael Rothschild, Plenary Presentation, 13th Annual Social Marketing in Public Health Conference, June 2003.

14   Michael Rothschild, "Accommodating Self-Interest," *Social Marketing Quarterly*, 8(2), Summer 2002, pp. 32–35.

15   Tools of Change Case Study, "Road Crew Reduces Drunk Driving," http://toolsofchange.com/English/CaseStudies/default.asp?ID=181 (accessed November 4, 2005).

16   Snohomish Health District, Washington State, Marketing Plan, April 2003.

17   Tendai Dhliwayo, "Taking you home," City of Johannesburg Official Web site, April 23, 2003, http://www.joburg.org.za/2003/apr/apr23_home.stm (accessed October 20, 2005).

18   City of Austin, "Scoop the Poop: Dogs for the Environment" Web site, http://ci.austin.tx.us/watershed/petwaste.htm (accessed November 18, 2005).

19   Kotler, Roberto, and Lee, *Social Marketing*, p. 308–309.

20   A.G. Greenwalk, C.G. Carnot, R. Beach, and B. Young, "Increasing voting behavior by asking people if they expect to vote," *Journal of Applied Psychology*, 72, 1987, pp. 315–318.

As described in D. McKenzie-Mohr and W. Smith, *Fostering Sustainable Behavior: An Introduction to Community-Based Social Marketing* (Gabriola Island, British Columbia, Canada: New Society, 1999), p. 47.

21   Doug McKenzie-Mohr, Quick Reference: Community-Based Social Marketing, www.cbsm.com.

22   D. McKenzie-Mohr and W. Smith, *Fostering Sustainable Behavior*, p 61.

23   Alan Andreasen, *Marketing in the 21st Century* (Thousand Oaks, CA: Sage, 2006), p. 11.

Chapter 10

1   AED Center for Environmental Strategies, "From Crisis to Consensus: A New Course for Water Efficiency in Jordan," 2004.

2   Causes & Effects, The Newsletter of Corporate Alliances with Charitable Causes, 19(8), August 2005, p. 1.

3   Philip Kotler and Nancy Lee, *Corporate Social Responsibility: Doing the Most Good for Your Company and Your Cause* (Hoboken, NJ: John Wiley & Sons, 2005), p. 5.

4   Ibid., p. 12.

5   Johnson & Johnson, "Johnson & Johnson Campaign Raises $7 Million for Nursing Shortage," Press Release, May 10, 2005, http://www.jnj.com/news/jnj_news/20050509_164453.htm.

6   http://www.jnj.com/home.htm.

7   American Express Company, "American Express Launches National Campaign to Help Reopen the Statue of Liberty; Pledges a Minimum of $3 million with Cardmember Support," News Release, November 25, 2003.

8   Kotler and Lee, *Corporate Social Responsibility*, p. 13.

9   Ibid., p. 106.

10   Tools of Change Case Study, "Back to Sleep—Health Canada SIDS Social Marketing Campaign," http://www.toolsofchange.com/English/CaseStudies/default.asp?ID=161 (accessed July 26, 2005).

11   Kotler and Lee, *Corporate Social Responsibility*, pp. 31–32.

12   Author interview with manager, Global Communications & PR, GE Consumer & Industrial Products, via email, September 2003. Kotler and Lee, *Corporate Social Responsibility*, pp. 152–153.

13   Motorola Inc., "Motorola: Leadership Programs to Protect the Environment," http://www.motorola.com/EHS/environment/ leadership / (accessed April 16, 2004).

14   Kotler and Lee, *Corporate Social Responsibility*, p. 217.

15   Ibid.

16   Casey Family Programs, "Public-private partnership to improve Wyoming's child welfare system," December 17, 2003, http://www.casey.org/MediaCenter/PressReleasesAnd Announcements/121703WyomingParnership.htm.

17   http://www.adcouncil.org/campaigns/.

18   Ibid.

19   http://www.Puravidacoffee.com.

20   Department of Homeland Security, "Secretary Ridge Addresses American Red Cross in St. Louis," May 21, 2004, http://www. dhs.gov/dhspublic/display?theme=44&content=3575&print=true.

21   Department of Homeland Security, "Homeland Security and American Red Cross Co-Sponsor National Preparedness Month 2005," Press Release, June 9, 2005, http://www.dhs.gov/ dhspublic/display?theme=43&content=4538&print=true.

22   New Zealand Injury Prevention Strategy, http://www.nzips.govt.nz/ priorities/drowning.html (accessed August 1, 2005).

23   Kotler and Lee, *Corporate Social Responsibility*, pp. 263–276.

Chapter 11

1   This project was carried out with the aid of a grant by Research for International Tobacco Control (RITC), an international secretariat housed within the International Development Research Centre (IDRC) in Ottawa, Canada.

2   Philip Kotler and Gary Armstrong, *Principles of Marketing*, 9th ed. (Upper Saddle River, NJ: Prentice Hall, 2001), p. 138.

3   Alan Andreasen, *Marketing Social Change: Changing Behavior to Promote Health, Social Development, and the Environment* (San Francisco: Jossey-Bass, 1995), p. 98.

4   http://factfinder.census.gov/home/saff/main.html?_lang=en (accessed March 26, 2005).

5   Andreasen, *Marketing Social Change*, p. 98.

6   Philip Kotler and Kevin L. Keller, *Marketing Management*, 12th ed. (Upper Saddle River, NJ: Prentice Hall, 2005), p. 104.

7   Ibid., p. 106.

8   Ibid., p. 111.

9   Kotler and Armstrong, *Principles of Marketing*, p. 152.

10   Ibid., p. 153.

11   Andreasen, *Marketing Social Change*, p. 105.

12   Alan Andreasen, *Marketing Research That Won't Break the Bank: A Practical Guide to Getting the Information You Need*, 2nd ed. (San Francisco: Jossey-Bass, 2002).

Chapter 12

1   Alan Andreasen and Philip Kotler, *Strategic Marketing for Nonprofit Organizations*, 6th ed. (Upper Saddle River, NJ: Prentice Hall, 2002), pp. 500–502.

2   U.K. Government News Network, "New Campaigns to Reduce Gum Litter," http://www.gnn.gov.uk/environment/detail.asp?ReleaseID=189651&NewsAreaID=2&NavigatedFrom Department=True (accessed March 13, 2006).

3   U.K. Department for Environment Food and Rural Affairs, "Local environmental quality: Chewing gum pilot campaigns," http://www.defra.gov.uk/environment/localenv/gum/pilot.htm.

4   U.S. Department of Labor, http://www.bls.gov/nls/#overview (accessed March 20, 2006).

Chapter 13

1   Joseph Perello, NYC Marketing, "The Fourth New York," Address to The Economist's 2nd Annual Marketing Roundtable, March 25, 2004, http://www.nyc.gov/html/nycmktg/html/cmo_ bio/economist.shtml.

2   Ibid.

3   Ibid.

4   Ibid.

5   Joseph Perello, "The Power of Being Unreasonable," *CMO Magazine*, September 2005, New York City, http://www. cmomagazine.com/read/090105/joseph_perello.html.

6   Philip Kotler and Kevin L. Keller, *Marketing Management*, 12th ed. (Upper Saddle River, NJ: Prentice Hall, 2005), p. 310.

7   Ibid.

8   Ibid.

ABOUT THE AUTHORS

Philip Kotler (M.A., University of Chicago, Ph.D., M.I.T.) is the S. C. Johnson Distinguished Professor of International Marketing at the Kellogg School of Management, Northwestern University, Evanston, Illinois. He published his 12th edition of *Marketing Management*, the world's leading textbook in teaching marketing to MBAs. He has also published *Principles of Marketing, Strategic Marketing for Nonprofit Organizations, Marketing Places, Kotler on Marketing, Marketing Insights A to Z, Lateral Marketing, Social Marketing, Museum Strategies and Marketing, Standing Room Only, Corporate Social Responsibility*, and several other books. His research covers strategic marketing, innovation, consumer marketing, business marketing, services marketing, distribution, e-marketing, and social marketing. He has been a consultant to IBM, Bank of America, Merck, General Electric, Honeywell, and many other companies. He has received honorary doctorate degrees from ten major universities here and abroad.

Nancy Lee, MBA, has more than 25 years of practical marketing experience in the public, private, and nonprofit sectors. This is the third book she has coauthored with Philip Kotler. She is an adjunct faculty member at the University of Washington and Seattle University where she teaches Marketing in the Public Sector, Social Marketing, and Marketing for Nonprofit Organizations. She is President of Social Marketing Services, Inc., founded in 1993, and consults with local, national, and international governmental agencies on strategic marketing planning, campaign development, and program evaluation. She is a frequent speaker at conferences, seminars, and workshops for public sector program managers and administrators.

INDEX